THE PHILOSOPHER'S ANNUAL

VOLUME IV – 1981

Editors

David L. Boyer
Patrick Grim
John T. Sanders

Ridgeview Publishing Company

Paper Text: ISBN 0-917930-61-4
Cloth Text: ISBN 0-917930-75-4

Published in the United States of America
By Ridgeview Publishing Company
P.O. Box 686
Atascadero, California 93422

Printed in the United States of America
By Ridgeview Letterpress & Offset Inc.
Independence, Ohio 44131

CONTENTS — Volume IV

Introduction   xi

A PERSPECTIVE ON MIND-BRAIN RESEARCH   1
Patricia Smith Churchland

THE EXPRESSION OF EMOTION IN MUSIC   25
S. Davies

LEGAL MORALISM AND FREEFLOATING EVILS   45
Joel Feinberg

RUSSELL'S SUBSTITUTIONAL THEORY   79
Peter Hylton

A PRIORI KNOWLEDGE   111
Philip Kitcher

MORAL DILEMMAS AND CONSISTENCY   133
Ruth Barcan Marcus

ON WORKS OF VIRTUOSITY   149
Thomas Carson Mark

SCIENTIFIC PROGRESS   167
Ilkka Niiniluoto

MODELS AND REALITY   203
Hilary Putnam

CAUSALITY AND PROPERTIES   223
Sydney Shoemaker

ACKNOWLEDGEMENTS

Churchland, Patricia Smith, "A Perspective on Mind-Brain Research", *The Journal of Philosophy*, 77, 4 (April, 1980), pp. 185-207. Copyright © 1980 by The Journal of Philosophy, Inc. Reprinted by permission.

Davies, S., "The Expression of Emotion in Music", *Mind*, 89, 353 (January, 1980), pp. 67-86. Copyright © 1980 by The Mind Association. Reprinted by permission.

Feinberg, Joel, "Legal Moralism and Freefloating Evils", *Pacific Philosophical Quarterly*, 61 (January-April, 1980), pp. 122-155. Copyright © 1980 by The University of Southern California. Reprinted by permission.

Hylton, Peter, "Russell's Substitutional Theory", *Synthese*, 45(1980), pp. 1-31. Copyright © 1980 by D. Reidel Publishing Company, Dordrecht, Holland. Reprinted by permission.

Kitcher, Philip, "A Priori Knowledge", *Philosophical Review*, 89, 1 (January, 1980). Copyright © 1980 by Cornell University. Reprinted by permission.

Marcus, Ruth Barcan, "Moral Dilemmas and Consistency", *The Journal of Philosophy*, 77, 3 (March, 1980), pp. 121-136. Copyright © 1980 by The Journal of Philosophy, Inc. Reprinted by permission.

Mark, Thomas Carson, "On Works of Virtuosity", *The Journal of Philosophy*, 77, 1 (January, 1980), pp. 28-45. Copyright © 1980 by The Journal of Philosophy, Inc. Reprinted by permission.

Niiniluoto, Ilkka, "Scientific Progress", *Synthese*, 45 (,1980), pp. 427-462. Copyright © 1980 by D. Reidel Publishing Company, Dordrecht, Holland. Reprinted by permission.

Putnam, Hilary, "Models and Reality", *The Journal of Symbolic Logic*, 45, 3 (September, 1980), pp. 464-482. Copyright © 1980 by the American Mathematical Society. Reprinted by permission of the American Mathematical Society.

Shoemaker, Sydney, "Causality and Properties", *Time and Cause*, edited by Peter van Inwagen, pp. 109-135. Copyright © 1980 by D. Reidel Publishing Company, Dordrecht, Holland. Reprinted by permission.

INTRODUCTION

The articles collected here represent our attempt to pick the ten best pieces from the philosophical literature of 1980. With the aid of a Nominating Board of prominent philosophers, representing a broad range of interest and expertise, we have tried not merely to assemble ten good articles but to assemble the ten best. Were one able to read only ten of the thousands of articles published during the year, these—it is hoped— would be the ones to read.

The great wealth of philosophical literature produced each year poses a serious practical difficulty for the working philosopher. No one is able to read every article which appears in every journal, even if he or she has access to them all; and unfortunately, it is often accidental features which determine what a given philosopher will read: the ready availability or prestige of the journal, the familiarity of the author's name, or the appeal of the title, As a result, less important and less worthy articles may attract a wider reading, while more important articles go relatively unnoticed.

Our attempt here is to compensate for this serious difficulty in some small way. *The Philosopher's Annual,* of which this is the fourth volume, is designed as a yearly collection of recent articles of special merit and worthy of special attention, recommended as outstanding by a group of prominent philosophers and judged by the editors to be the finest of a fine lot.

Our procedure is as follows. Each year, the members of our Nominating Board are asked to suggest three outstanding articles which appeared in print for the first time that year. No limitations are placed on sources from which articles may be nominated, on subject matter, or on mode of treatment. Though our nominating editors are selected so as to represent a wide spectrum of interests and areas of expertise, no one is asked to nominate articles from any particular area.

Despite occasional duplications, this leaves the editors with a ponderous pile of nominations. Each of us then reads each of these with care, and the collection is progressively whittled down to ten selections by discussion and argument—often heated argument—among the editors. Our aim is to convince each other of overlooked virtues or disguised vices by force of argument, rather than to accept convenient compromises or to resort to log-rolling or trade-offs. Philosophical argument regarding the philosophical merits of various pieces is to count for everything. Authorship, area, original source of publication and the eventual distribution of areas or sources within the final collection are to count for nothing. Our aim is simply to select from among the nominations those ten which we can convince each other are the best of the lot.

Can we claim to have succeeded in selecting the ten best articles of the year? Surely not without nagging doubts, and surely not short of controversy. There are of course articles published each year which neither we nor any of our nominating editors reads, and these will inevitably slip through our net. There may also be virtues we fail to see and vices we overlook. And each of us may harbor doubts as to whether this or that aspect of a particular piece was *that* good, or as to whether we argued as strongly as we did for a particular article only because of its importance for our own current research.

Any attempt to choose the best of a year's contributions, moreover, will raise some major philosophical questions. How philosophy ought to be done is itself a philosophical issue, and it must be admitted that the collection of these papers here indicates a conviction that there are philosophical virtues they exhibit and philosophical vices they avoid. Some such virtues may be fairly uncontroversial and fairly easily listed. Clearly written articles have something in their favor which obscurely presented articles do not; papers which approach the literature fairly are to be preferred over those which ignore it; it is a virtue to isolate and concentrate on central rather than peripheral points; and innovation is to be applauded. Not all proposed virtues will be as uncontroversial or as easy to characterize, however, and even general agreement on listed virtues and vices is of little help if it is open to question whether they are exemplified by a particular piece.

Thus an edge of controversy will inevitably remain. This, perhaps, is as it should be. Our attempt is to alleviate to some extent the confusion engendered by an unmanageable wealth of annual literature, and in some small measure to direct discussion by making more widely accessible a limited number of worthy articles. That any selection will itself involve a degree of intellectual controversy is perhaps as desirable as it is unavoidable within a discipline to which intellectual controversy is essential.

David L. Boyer

Patrick Grim

John T. Sanders

PATRICIA SMITH CHURCHLAND

A PERSPECTIVE ON MIND-BRAIN RESEARCH *

THERE is a fairly widespread conviction among philosophers that direct study of the brain is not likely to be
very fruitful in the endeavor to get a theory of how the
mind-brain works. Surprisingly, this opinion concerning brain research appears to be shared among philosophers who otherwise
have starkly incompatible views about the nature of the mind. On
the one hand are the dualists and phenomenologists who take the
mind to be a nonphysical entity and who believe that mainly by
introspection can we come to understand such things as perception,
memory, consciousness, and the like. Their reservations concerning
the value of brain research are understandable, however lament-
able. Less easy to understand are the reservations of some physicalists. Yet it is apparent that many physicalists, including not
only philosophers,[1] but also psychologists [2] and artificial-intelli-
gence researchers,[3] are frankly skeptical concerning what neuro-

---

* I am particularly indebted to Paul Churchland, Michael Stack, Larry Jordan,
and Daniel Dennett for inspiring conversation.

[1] Cf. J. A. Fodor, *The Language of Thought* (New York: Crowell, 1975);
Hilary Putnam, "The Nature of Mental States," in David M. Rosenthal, ed.,
Materialism and the Mind-Body Problem (Englewood Cliffs, N.J.: Prentice-Hall,
1971); Daniel C. Dennett, "Artificial Intelligence as Philosophy and as Psychology," in his *Brainstorms* (Montgomery, Vt.: Bradford, 1978), pp. 109–126.

[2] Cf. John R. Anderson, *Language, Memory and Thought* (Hillsdale, N.J.:
Erlbaum, 1976). Anderson says:

> Obviously one would be foolish to claim that physiological data will never
> be of use to the cognitive psychologist. However, one would be equally
> foolish to expect that physiological data will help decide current issues
> about internal structure and process (14).

See also Zenon Pylyshyn, *Cognition and Computation* (in progress), and Julian
Jaynes, *The Origin of Consciousness in the Breakdown of the Bicameral Mind*
(Boston: Houghton Mifflin, 1976), p. 18.

[3] Cf. Joseph Weizenbaum, *Computer Power and Human Reason* (San Francisco: W. H. Freeman, 1976).

1

science can tell us about how the mind-brain works. Their reservations are prima facie startling, in light of the fact that the central
tenet of physicalism is that mental states are physical states, and
given that we humans have brains, our mental states are brain
states. This skeptical attitude on the part of physicalists has frequently come to my notice insofar as my own studies in neuroscience have often been met with bemused incredulity, as though
knowledge of neuroscience was probably no more nor less valuable
to a philosopher of mind than, say, knowledge of cartography or
soil science—it might provide entertaining and even useful examples, but it will not do more. I have therefore tried to inquire
into the nature and justification of the physicalist's skepticism toward the value of neurological research. In so doing, I have discovered that this skepticism should really be distinguished into two
basic kinds, one of which I shall call *principled skepticism* and the
other *boggled skepticism*. As will be seen, sometimes principled
skeptics share doubts with boggled skeptics, but the distinction is
meant to correspond to two distinct rationales. Briefly, the principled skeptic believes, for reasons presently to be adumbrated,
that the kind of explanation available through neurological research will always, given the nature of the case, be inappropriate
to our understanding of such things as perception, memory, and
consciousness. The boggled skeptic, on the other hand, tends to be
awestruck by the 10^{12} neurons and the very considerable complexity of the nervous system. He allows that perhaps, in the far, far
distant future, brain research might be revealing, but thinks that
for the foreseeable future, it is only remotely possible that brain
research will yield anything of interest to the psychologist or the
philosopher. Both types of skepticism seem to me to be in error and
to stand in need of dislodging. The guiding aim of this paper is
to provide each with a bit of a jar.

Assuming that the cognitive activity of organisms is brain activity, why should brain-based theories of such activity be thought to
be the wrong kind of theory—indeed, how could they fail to be the
right sort of theory? The currently bruited answer that engenders
spirited spurning of neuroscience proceeds in this vein: at best,
neuroscience can provide only a *structural* theory, as opposed to
the *functional* theory sought; at most, it will give us the engineering minutiae as opposed to the design configurations we want. It is
in the nature of the case that neuroscientific theories will fall short,
because cognitive states and processes are properly understood as
functional states and processes, and the research program for psy-

chology, precisely in contrast to neuroscience, is to determine the functional organization that accounts for cognitive activity. To be sure, cognitive states are, at least in ourselves, also brain states, but what is interesting about them qua cognitive states is their functional role, not their neuronal instantiation. This can be seen by reflecting on the following considerations: (1) there will be a one-many mapping of functional states onto physical realizations of those states, because functional states can be realized in a variety of material bases. Furthermore, within one species, or even within one organism across time, different batteries of neurons will be recruited for a type-identical task, say, computing the sum of 67 and 59. (2) Neuroscience will yield generalizations orthogonal to cognitive explananda. Simply put, it will give us the wrong generalizations.[4] The type-identical state consisting of the belief that hens molt may be produced in one person by his having read that hens molt, in another by his having been told, in another by his observation of molting hens, in another by deduction from other biological beliefs, and so on. As a result of this belief, together with the belief that molting hens do not lay and the common desire to maximize egg-laying in the hen-house, each of the persons may perform the same action, to wit, wringing the necks of the molting hens. But the neuronal, causal stories will be totally different, given the distinct acquisition of beliefs, and, consequently, the crucial cognitive similarity between the persons will be hopelessly unavailable from the neuronal story. Structurally based as it is, neuroscience will not have the resources to be sensitive to the important cognitive similarities. In contrast, cognitive psychology, faithful to the explananda by deliberate design, will provide the right sort of generalization, if anything can.

Having thus delineated the nature of the research problem, the functionalist naturally enough sees the appropriate research strategy as exclusively top down.[5] Briefly, it will consist in explaining

[4] Pylyshyn advances essentially this objection in *Cognition and Computation*.
[5] Thus Barbara von Eckardt Klein says:
. . . in general, research must proceed from psychology to neurology. The reason is simple. We will not be in a position to discover how language-responsible cognitive structure is realized neurologically until we know what is so realized. In other words, evidence of the neurological realization of language-responsible cognitive structure cannot be properly evaluated except in the context of linguistic and psycholinguistic models of language-responsible cognitive structure (5).
in "What Is the Biology of Language?," in E. Walker, ed., *Explorations in the Biology of Language* (Montgomery, Vt.: Bradford, 1978). See also Pylyshyn, "Computation and Cognition," *The Behavioral and Brain Sciences*, III, 1, forthcoming.

such top-level, abstract, and familiar processes as intelligent choice and hypothesis testing as the outcome of less abstract and less complex processes on the part of a suitably organized collection of lower-level functional components. This is captured in Zenon Pylyshyn's claim that the appropriate type of explanation is explanation by functional decomposition.[6] Common-sense psychology, we are told, constitutes the correct first stage of cognitive theory, and essentially what is needed is an extension and development of common-sense psychological theory. From this point of view, the intelligent organism is a sentential automaton,[7] whose behavior is the outcome of a sequence of mental states (beliefs that p, desires that p, etc.), and the processing will be described in terms of the *semantic and syntactic* relations among the content-specifying sentences.[8]

The adequacy of the aforementioned complaints against the ambitions of neuroscience rests substantially on the adequacy of the central assumption, namely, that common-sense psychology is an essentially correct, if fragmentary, theory of how the mind-brain works. That common-sense psychology is indeed a theory, and as such might be seriously misdirected or significantly misconceived, is occasionally recognized as an empirical possibility, but it is nevertheless considered handily dismissible as a *mere* possibility.[9] Such resolute confidence notwithstanding, there are weaknesses in common-sense psychology, weaknesses which threaten to sully attempts to develop it into a scientific psychology. In what follows, I shall first provide a summary discussion of some of these weaknesses. I shall then turn to a discussion of a selection of examples of neuroscientific research which indicate the promise of a quaquaversal, or multi-directional, approach.

There is, to begin with, what I shall call the *infralinguistic catastrophe*. Nature abounds in infraverbal intelligent activity, the most spectacular of which is perhaps to be found in the aspiring infant hominid, lisping his way to linguistic fluency and worldly wisdom. Intelligent behavior is no more unique to humans than is a nervous system, and undoubtedly many nonverbal nonhumans display im-

---

[6] Pylyshyn, "On the Explanatory Adequacy of Cognitive Process Models," mimeo; parenthetical page references to Pylyshyn are to this paper.

[7] See my "Fodor on Language Learning," *Synthese*, xxxviii, 1 (May 1978): 149–159.

[8] For a fuller description, see my "Language, Thought, and Information Processing," forthcoming in *Noûs*; and Fodor, "Computation and Reduction," in C. Wade Savage, ed., *Minnesota Studies in the Philosophy of Science*, vol. ix (Minneapolis: Univ. of Minnesota Press, 1978): 229–260.

[9] For example, Fodor, *The Language of Thought* (New York: Crowell, 1975), ch. 2.

pressive intelligence. The belled elephant who sneaked into the banana plantation after stuffing her bell with mud exhibits a capacity which deserves to be called cognitive. The question is, how best to model the infraverbal information processing underlying the behavior? As Jerry Fodor (*ibid.*) incisively points out, the only model available within the top-down approach is explicitly and unrepentantly linguistic. Thus, in order to explain infraverbal activity, a nonverbal innately understood language (Mentalese) is posited, and the infraverbal representations are accounted for as Mentalese representations. The infraverbal is not, on this view, *infralinguistic*; where there is cognition, there also is linguistic representation, no matter how far, phylogenetically or ontogenetically, the creature is from overt language. As to language learning, it is explained within the confines of this approach as nothing other than translation between Mentalese and the target language. As if all this were not bad enough, hard on the heels comes the consequence that there is no such thing as concept learning (*ibid.*). On this view, hard-wired in the organism are the conceptual "atoms," and the old war horse, logical atomism, is wheeled out to explain how we acquire—but do not learn—complex concepts, including, presumably, such concepts as meson, charmed quark, and force field. The analogy with the ultraviolet catastrophe in pre-quantum physics is regrettably apt.[10] In both cases, the consequences of the theory are impossible to digest. The recalcitrant result, alas, is no trifling oddity that can be trussed up and eased into the existing theory by minor adjustment. Rather, it presages the advent of a quite different theoretical paradigm.

The linguistic model for explaining infraverbal representation does have the advantage of being available, but the fact that it is inconsistent with genuine concept learning renders mere availability a diminishing virtue. True enough, language is the most powerful system for representing that we know anything much about. The system we do not yet understand is the system that is in fact used by the brain. Although it is natural enough initially to hypothesize that the system we do *not* know is similar in the relevant respects to the system we *do* know, the infralinguistic catastrophe reveals the perils attending that hypothesis.

Common-sense psychology is beleaguered with yet further woes. The companion concepts of belief and desire are to function as the coping stones of the envisaged scientific psychology, but it now ap-

[10] For an account of the ultraviolet catastrophe, see J. Andrade e Silva and G. Lochak, *Quanta* (New York: World University Library, 1969), ch. 2.

pears doubtful that they have the theoretical integrity to so function. There are difficulties with deductive closure, which, as Daniel Dennett [11] argues, are not readily solvable by positing a deducer mechanism to handle beliefs *in potentia*; there are difficulties in determining which beliefs and desires are causally in the picture, difficulties attending individuation of beliefs and specification of content (39 ff) and difficulties with determinateness when the content is specified sententially (39 ff). Stephen Stich [12] has produced several remarkable results which indicate a disastrous mismatch between scientific psychology's need to postulate causally efficacious cognitive states and common-sense psychology's ability to specify content for beliefs and desires. From a rather different standpoint, Paul Churchland [13] has adduced general considerations which indicate that the linguistic model is decidedly parochial and that how evolution solved the problems of information *processing* is probably quite different from how it solved the problem of information *exchange*. In a similar spirit, C. A. Hooker [14] stresses the communicative function of language, and argues that it is a relatively superficial phenomenon in the information-processing story. To argue these views here is neither appropriate nor necessary, but to cite them is important in dispelling the comfortable illusion that, apart from a superficial blemish or two, common-sense psychology will do nicely. Together with the infralinguistic catastrophe, these difficulties bespeak the need for conceptual innovation, and to suppose that the work of neuroscientists must be irrelevant here is self-defeating. If in search of a scientific psychology we confine ourselves to working top-down, it may be every bit as constraining as trying to determine explanations of chemical behavior from within alchemical theory, or the nature of life from within vitalism.[15]

Before considering the remaining arguments of the principled skeptic, I want to dramatize my point by showing how results from neuroscience can bear not just upon the details of top-down theory, but, more critically, upon the very top-down criteria employed to test the adequacy of top-down theories. In this way I hope to show

[11] Dennett, "Brain Writing and Mind Reading," in *Brainstorms, op. cit.,* pp. 39–50.

[12] "Do Animals Have Beliefs?," *Australasian Journal of Philosophy* LVII, 1 (March 1979): 15–28; and "Autonomous Psychology and the Belief-Desire Thesis," *The Monist,* LXI, 4 (October 1978): 573–591.

[13] *Scientific Realism and the Plasticity of Mind* (New York: Cambridge, 1979).

[14] "The Information-processing Approach and Its Philosophical Ramifications," *Philosophy and Phenomenological Research,* XXXVI, 1 (September 1976): 1–15.

[15] For a critique of dominant top-down strategies in epistemology, see Paul M. Churchland, *op. cit.*

that the orderly transition from the top to deeper and deeper psychological levels may be threatened, and to demonstrate the risk in counting on the security of any scaffolding in the abstract structure that is our current and prevailing cognitive theory. In consequence, I hope to render more reasonable the idea that bottom-up research should be an important ingredient in top-down research.

In "Towards a Cognitive Theory of Consciousness," [16] Dennett succeeds in giving the flavor of functional organization at a level down from the level at which one standardly conceives of oneself when, for example, one thinks of oneself as a unified conscious being. Psychology at the *subpersonal* level, as Dennett puts it (153), explains activities of *persons* as the outcome of complexes of activities carried out by functional parts or faculties which conjointly are the person. A theory at the subpersonal level will posit a functional organization of modules each of which deals with information in certain specified ways: they may operate on information received, exchange information, and some will put out behavior commands. Admittedly, the painting is in bold strokes, but these are the sort of features borne by a cognitive theory in its nascent stages and proceeding top-down. Dennett's aim in the paper is to construct a functional organization such that it would be reasonable to say that anything that instantiates that particular functional organization is conscious. As such, it will be a theory about what it is to be conscious, and *eo ipso* about what consciousness is (TCC 149). It seems to me that Dennett's is a decidedly worthy theory—it is eminently plausible and highly sensible, at least viewed from the vantage point of the abstract heights of top-down research. What I wish to focus on here are two fundamental claims Dennett makes, drawn from our *personal*-level psychological theory, which he deems so safe as to be used to test the adequacy of his subpersonal-level theory. The first criterion is this: "if one can say something about [i.e., report observationally on] some current feature of the perceivable world, one has experienced it" (TCC 158). The second criterion is this: someone experiences something if and only if he is conscious of it (TCC 149).

Both claims seem as safe as houses, and it is fair to say that both are quite highly entrenched in common-sense beliefs about consciousness and conscious beings. From *within* the prevailing psychological paradigm, these propositions might well be graced with the

[16] *Brainstorms, op. cit.,* pp. 149–173; hereafter referred to as "TCC."

status of conceptual truths, but from without it can be seen that at least one is false. Here is why.

It is well known that in higher primates, including man, damage to the primary visual cortex results in blindness. However, recent tests conducted under rather special circumstances show that monkeys whose primary visual cortex had been destroyed nonetheless have a residual capacity for visual discrimination, and a rather impressive residual visual acuity. Since the monkeys could not report on their visual awareness or lack of same, it remained a possibility that they were not in fact blind.[17] As luck would have it, in 1974 L. Weiskrantz et al.[18] were able to garner information on "blind-sight" from a human subject. The case involved D.B., who for medical reasons had the major portion of the primary visual cortex on the medial surface of the right hemisphere removed. As a result, he was blind in his left visual field in both eyes (i.e., homonymous hemianopia). According to D.B., he had no visual perception in that field. When tested for visual discrimination in that field, he protested that he could see nothing in the left field, and his examiner therefore asked him to guess his answers. Astonishingly, it was found that D.B. was indeed able to make discriminations with respect to gross features of his environment, and could do so with a very considerable accuracy. So long as the presentations were not too small, and the duration of the presentation not shorter than about .0625 seconds,[19] he could correctly discriminate horizontal bars of light from vertical bars (accuracy of 30/30, 29/30), diagonal bars from vertical bars, X's from O's, red lights from green lights, and in addition he could point with great accuracy to where in the *blind visual field* a light was shining. It was incontestable that his "guessing" was no mere guessing and that he was making use of visual information to form a judgment, despite the fact that he did not have consciously accessible visual information. Weiskrantz does not yet have an explanation for this phenomenon, but a speculation worth pursuing is that, in addition to the well-known geniculostriate visual pathway, there is a phylogenetically older pathway involving the superior colliculus and the visual association cortex, and that perhaps this route carries the visual information that makes "blind-sight" possible.[20]

[17] N. K. Humphrey and L. Weiskrantz, "Vision in Monkeys after Removal of Striate Cortex," *Nature*, ccxv (1967): 595–597.

[18] "Visual Capacity in the Hemianopic Field following a Restricted Occipital Ablation," *Brain*, xcvii (1974): 709–728.

[19] For a complete account of the data, see Weiskrantz, *op. cit.*, p. 716.

[20] *Ibid.*, pp. 720–727. For recent work on "blind-sight" in other subjects, see

What is wondrously intriguing about the case of D.B., of course, is that he was providing visual reports on features of his environment, yet he was not doing so on the basis of visual experiences. Indeed, from the account Weiskrantz gives, evidently D.B. was not reporting on the basis of any experiential phenomena at all. Perhaps one might balk at my description here, and suggest that he was reporting on the basis of experiences, but that these experiences were not conscious. However, which description is preferred matters not at all to me. What is important is that on *either* description, one of the "safe" assumptions goes to the wall. Either we *can* make perceptual judgments about some current feature of the perceivable world even though we have not experienced it, or some of our experiences are such that we are not conscious of them. In the top-down approach, it is our intuitions, drawn from commonsense psychology, which play the prominent theoretical role, and the moral of the Weiskrantz story is that our intuitions, even at their best, are frail and vulnerable hypotheses.

The principled skeptic's objection that neuroscience cannot provide explanantia for the desired cognitive explananda is, therefore, enfeebled by the examination of whether the cognitive explananda are theoretically sound enough to stand as the unsullied end of scientific pursuit. If we cannot assume the adequacy of the cognitive explananda, then we cannot fault a strategy that seeks explanations which may fail to converge upon those explananda. However, should there really be a unity underlying cognitive explananda (e.g., the belief that hens molt), then neuroscience may well describe that unity, not of course in terms of the behavior of the peripheral sensory neurons, but in terms of informationally similar structures in the central system. Here it needs to be stressed that neuroscience is not limited to talking about structural minutiae, such as the spiking frequency of individual neurons, but can and does use network concepts (*neurofunctional* concepts), and aspires to the construction of higher-order network concepts. (For more on this, see below, pp. 204–207.) On the other hand, the ostensible unity implied by the cognitive description may in fact have no reality. In that event, what may happen is that neuroscience, initially making use of common-sense concepts, will make discoveries that transmogrify them. Neuroscience is as able to bootstrap as any other science.

also M. T. Perenin, "Visual Function within the Hemianopic Field following Early Cerebral Decortication in Man—II. Pattern Discrimination," *Neuropsychologia*, xvi, 6 (1978): 697–707.

Before going further, I want to make a clean breast of the fact that I have knowingly used 'information', 'representation', and their cognates in what must be described as an imprecise fashion. The imprecision, however, is owed not so much to my willful woolliness as to the state of the sciences concerned. The question of how to characterize information processed by the mind-brain and how to characterize the processing of information is a matter for *theory*, and it cannot yet be said that there is an anointed theory. In obvious but precarious contention is the theory of top-down advocates, which sees cognitive representation as inescapably sentential and which sees information processing as primarily a matter of inference within the frameworks of deductive and inductive logic. A rather different and more abstract conception is that of C. E. Shannon and W. Weaver [21] as embodied in the mathematical theory of communication, in which the "information" associated with an arriving signal is a measure of the reduction it effects in the uncertainty among a set of possible "messages." In this case, "information" processing can consist of transformations that bear no relation to those of deductive and inductive logic, e.g., amplification, filtering, averaging, integrating, etc. Further, a close and provocative relative of this notion of 'information' emerges naturally from statistical thermodynamics, wherein "information" is identical with negative entropy.[22] The identity is provocative because statistical thermodynamics provides the physical basis for understanding the evolution of semi-closed systems toward progressively greater order.

For *pre-theoretic* purposes, "information" may simply be conceived of in the following way: the state S of an object O contains the information that P just in case O would not be in S unless P. Neuroscientists for the most part are wililng to content themselves provisionally with some such vague sense of 'information', a sense sufficiently palpable only to underwrite the claim that information processing is what wants investigation and is what we need a theory of. This method is surely sensible, and certainly there is no reason for them to quit their laboratories until 'information' is well defined. On the contrary, it is the aim of neuroscience to *discover* how the mind-brain represents, how information about the world is filtered, stored, and transmitted, and, in so discovering, to pro-

[21] *The Mathematical Theory of Communication* (Urbana: Univ. of Illinois Press, 1949).

[22] L. Brillouin, *Science and Information Theory* (New York: Academic Press, 1956).

vide a theory characterizing "information" and "information processing." Consider, for suggestive example, the following characterization from A. Pellionisz and R. Llinas: [23]

> . . . the internal language of the brain is vectorial (330).
>
> Thus, the cerebellar cortex is represented as a system which receives vectorial inputs and emits vectorial outputs and where 'information processing' is indeed a transform of a mossy fiber input status vector (row vector of I-elements) into a Purkinje cell activity vector (row vector of I-elements) into a Purkinje cell activity vector (row vector of J-elements). The transform is determined by a network tensor which is, in this particular case, technically a matrix of I rows and J columns (333).

Later in the paper I shall discuss this work, but here my main point is that the desired definition of 'information' awaits theoretical development. A theory of how the mind-brain processes information and a definition of 'information' will emerge *en deux*.

The common-sense conception of our mind-brains and how they work does have an immensely powerful hold on the imagination, and a particularly tenacious conviction which fuels principled skepticism claims that, no matter how sophisticated explanations of human behavior become, no matter how "far down" our explanations go, if they are to succeed in explaining cognitive activities as successfully as our current explanations, they must, unavoidably, advert to representations (interpretations, meanings). Allegedly, no structural description can possibly do what a description in terms of representation can do. Pylyshyn, for example, argues that for nonpsychological things, the downward reduction terminates 'when the functional specification of a component can be mapped on to a physical law'. In contrast, for things which do have psychological processes, Pylyshyn says that "the functional reduction of cognitive functions should come to rest on cognitive laws," not, he insists, on neurophysiological laws (5). His reasons are interesting:

> In the psychological case the functions performed as well as the inputs and outputs of components must be interpreted in terms of what they *represent* in order for the description to address cognitive phenomena . . . the upshot of this feature of symbolic systems (including of course computers) is that although components function according to physical principles, the explanation of *what they are*

[23] "Brain Modeling by Tensor Network Theory and Computer Simulation. The Cerebellum: Distributed Processor for Predictive Coordination," *Neuroscience*, IV (1979): 323–348.

doing must make reference to what the symbols represent. Thus explanation by reduction cannot come to rest on physical laws (4).

The reservation Pylyshyn has here can perhaps be demonstrated by the following: Suppose someone says, "That chimney is on fire," and runs and telephones the fire department. According to the principled skeptic, no strictly physical explanation of what the person did will be as good as an intentional explanation, because, for starters, no physical account can do justice to the meaning of the utterance. The meaning of the utterance cannot be specified via a structural account of the equivalence class of utterances that have that meaning. The same message would have been contained whether it had been screamed, whispered, semaphored, given in American Sign Language, or sung to the strains of Pagliacci. Accordingly, explanations drawn from neurophysiology will always be defective in one decisive respect—they will have no truck with representation, sententially conceived.

The way to begin to defeat this objection is to reflect on the over-arching aims and methods of neurophysiology; for it is easy to be dumb-founded by papers with such titles as "Command Neurons in Pleurobranchaea Receive Synaptic Feedback from the Motor Network They Excite," [24] and to wonder how such studies could possibly come to connect with the problems we face in figuring out how we perceive and how we can use language to represent the world. A neurophysiological account of how an organism processes information will include hypotheses about what really *is* the information contained in certain neuronal states at various levels from the periphery, what information is filtered in and what filtered out, and how information is integrated. Given the nature of the case, these hypotheses will be sensitive on the one hand to our understanding of the sort of behavior the states are found to lead to, as well as to our physical and biochemical theory which we shall draw upon in determining what brings about a change in neuronal state. So long as the route from the peripheral input to the behavioral output is pretty direct, the hypotheses concerning what information is borne will be more or less straightforward. Alas, in true life the route is seldom simple and direct, though, when it is, we call the behavior a reflex, and, not needing to ascribe representations to so simple a system, we cheerfully characterize the information contained by appealing to biochemical theory and the overt details of the physical circumstance. The complexity enters when the input

24 R. Gillette *et al.*, *Science*, CIC, 4330 (1978): 798–801.

to, say, a motoneuron, comes from an extensive array of sources, some of which themselves contain highly integrated information from a variety of sources and some of which contain "internal" information. Evidently when the internal information transmitted to a neuron is very rich, it becomes profoundly difficult to specify precisely what information is contained in its various states. To the extent that it is difficult, we may tend, provisionally, to talk not about the information in the neuronal states, but about the animal's representations. The methodological point is that a demonstrably useful way to track down and converge upon what information is contained is to find out where the neuron set gets its information (e.g., from the cochlea, from the hypothalamus etc.), to find out what kinds of information the neuron is sensitive to, to find out what happens when you give it certain kinds of information, to find out what happens to other parts of the system when it transmits information or when it is prevented from transmitting information, and then to fit this in with whatever else one knows about the nervous system. Nobody thinks this child's play, but these are the things standardly done in the neurosciences to render the complexity tractable. In this fashion then does neuroscience put the squeeze on representation explanations of behavior. The increase in complexity in the nervous system as one moves up the phylogenetic scale is admittedly breath-taking, but there is no reason to suppose that the increased complexity is anything more than increased complexity or to suppose that representing is an emergent property absolutely inexplicable in terms of the underlying physical structure. Representation explanations are explanations we employ either out of ignorance or out of convenience; they are not explanations we employ by dint of the *sui generis* nature of intelligence. The explanation of how the human brain represents will turn out to depend on a theory of what information is contained at various levels and of how, by virtue of physical changes wrought in the system, information is transmitted. Though we surely cannot now say what this theory will look like, progress in the task has been spectacular in the last twenty years, and it does suggest that a solution is not in principle beyond our grasp.

The story of how language represents the world will undoubtedly be a late-comer, for it will be dependent upon our account of how the brain represents generally. There is no reason at this stage of inquiry to believe that the representation typical of linguistic behavior should constitute a unique and inexplicable case of representation. To be sure, social considerations will enter the story, for, as Quine has put it, language is a social art, and so that will add a dimension of complexity. The problem of the "equivalence class" in linguistic behavior (see above, p. 196) is not, I suspect, the bugbear for neuroscience that the principled skeptic imagines. Naturally the neuroscientist bent on getting a theory of how the brain represents would be foolish to try to specify the meaning of an utterance in terms of the physical properties of the utterances themselves or of the external stimuli to which they are related. Rather, the relevant specification will surely be in terms of informationally similar brain structures which figure in the etiology of the behavior. There is certainly no need for the neuroscientist to be red in the face about not *now* being able to provide the description, for it would be astonishing if we had more than common-room guesses at this stage of the endeavor. The equivalence-class problem can be deprived of such steam as it has by noticing that neither can the equivalence class of much *nonlinguistic* stimuli for *simple* animals be specified *in the way held out by the principled skeptic.* That is, if we consider a simple creature with respect to whose processing we do not feel compelled to invoke representation, we still have an equivalence-class problem so far as specifying what evokes flight behavior, feeding behavior and so forth, if we look to the purely intrinsic properties of the relevant conditions. The weakness with the equivalence-class objection is that it rests on a withered and parochial conception of how we might specify the meaning or the telos of behavior.

Though it is certainly a fool's errand to try to summarize in short compass the recent progress in brain research, in a spirit of *faute de mieux* I offer several examples which I think give some indication of how brain research puts the squeeze on representation explanations and contributes to our knowledge of how the brain processes information. My presentation will be ruthlessly synoptic, and it should be borne in mind that a proper appreciation of the significance of these examples does of course require a much more detailed discussion than I can hope to provide here.

Aplysia Californica is a humble sea slug with an approachable nervous system of about ten thousand neurons. This number is, relatively speaking, a mere thimbleful, and this fact, in conjunction with the relative accessibility of its nervous system and a plentiful supply of specimens, makes *Aplysia* a highly prized preparation. Indeed, *Aplysia* may be for neuroscience what *Drosophila* was for genetics. The strategy with *Aplysia* has been to try to get the full story on its entire neuronal organization, and thus to have, in at least one simple case, a complete account of what information its nervous system is sensitive to, how that information is filtered and transmitted, what information it stores and exactly how it stores it, how its behavioral repertoire is produced and exactly what changes are responsible for such behavioral modification as it displays. Naturally it is to be expected that there will be differences between vertebrates and invertebrates, but certainly there are similarities, some of which are well known (e.g., the formation of connections in the visual system). By exploiting the similarities, the job in the complex case can be made much less daunting, and thus the full story in the relatively simple case may well provide the basis from which to make gains in the complex case.

So far the strategy must be counted as having had brilliant success. The simple behaviors, such as gill-withdrawal, inking, locomotion, and egg-laying, are now largely understood in terms of the biophysical properties of identified cells and their invariant connections with each other and with effector organs.[25] This in itself is an extraordinary accomplishment; but perhaps more impressive are the results pertaining to behavioral plasticity, and on this matter I shall now focus.

Habituation is a gradual decrease in the amplitude or in the probability of a response to a repeated presentation of a particular stimulus, and is commonplace in organisms generally. It is an important component in acquiring familiarity with the environment and in learning on which stimuli not to bother expending energy. So, for example, a dog may initially be startled by the sound of gunfire, but in time loses his gun-shyness as he comes to appreciate that the stimulus is not harmful to him. As Eric Kandel explains, "the elimination of responses that fail to serve useful functions is as important as the development of new ones. . . . As a result of habituation to common, innocuous stimuli, an animal can put a large number of stimuli that do not affect its survival beyond its attention. The animal can focus on stimuli that are novel or that become associated with either satisfying or alarming consequences" (539). Ceasing to pay attention to the drone of one's air conditioner, the normal beat of one's heart, and the barking of a neighbor's dog are familiar examples of habituation in humans. In short, habituation serves to cull out responses not keyed to reward and satisfaction, and permits the expression of responses that are more

---

[25] For a very thorough and readable discussion of recent *Aplysia* research, see Eric R. Kandel, *The Cellular Basis of Behavior* (San Francisco: W. H. Freeman, 1976); parenthetical page references to Kandel are to this book.

useful. *Aplysia* too is blessed with the capacity for habituation, and the attempt to determine the nature of that capacity has been undertaken.

When *Aplysia* is squirted with a gentle spurt of sea water on its siphon skin, the gill muscle contracts and the gill is withdrawn, an obvious protective maneuver. After several repetitions of this mild and innocuous stimulus, the response habituates, and the habituation lasts for some thirty minutes (532 ff). Knowing in detail the circuitry for gill withdrawal, the investigators compiled a list of the nine possible means by which the habituation could take place, and each of the nine was systematically tested. It has now been demonstrated that the habituation was due not to fatigue of the gill muscle, not to sensory adaptation of the mechanoreceptors on the siphon skin, not to decreased sensitivity of the motor neurons, and so on. The changes that do account for habituation of the gill-withdrawal response have been traced directly to changes in the amount of excitatory neurotransmitter passed from the sensory neuron synapse to the motor neuron receptor sites (557–575). Moreover, long-term habituation, *circa* three weeks, has also been traced to synaptic depression,[26] and the neuronal story for dishabituation by a strong stimulus has also been painstakingly uncovered (Kandel, *op. cit.*, 575 ff).

The attempt to map the whole *Aplysia* is only one route among many others into the manifold mysteries of nervous systems, and it needs to be seen in the context of a broad spectrum of activities in the business of contributing answers. These activities range from research on the chemical affairs of cells, to the determination of tracts and pathways in the nervous systems of a wide array of organisms, to the localization of functions in the human brain by measuring differences in glycogen and oxygen uptake during the performance of different tasks.[27] The results from the *Aplysia* studies on habituation are exciting because, in giving us the precise locus of habituation in the nervous system of *Aplysia*, they give us a tremendous lead into a theory of simply learning. Not, indeed, a complete theory of simple learning, for there are many remaining questions. The cellular changes underlying alterations in the volume of neurotransmitter are not yet understood, and the sensory dimension of *Aplysia*'s life is on the whole less well understood

26 V. F. Castellucci, T. J. Carew, and E. R. Kandel, "Cellular Analysis of Long-term Habituation of the Gill-withdrawal Reflex of *Aplysia Californica*," *Science*, ccii, 4374 (1978): 1306–1308.

27 This work is beautiful, and I should have discussed it but for lack of space. See Niels A. Lassen, David H. Ingvar, and Eric Skinhøj, "Brain Function and Blood Flow," *Scientific American*, ccxxxix, 4 (1978): 62–71.

than the behavioral. The question of the generality of the results is pertinent, and some there are who find it positively insulting to suppose that human learning or even human habituation might have anything at all in common with habituation in a vulgar, low-born slug. Insulting or not, it may turn out to be fact, much as it turned out that the exalted and humble alike share in DNA and that what ultimately distinguishes the two are merely different articulations of the same basic structural elements. The serious generality question is this: Is there reason to think that the story on gill-withdrawal habituation in *Aplysia* applies elsewhere? There is evidence, though less conclusive than for *Aplysia*, that the same style of underlying neuronal change is to be found in crayfish (Kandel, 649), and preliminary analysis of cellular changes in vertebrates (cats and frogs), though not yet conclusive, points to the same sort of mechanism (600). It is still too early to say very much here, because the habituation analysis in *Aplysia* is very recent. What should be underscored is how important the knowledge of the simple case is in approaching more complex systems: if there is more to vertebrate habituation, it may now be possible to track down what that more is; if there are differences, having one theory in hand will the better allow us to converge upon those differences; if habituation does figure in more complex learning, knowing the neuronal story for habituation will be invaluable.

In "Why Not the Whole Iguana?," [28] Dennett wistfully hankers after a complete model of a simple organism, but decides that, since what a cognitivist wants anyhow are the abstract, functional principles of information processing, it would be preferable to ignore on-the-hoof information processors, and instead create a whole cognitive beast, guided in one's manufacture by top-down theory:

> . . . one does not want to get bogged down with technical problems in modeling cognitive eccentricities of turtles if the point of the exercise is to uncover *very* general, *very* abstract principles that will apply as well to the cognitive organization of the most sophisticated human beings. So why not then *make up* a whole cognitive creature, a Martian three-wheeled iguana, and an environmental niche for it to cope with? I think such a project *could* teach us a great deal about the deep principles of human cognitive psychology, but if it could not, I am quite sure that most of the current A.I. modeling of familiar human mini-tasks could not either (103/4).

I am less troubled by the suggestion that such construction might teach us something than I am with the corresponding presumption

[28] *The Behavioral and Brain Sciences*, I, 1 (1978): 103–104.

that the neuronal story of a simple organism will *not* teach us anything much. As Paul Churchland has argued,[29] this is analogous to supposing it is preferable to determine the nature of life by forsaking the investigation of the microstructure of actual living things and favoring exclusively the construction of functional models satisfying common-sense constraints about what living things do. This program for biology might conceivably have been useful, and who knows, Dennett's suggested program might possibly be useful. But to deny that the complete neuronal story of an organism will be useful is to deprive oneself to no purpose. True, humans do not exhibit gill-withdrawal, for want to gills to withdraw. However, habituation we certainly do exhibit, of complex behavior as well as of spinal reflexes. Dennett's desire for a complete story in at least one case is widely shared by neuroscientists, though they favor study of actual information processors, and *Aplysia* seems to be the front runner. Undoubtedly, *Aplysia* habituation, *Aplysia* information storage, *Aplysia* information transfer, etc., will inform the investigation of fancier nervous systems.

My second example is drawn from vertebrate research, and is chosen to illustrate the kind of progress that is being made on a problem which, *a priori*, might have seemed too "cognitive" or too high-level to be tackled by neuroscience. In a recent paper, Vernon Mountcastle [30] is concerned to investigate the brain mechanisms for directed attention, and, since the results of lesion studies clearly implicate structures in the parietal lobe, Mountcastle *et al.* set out to see what the neurons of the parietal cortex do when the animal is visually attending to an object of interest. The major behavioral elements in visual attention are saccadic movement, fixation, and visual tracking. The investigators implanted recording electrodes in the parietal cortex of monkeys, and found a rather remarkable neuronal organization. The results of the recordings revealed quite distinct functional units of neurons: (1) light-sensitive neurons, (2) saccade neurons, (3) visual-fixation neurons, and (4) visual-tracking neurons (active during and only during tracking, inhibited during saccades). Moreover, given the data, the orchestration of activity in these neurons appears to be this:

(1) activation of the light-sensitive cells by the appearance of an eccentrically placed target, with a latency of about 80 milliseconds.

[29] Paul M. Churchland, "Is *Thinker* a Natural Kind?," mimeo.
[30] "Brain Mechanisms for Directed Attention," *Journal of the Royal Society of Medicine*, LXXI (1978): 14–28.

(2) conditional discharge of the saccade neurons which follows the onset of activity in the light-sensitive neurons by about 50 msec.

Mountcastle suggests that:

> . . . during that 50 msec. a matching function is executed between the neural signals of the nature of the visual target and those of the internal needs of the organism. I cannot specify this mechanism, but recall the heavy reciprocal connections between the parietal association cortex and the limbic lobe (24).

(3) Provided that the saccade cells discharge, the tracking begins after a delay of 73 msec.

> Once the saccadic movements foveate the visual target, the powerful fixation mechanism comes into play, with its tracking appendage. These commands drive a tenacious visual grasp of objects of interest—the essence of selective or directed visual attention. The activity of fixation/tracking neurons is broken only by the suppression which precedes a subsequent saccadic movement to a new target (24).

Since it is well known that brain-stem structures have a role in eye movement and position, Mountcastle then proceeds to relate the function of the brain-stem oculomotor mechanism to that of the parietal cortex, aided by additional anatomical information about the projections of the parietal lobe neurons to brain-stem oculomotor neurons. His hypotheses concerning command function with respect to visually directed attention are worth quoting;

> The development in primates of a foveal vision with great resolving powers is accompanied by that of an elegant brain-stem apparatus for controlling oculomotor operations. It is my hypothesis that there has developed congruently in the parietal lobe and its distant connections a neural apparatus for the integration and governance of these events. This command source is itself sentient to a continually updated image of the position of the body, head, and eyes relative to the immediate surround and the gravitational field; it is linked to neural signals of the internal drive state of the organism; and from time to time generates commands for the fixation of gaze upon objects of interest—the first step in directed visual attention. I emphasize the general nature of this idea, for there must exist in the brain many sources of command for the direction of gaze (26).

Having plucked for display several pieces of research from the massive mosaic of which they are a part, I can hardly expect immediate and hearty concurrence in my view that they are exemplary of a useful way to proceed. Nevertheless, I do believe the results to be sufficiently striking to give the principled skeptic pause. I suppose reasons might be found for looking askance at these sorts of study, but I do not see how it can be seriously argued that such study is not likely to be useful in revealing the mysteries of mind-brain operation.

With these remarks I shall put aside for a moment my case against the principled skeptic, and I turn my efforts to the task of nudging the boggled skeptic who, recall, doubts that much of significance will be revealed by bottom-up research in the foreseeable future. Something should of course be conceded the boggled skeptic, for indeed the number, size, interconnectedness, and plasticity of neurons in the human nervous system means that neurological research *is* very difficult. Additionally, for many questions concerning the nature and function of normal human living brains, we cannot, for ethical reasons, study normal human living brains. What must be conceded to the skeptic is, however, a good deal shy of blank despair. Progress in the neurosciences, especially since the fifties, has been nothing short of awesome, partly because technological progress has made possible certain kinds of probing hitherto undreamt of. The electron microscope, micropipettes, microelectrodes, freeze-fracturing techniques, radioimmunoassay, the isolation of such substances as acetylcholine and dopamine (to give a handful of examples), have been of the utmost importance to the nascent science. I do not suppose any sober neuroscientist wants to claim that the teeming mysteries of the brain are about to disclose themselves or that the full story of how the human brain works is close at hand. The progress to date in neuroscience does not warrant that kind of unbridled enthusiasm. Yet, on the other hand, the progress demonstrably is sufficiently impressive to make outright skepticism equally inappropriate. A particularly striking example of the fruitfulness of bottom-up research concerns work done on the cortex of the cerebellum, and I shall provide a short discussion of this work in hopes of winning the skeptic over to a position of cautious optimism. Because my discussion of the structure of the cerebellum is all too brief, I refer the reader to the brilliant and eminently readable paper, "The Cortex of the Cerebellum" by Rodolfo Llinas.[31]

The cerebellum is the deeply wrinkled lump tucked under the end of the cerebrum, which consists of immense numbers of neurons and whose size is progressively larger the higher the brain on

[31] In *Scientific American*, CCXXXII, 1 (1975): 56–71.

the phylogenetic scale. A good deal is known about the sort of behavioral deficits caused by cerebellar lesions and about the sort of information that goes into this brain structure, which permits the hypothesis that the cerebellum is a central control point for the organization and orchestration of movement. It is to the neural structure of the cerebellar cortex that we must look in order to determine more exactly what the cerebellum does and *how* it does what it does.

The cerebellar cortex is a splendidly organized part of the brain. To begin with, there are just seven types of neurons, and their respective positions, interconnections, and electrical properties are known in great detail. For example, the Purkinje cell is the sole output cell; its output is inhibitory; it is always oriented in a particular manner; it is associated with precisely one climbing fiber; a fine row of dendrites of a set of Purkinje cells receives input from parallel fibers, etc. The neurons of the cerebellar cortex are arranged in a highly orderly and regular fashion which has been well documented, and, accordingly, *it has been possible to hypothesize a wiring diagram describing in a general way the function of the cerebellar cortex, based on the detailed information concerning the structure of its components.*[32]

That neuroscience has come so far in understanding this part of the brain is obviously enormously exciting, and recently Llinas *et al.* have gone much further in an attempt to characterize the details of the processing in the cerebellar cortex and to determine second-order concepts that will describe network properties.[32] They have "grown" a frog cerebellar cortex in a computer, based on functional and morphological facts about cortical neurons. The computer model consists of 8285 Purkinje cells, 1.68 million granule cells and 16,820 mossy fibers. The simulation is a remarkable tool because it makes the information concerning precisely what happens to input in the cerebellar cortex infinitely more accessible, and of course it renders manageable the "unmanageable numbers." By using the computer model, Llinas has made discoveries concerning network properties which had not been expected and which he subsequently confirmed in tests on actual cerebellar cortices. I emphasize these accomplishments because they are highly interesting not only for what they tell us about the cerebellum, but also for the challenge they represent to the boggled skeptic. Llinas's

---

[32] A. Pellionisz and R. Llinas, "A Computer Model of Cerebellar Purkinje Cells," *Neuroscience*, II, 1 (1977): 37–48; and A. Pellionisz, R. Llinas, and D. H. Perkel, "A Computer Model of the Cerebellar Cortex of the Frog," *ibid.*: 19–36.

work is an example of the sort of means by which function can be winnowed out of facts concerning appallingly complex structure.

These remarks should be addressed to the principled skeptic as well, and a more recent paper by Pellionisz and Llinas [33] illustrates the manner in which a knowledge of the micro-architecture of the neuropil can suggest general, mathematical models to characterize the functions being discharged. For example, citing the connection in parallel of small groups of Purkinje cells in the cerebellar cortex, cells whose output (firing frequencies) converge upon a nuclear neuron, Pellionisz and Llinas give a most convincing reconstruction of the activity of such a battery in terms of the approximation of some specific function with a Taylor series. Given their common input, the output firing frequencies of the respective Purkinje cells correspond to the values of the first several elements in a Taylor series, and their summation at the nuclear neuron provides the relevant functional approximation.

Turning to more extensive neural networks, and inspired by the patently vectorial nature (specific firing frequencies along specific weighted paths) of their manifold input and output, Pellionisz and Llinas propose tensor analysis as the relevant mode of representation. The brain, they affirm, is a tensorial entity, and as such is subject to universal tensorial laws. Aside from its explanatory power with regard to coordination of behavior, the authors point out that on this hypothesis:

> ... the genetic code would provide "only" the ontogenetic guidelines for building a tensor in a general sense, leaving the particular selection of the frame of reference and the establishment of the corresponding numerical values of connections to the individual epigenetic development, i.e. determined by "local" thermodynamic processes. As a result, by encoding reference-invariant tensors, not particular matrices, genetic specification is relieved from the awesome task of determining each and every neural connection in the brain (330).

It is not possible to evaluate these claims properly here, though it can be conjectured that the work may constitute a major breakthrough in the attempt to describe neuro-functional concepts.[34] The point I wish to make is that it should be plain, even to the most principled of skeptics, that the search for adequate *func-*

---

[33] "Brain Modeling by Tensor Network Theory and Computer Simulation. The Cerebellum: Distributed Processor for Predictive Coordination," *Neuroscience*, IV (1979): 323–348.

[34] See the comments by Theodore Melnechuck, "Network Notes," *Trends in Neuroscience*, II, 4 (April 1979): 6–8.

tional characterizations can proceed very profitably indeed from a bottom-up direction. And surely it is better to be guided here by the empirical *facts* about brain activity, as discovered by neuroscience, than to be guided by the ancient and ramshackle *theory* of cognitive activity embedded in the intentional idiom of common sense.

I shall conclude with two observations. First, it will be obvious from the diversity of techniques, problems, and subject matter in the examples that "bottom-up" does not distinguish a unique approach and that what constitutes the "bottom" is loosely delimited. For purists, the real bottom will of course belong not to neuroscience but to physics. It is only by contrast with the top-down character of cognitive psychology and conceptual analysis that the neuroscientific approaches are called "bottom-up," and these approaches are more accurately called "quaquaversal," to reflect the variety of routes into the problem of how nervous systems do what they do.

Secondly, what finally motivates my thesis is the insight, owed to Quine, Sellars, and others, that our conception of ourselves is, after all, *concept-mediated*, and, insofar, it is questionable whether those concepts permit us an adequate understanding of the facts. Once the question is asked, and once it is seen that common-sense psychology must be evaluated as a theory, not taken for granted because it is "dead obvious," the certitude of the exclusively top-down approach pales. I think this is on the whole a most salutory thing, for common sense may have no better a line on mind-brain function than it did on the nature of motion or heat. What we are and how our mind-brains work remains to be discovered, and those discoveries may depend on our willingness to see ourselves in the light of evolutionary dynamics and nervous-system kinematics; in short, to see ourselves as part of the natural order. In the words of Aldous Huxley,[35] psychology has no more right to be anthropomorphic than any other science.

PATRICIA SMITH CHURCHLAND

University of Manitoba

---

[35] *Eyeless in Gaza* (New York: Penguin, 1936), p. 19.

The Expression of Emotion in Music

S. DAVIES

In this paper I will attempt to analyse the expression of emotion in music. The field of interest is restricted in two ways. First by distinguishing between the expression of emotion *in* music and the expression of emotion *through* music. Here we are concerned only with the former; that is, with the emotions that music may be said to express in itself and not with the emotions that may be given expression through the act of composition, or through the performance of music, or through a dramatic context in which music plays a part. This distinction suggests a second restriction, this time on the type of music to be discussed. If there is a problem in claiming that emotions may be expressed in music then it is one which will be at its most obvious and acute in 'pure' music which is unencumbered by drama or words which may be expressive in themselves. For this reason opera, ballet, song, music with literary titles such as *La Mer*, and so on are specifically excluded from the discussion.

The difficulty in claiming that emotions may be expressed in music consists in this: In the non-musical paradigmatic cases something that *is* sad *feels* sad. Since no-one who says that a particular musical work is sad believes (or knowingly imagines) that the music feels sad, how is it possible to claim that music is sad and, at the same time, maintain that the word 'sad' retains here a use which preserves its meaning? Clearly we cannot say, as in the views that purely musical emotions are expressed in music or that disembodied mental states are expressed in music, that in their application to musical works emotion words have a uniquely aesthetic secondary use. For then we would be unable to explain why it is that, say, musical sadness interests and moves us as it does. What is interesting about 'sadness' that is divorced from and in no way reflects upon the world of felt-emotions? Why does musical expressiveness compel from us emotional responses if that expressiveness is not related to the expression of human emotions? If the expression of emotion in music is seen as one of music's most important features then it can only be because we recognise a connection between the emotions expressed in music and in life, because musical expressiveness reflects and reflects upon the world of emotions. These considerations demand that, in its application to music, emotion words retain the meaning that they have in their primary use. One way we could demonstrate this is by showing that (a) there is a secondary use of emotion words in the description of human behaviour and that (b) the use of emotion words in descriptions of music is significantly analogous to their use in (a). Thus we could demonstrate that, although the use of emotion terms in describing music is secondary, it is a use which also finds application in the description of human behaviour, and, via the parasitic connection between (a) and the primary use of emotion terms, we could establish a connection between the emotions expressed in music and the emotions felt by sentient beings. This then is the route by which we hope to analyse the nature of musical expressiveness.

The emotions expressed in music differ from the emotions felt by people in that they are unfelt, necessarily publicly displayed and lack emotional-objects. Do emotion terms have a secondary use in descriptions of human behaviour in which they refer to 'emotions' that are similarly unfelt, necessarily publicly displayed and lacking in emotional-objects? As the following case indicates, the answer is yes. We frequently describe the character of a person's appearance or bearing by the use of emotion terms. We say 'He is a sad-looking person' or 'He makes a sad figure'. In such cases we do *not* mean that he now *feels* sad or even that he often feels sad; we are referring not to any emotion, in fact, but to the look of him, to what I will call 'emotion-characteristics in appearances'. Because this use of emotion terms involves reference to appearances and not to feelings, the sadness of a person's look cannot not be displayed, nor does it take an emotional-object as his feeling of sadness normally does. Although we may sometimes be justified in over-ruling first-person reports of felt-emotions we are obliged to take such reports seriously and, in some cases, as definitive. We are under no such obligation when a person reports on the emotion-characteristic worn by his appearance. He is as liable to be mistaken about that as is anyone else (if not more so). The emotion-characteristics in a person's appearance are given solely in his behaviour, bearing, facial expression and so forth. And, as a person's felt-emotion need not be expressed, it can be privately experienced in a way in which the emotion-characteristics in appearances can never be. A person who changes or suppresses the behaviour which made him a sad-looking figure ceases to be sad-looking. Emotion-characteristics in appearances do not take objects in the way that felt-emotions do; to say that someone makes a sad figure is not to say that he has something to be sad about or about which he feels sad. The emotion-characteristics in a person's appearance may be socially appropriate or inappropriate to a context, but they are not appropriate or inappropriate to an object.

Of course it will sometimes be the case that a sad-looking person looks sad because he feels sad or because he is a person who is prone to feel sad. The point that I wish to make here is that there is a legitimate and common use of the word 'sad' in such sentences as 'He is a sad-looking person' where we do not imply that the person feels sad or is prone to feel sad and, therefore, we are not referring to the person's felt-sadness or proneness to feel sad. In this no-reference-to-feeling use we refer solely to the person's look. That is, emotion words can be used, are regularly used, and can be understood by others as being used without even implicit reference to the occurrence of feelings. Despite the fact that such sentences as 'He is a sad-looking person' may also be used implicitly to refer to the person's feelings, I wish to distinguish the no-reference-to-feeling use as a distinct use. In this latter use emotion words refer solely to what I have called emotion-characteristics in appearances. The distinction invoked does not depend upon a difference between verbal forms; for example, between 'He looks sad' and 'He is a sad-looking person'. The distinction drawn points to a difference in use and the same verbal form may lend itself to both the uses that we wish to distinguish. Where 'He is a sad-looking person' involves implicit reference to that person's feelings it does not point to an emotion-characteristic in his appearance as we have now restricted that term's use.

The distinction that we have made above and our consequent restrictions upon the use of the term 'emotion-characteristics in appearances' are not arbitrarily imposed. This distinction is apparent in and gains its force from the ways in which expressions of emotions and emotion-characteristics are discussed in everyday language. If when a person looks sad he feels sad, then his look expresses or betrays his felt-emotion. By contrast, an emotion-characteristic in appearance is 'worn' by, say, a face; it is not expressed by the face, nor does it express a feeling. When we use emotion words in describing people it is normally clear from the context, whatever verbal forms that we employ, whether we are referring to their feelings or merely to the look of them. If this is not clear we can sensibly ask for clarification. The need for this distinction is obvious. A person need not look the way that he feels and therefore an interest in the way that he feels need not be an interest in the way that he looks. The criteria for sad-lookingness are given solely in appearances; it makes no difference whether the appearance is consciously adopted or worn naturally. A person who consciously adopts a sad look may attempt to deceive us into believing that he feels sad (or into thinking that he is a naturally sad-looking person) and, as a result, we may make false predictions about his future behaviour (or future deportment). By this ruse he may mislead us about his feelings, but he could not deceive us about the emotion-characteristic worn by his appearance. We may be mistaken in thinking, for example, that a person is sad-looking, but we are never mistaken about this as a result of that person's deception. A person who 'pretends' to be sad-looking cuts as sad a figure as someone who is naturally sad-looking. Strictly speaking a person cannot *pretend* to be sad-looking or be *sincere* in being sad-looking except in respect of what he actually feels. Many of the notions—sincerity, pretence, the non-expression of felt-emotions—on which our ordinary discussions of emotions centre rely upon the distinction we have formalised above in our definition of an emotion-characteristic in appearance.

The use of emotion words in attributing emotion-characteristics to appearances is secondary and parasitic upon the use of such terms in referring to felt-emotions. It is not difficult to see how the meaning of emotion words has been extended to this secondary use. The behaviour which gives one's appearance its emotion-characteristic is the same as the behaviour which gives 'natural' expression to the corresponding felt-emotion. To be a sad-looking person is to look as if one is feeling sad. Thus it is the behaviour which characteristically and naturally expresses a felt-emotion which, in other contexts, gives rise to the corresponding emotion-characteristic in an appearance. It is because of this that emotion words retain the same meaning although they have a non-primary use in referring to the emotion-characteristics in appearances.

There are three points which emerge from the relationship

between the behaviour that gives rise to emotion-characteristics in appearances and the behaviour which betrays or expresses the corresponding felt-emotions. These points are:

(1) Some behaviour which could give expression to a felt-emotion could not also give rise to the corresponding emotion-characteristic. Much behaviour which can be seen as expressive is seen as expressive because it serves to identify the emotional-object of a person's emotion or the desires that he entertains towards that object. In other contexts this same behaviour would not be seen as expressive of any emotion. It is only what we have called naturally expressive behaviour, that is behaviour which can be seen as expressive without further knowledge of emotional-objects or without evincing emotion-appropriate desires, which can give rise to emotion-characteristics in appearances. This is important because many emotional states lack characteristic modes of behavioural expression. It might be possible to distinguish between emotions 'proper' (sadness, joy, etc.) and what are generally called feelings (embarrassment, hope, acceptance, despair, puzzlement, annoyance, amusement, nervousness, etc.) by the fact that some of the behavioural expressions of the former can usually be seen as expressive of emotion although we lack a knowledge of the emotion's emotional object, cause and context, whereas the behavioural expressions of the latter are not self-evidently expressive to those who lack such knowledge. The range of possible emotion-characteristics in appearances corresponds with only one class of possible emotional states. There are no emotion-characteristics in appearances which correspond to felt-hope, felt-despair, felt-acceptance, and so on. To say that a person is 'hopeful-looking' is to indicate either that we believe that he feels hopeful, or that we believe that he is a person who tends to feel hopeful, or that we are entertaining without belief the thought that he feels hopeful. To say that a person is 'hopeful-looking' is not to attribute to his appearance an emotion-characteristic as something which pays no regard to how he feels, for the hopefulness is only apparent in his look when we believe that he feels or is inclined to feel hope or where we entertain without belief the thought that he feels hope.

(2) Not all the behaviour which might naturally express a felt-emotion is equally as likely to occur in the corresponding emotion-characteristic in appearance. A person who continually weeps (without cause and without feeling sad) is sad-looking, but

usually sad-looking people continually frown, say, rather than continually weep. The features of behaviour which is naturally expressive of felt-emotions which are most likely to occur in the behaviour which gives rise to the appearance of the corresponding emotion-characteristic are, one suspects, those features which a face, gait or deportment might fall into without intentional pretence or genuine feeling. Whilst a person may consciously attempt to adopt an appearance displaying a particular emotion-characteristic, by no means all such appearances are consciously adopted.

(3) It need not be necessary that we are able to identify uniquely a felt-emotion on the basis only of the behaviour that naturally expresses that emotion if that behaviour, in other contexts, is to give rise to an emotion-characteristic in an appearance. If several felt-emotions have the same or similar natural behavioural expressions then, in other contexts, that behaviour may give rise to the appearance of one or more of the corresponding emotion-characteristics. But of course this is not to say that just any naturally expressive behaviour can give rise to just any emotion-characteristic in appearance. We justify our perception of the emotion-characteristic in an appearance by arguing that the behaviour which gives rise to it would, in appropriate contexts, naturally express the corresponding felt-emotion. Where the naturally expressive behaviour could be expressive equally of more than one felt-emotion then we could justify equally seeing that behaviour as giving rise to the different corresponding emotion-characteristics in an appearance, but not to just any emotion-characteristic. If the natural behavioural expressions of felt-happiness and felt-joy are similar then we may be able justifiably to support the claim that someone's appearance is both joyous-looking and happy-looking, but, given that the natural behavioural expression of felt-sadness differs from that of felt-joy and felt-happiness, we could not justify the claim that the appearance was sad-looking.

The perception of an emotion-characteristic involves the recognition of an aspect of the appearance which bears the emotion-characteristic. As with other instances of aspect-perception, it is sometimes possible to see an appearance as presenting first one emotion-characteristic and then another. Because of the possibility that the same material object of perception may be seen under more than one aspect, aspect-perception differs from 'ordinary' seeing whilst remaining a perceptually-based experience. To say that someone is 'hopeful-looking' where one believes that he feels hopeful or is prone to feel hopeful is to report an 'ordinary' perceptual experience. To say that a person is 'hopeful-looking' where one entertains without belief the thought that the person feels hopeful or is prone to feel hopeful is to report an experience of aspect-perception. But this case involves what we might call 'seeing as if', whereas the perception of an emotion-characteristic in an appearance involves what we might call 'seeing as'. Amongst the differences between these modes of 'seeing' is the fact that 'seeing as' does not involve the (willing) suspension of belief whereas 'seeing as if' does. When we see a person's appearance as wearing an emotion-characteristic our beliefs about his feelings are irrelevant.

It follows from the fact that the perception of the emotion-characteristic in an appearance involves aspect-perception that the emotion-characteristic is like (without being) a simple property of the appearance in that there are no specifiable rules for its occurrence. There are no generalisable rules of the type: 'Whenever the ends of the mouth droop the person is sad-looking.' Although the behaviour that gives rise to an emotion-characteristic in an appearance is necessarily similar to the behaviour which naturally expresses the corresponding felt-emotion, and although we might draw attention to analogies between the two in aiding another to perceive the emotion-characteristic worn by the appearance, the perception of the emotion-characteristic does not depend upon the noticing of analogies. No amount of analogical evidence will entail that another who accepts the 'evidence' will perceive the appearance as wearing the emotion-characteristic.

Let us now consider whether there are any important respects in which music is like human behaviour. Our concern is not to show that music may imitate or represent human behaviour but, rather, to demonstrate that music is experienced as having features displayed in human behaviour, especially the features of behaviour which give rise to the emotion-characteristics in appearances.

We can begin by pointing out that music, like behaviour, is dynamic. It is a straightforward fact about hearing that two notes an octave apart are heard as the same and that notes are heard as relatively high or low. The relative highness and lowness of

notes provides a dimension in aural 'space' within which music
may move through time; that is, we hear movement between
notes. Furthermore, like the behaviour that gives rise to emotion-
characteristics in appearances, musical movement is non-teleo-
logical. (Whilst notes may move, say, towards a tonic, the notion
of a 'tonic' must be defined in terms of the course of musical
movement.) In this respect both are unlike the behaviour which
expresses a felt-emotion which, because most such emotions take
emotional-objects, is frequently teleological.

But the similarity noted above between musical movement and
the behaviour that gives rise to emotion-characteristics in appearances is hardly striking enough to establish our case. Much more
important is the need to show that music displays the kind of
intentionality upon which the expressiveness of human action
depends. As the product of human actions, music does display
intentionality, but this does not yet substantiate the sort of claim
that we wish to make, for the movements of a machine exhibit
intentionality in this sense without being regarded as like human
behaviour in such a way as to be intrinsically expressive. The
important difference between the movements of the machine and
human behaviour consists in this: to explain the movements of
the machine we refer to its creator's intentions and to causal
mechanisms. To describe the causal mechanisms is to show how
the machine's movements are determined and therefore to explain
fully those movements. This is all the explanation consists of;
nothing else is needed. But this is not the case when we explain
why a person behaves as he does; here a further dimension is
apparently required. By referring to a person's motives, desires,
feelings and intentions we can give the causes of his behaviour
but, at the same time, we recognise that these causes do not
determine his behaviour in the way that causal mechanisms determine the machine's movements. His behaviour could have been
other than it was and, what is more, it could have been other than
it was and yet still be explained by the same motives, feelings, etc.
In this way human behaviour goes beyond the reasons which
explain it in a way that mere movement does not (which is not to
say that explanations of human behaviour are in some sense
incomplete). Explanations of human behaviour do not stop short
at the specification of causal mechanisms and entertained intentions. The difference between human behaviour and mere
movement is reflected in the terms in which they are discussed.

A machine may move jerkily, quickly and so forth, but it cannot move with hesitation, vivacity, abandonment; it cannot hurry. 'Hesitation' connotes behaviour and not mere movement.

Returning to the case of music, it is possible to argue that music displays the type of intentionality which is characteristic of human behaviour. Unlike an explanation of the movements of a machine, an explanation of the movement of music is incomplete if it refers merely to causal mechanisms and the composer's intentions. Much more to the point in such an explanation is an account of the reasons why the musical movement takes the course that it does. We say, for example, 'This section develops the preceding motive and foreshadows the melody which follows.' The reasons for the musical movement are to be sought in the music itself; if the music makes 'sense' then its sense is given in the course of the music and an appreciation of the composer's intentions is not yet an appreciation of the musical sense. We recognise that the course of the music may have been other than it is; the possibility of alternative courses comes with the notes themselves. No causal mechanism determines the outcome. As in explanations of human behaviour, we recognise that the reasons that we give in explaining why the music takes the course that it does could count equally well in explaining other courses which the music might have taken. The movement of music is not governed by natural laws. At any moment a musical work could pursue a number of different courses each of which would be consistent with and explained by the music which preceded that moment. Like the intentionality of human behaviour and unlike the intentionality displayed by the movements of a machine, the intentionality of musical movement does not derive directly from the fact that the music is the product of its creator's intentions. The analogy between musical movement and human behaviour goes much deeper than the analogy between human behaviour and the movements of a machine. It is noteworthy that the adjectives listed above as connoting behaviour rather than mere movement find ready application to music.

Our claim is that, because musical movement can be heard as making sense and because that sense is not determined solely by the composer's intentions, musical movement is sufficiently like the human behaviour which gives rise to emotion-characteristics in appearances that musical movement may give rise to emotion-characteristics in sound. Of course, musical movement can only

be like human behaviour which is indifferent to sentience in the
way in which the human behaviour which gives rise to emotion-
characteristics in appearances is indifferent to sentience. 'That is
a sad-looking face', where it involves no implicit reference to
feelings, is not reducible to a statement about the way that any
particular person will look if he is sad-feeling and shows it, nor
does it contain an implicit reference to an intention to wear any
particular facial expression even where the expression was
consciously adopted. Our point is this: Anything that can wear
an expression or have a gait, carriage or bearing in the way in
which a person's behaviour may exhibit these things can present
the aspect of an emotion-characteristic in its appearance. Few
non-sentient things will be able to meet these requirements, but,
amongst these few, music will find a place.

Now we can look more closely at the 'mechanics' of the process
by which music comes to wear emotion-characteristics. As we
have already indicated, our appreciation of music's dynamic
nature is essential to our appreciation of the analogy between our
experiences of music and human behaviour. This is apparent
when we consider how we would attempt to get another to
experience the sadness, say, that we hear in a musical work. At
first we might describe the music as dragging and forlorn. If he
could not hear the music in this way we would describe the
dynamic character of the music in a way which would encourage
him to hear the musical movement as dragging and forlorn. For
example, we would draw his attention to the slow tempo, the
faltering and hesitant rhythms, the irregular accents on unexpected discords, the modulations to 'distant' keys, the dense
texture, and so forth. That is, one would encourage him to
experience the musical movement as analogous to (which is not to
say imitative of) movements which, as part of a person's behaviour,
would lead us to describe that behaviour as dragging and forlorn.
Having led him to experience the music in this way one would
expect him to hear the sadness in the music, just as a person,
seeing the appearance of human behaviour as dragging and
forlorn, would see that behaviour as wearing the sadness-char-
acteristic in its appearance. Of course no amount of such evidence
entails that the person we are trying to convince will be able to
hear the music as dragging and forlorn, or to hear the sadness in
the music. He may be able to hear all the musical features to
which we draw his attention without being able to hear the

sadness in the music. To that extent the analogy between human behaviour and musical movement is irreducible. But to acknowledge this irreducibility is not to accept that it is impossible to help another to experience the sadness in the music by pointing out to him musical features. To say that the only evidence available cannot entail that the other hears the sadness when he accepts the evidence is not to say that we have no evidence at all and that argument and discussion are therefore irrelevant. The relevance if not the conclusiveness of the evidence is apparent from the following example. Would it be possible to argue that the brisk tempo, driving rhythm, open texture, bright scoring, etc. in the overture to Mozart's *Marriage of Figaro* was evidence that the overture was expressive of sadness? Would this not be like claiming that movements which, as behaviour, would be described as vivacious and energetic could betray felt-sadness? Even if our hearing of the musical features of slowness etc. in a musical work does not entail that we will also hear sadness in that work, these features may be relevant to our experience of the music's sadness. They could not be used to support the mistaken claim that the music expresses happiness in the way in which they may be used to support the claim that the music expresses sadness. The fact that the analogy between musical movement and human behaviour is ultimately irreducible does not preclude the possibility of drawing out the analogy in an instructive way and thereby helping others to experience expressiveness of which they were previously unaware in music. When there is disagreement about the expressiveness of a musical work the debate centres on the applicability of the descriptions offered of the musical movement, not on the appropriateness of describing musical movement in terms more relevant to the description of human behaviour than to the description of mere mechanical movement.

If the theory that in hearing the emotions expressed in music we are hearing emotion-characteristics in sounds in much the way that we see emotion-characteristics in appearances is correct, then we might expect that the limited range of emotion-characteristics that can be worn by appearances corresponds with the limited range of emotions that may be expressed in music (by contrast with the wider range of emotions that can be expressed through music). Indeed, I do wish to make this claim, but because this correspondence is undemonstrable the claim will remain a controversial one. Not all the emotions which music may be said 'to express' (which can be expressed through music) can also be said 'to be' in music (can be expressed in music). Music can be said to express (someone's) sadness and can also be said to 'be sad'; sadness may be expressed both through and in music. But whilst music can be said to express hope it cannot be said to 'be hopeful'; hope can be expressed through but not in music. To say that hope is expressed in music is to refer implicitly to someone's felt-hope expressed through the music. The acceptability of the above claim depends upon our providing an independent line of proof of the theory's correctness. For the moment we will assume the truth of the theory and consider how it might accommodate possible exceptions to the claim made above. In the case of some musical works, if not in many, we may reasonably wish to say that hope is expressed in rather than through the music. How are such exceptions to be treated?

It is arguable that, *as feelings,* emotions have natural progressions; for example, from slightly hysterical gaiety to fearful apprehension, to shock, to horror, to gathering resolution, to confrontation with sorrow, to acceptance, to resignation, to serenity. Such progressions might be used by the composer to articulate in his music emotions other than those which can be worn by appearances without regard to feelings. Thus, by judiciously ordering the emotion-characteristics presented in an extended musical work the composer can express in his music those emotional states which are not susceptible to presentation in mere appearances. These emotional states belong naturally within the progression of emotions whose characteristic appearances are given in the music. In this way hope, for example, may be expressed in music, although hope cannot be presented as the emotion-characteristic in an appearance. Thus the range of emotions which can be expressed in music, that music can be said 'to be', goes beyond the range of emotion-characteristics that can be worn by appearances. Nevertheless, the expression of such emotional states as hope in a musical work depends directly upon and is controlled by the emotion-characteristics in sound presented in the musical work. Before hope can be expressed in a musical work that work must have sufficient length and expressive complexity to permit the emotions presented in its 'appearance' to form a progression in which hope occurs naturally. The close relationship between the emotion-characteristics that can be worn by appearances and the emotions that music can be said 'to be' remains essentially unbroken by the counter-example we have been considering. We would allow, I think, that saying a musical work 'is hopeful', or 'is accepting' or 'is longing-ful' etc. is unusual in a way that saying a musical work 'is sad' is not.

What evidence is there to support the theory that the emotions heard in music are presented to the listener as emotion-characteristics in the 'appearance' or sound of the music? The most striking confirmation of the theory is provided by a consideration of the listener's emotional response to the expressiveness that he hears in a musical work. Not only is there a close parallel between that response, where it is an aesthetic one, and a person's emotional response to the emotion-characteristic that he perceives in another's appearance, but also we can argue that the nature of the listener's response as an *aesthetic* response can be accounted for only as a response to an emotion-characteristic he hears presented in the music. That is, we can only understand the listener's emotional response as an aesthetic response, as a response to the musical work which may be justified by reference to features of the music, when we regard it as a response to an emotion-characteristic presented in the sound of the music. In the remainder of this paper we will pursue this line of the argument.

How do we respond to the emotion-characteristics displayed in human appearances? We can begin by noting that, in so far as an emotion-characteristic observed by B in the appearance of A may be believed (or knowingly imagined) by B to instantiate—if we may borrow Kenny's term—the formal object of some emotion, then it will be possible for B to respond to the emotion-characteristic seen in A's appearance by feeling the appropriate emotion. Thus, for example, B may be annoyed by happy-looking A because B does not think that anyone should be happy-looking, whether he feels it or not, at a funeral. Such emotional responses, in which the emotion-characteristic in appearance supplies the emotional-object of the emotion felt are quite unproblematic and, from our point of view, uninteresting. However, other emotional responses to the emotion-character-istics in appearances are possible. That is, surprisingly, when we have covered all the emotional responses for which the emotion-characteristic in an appearance supplies the emotional-objects of the emotions felt we have not yet exhausted all the emotional responses which can be made *appropriately* to the emotion-characteristic in an appearance. There are several points to be made about these other responses, which take the emotion-characteristic in the appearance as their perceptual-object but not as their emotional-object. They are typical of the responses to emotion-characteristics in appearances. They are typical in the sense that emotional responses of this form are characteristic of responses to emotion-characteristics in appearances where they are not characteristic of responses to the felt-emotions of others. Thus it might be an identifying feature of emotion-characteristics in appearances that they invite emotional responses of this form.

The form of these 'typical' emotional responses to emotion-characteristics in appearances is as follows: Provided that there are no intervening factors, when one has an emotional response to an emotion-characteristic in an appearance one will tend to respond by feeling the emotion that is worn by the appearance. The 'intervening features' are just those things which, if believed or knowingly imagined, would make the emotion-characteristic in an appearance the emotional-object of one's emotional response. If one responds to an emotion-characteristic in an appearance without taking that appearance (or any other thing) as the emotional-object of one's response, then the felt-emotion with which one responds will mirror the emotion-characteristic displayed in the appearance. In support of this claim we can mention that if one wished to feel happy one might attempt successfully to do so by surrounding oneself with happy-looking people. The fact that one need not believe that the happy-looking people feel happy before their appearance can have a cheering affect on one, and that no belief that they felt happy would have this affect on one if they never showed their happiness indicates that emotional responses of this kind are made to emotion-characteristics in appearances rather than to felt-emotions *per se*. The mood of a look is often contagious. Quite simply, happy-lookingness is extremely evocative of happy-feelingness.

Obviously the typical emotional response to an emotion-characteristic in an appearance takes the appearance as its perceptual-object but not as its emotional-object. The emotion-characteristic is not the emotional-object of the typical response and nor is anything else. It follows therefore that we cannot justify the typical response to an emotion-characteristic in an appearance; or, at least, not in the way that we would justify a response which has an emotional-object. To say that one believes that the object towards which one's felt-sadness is directed instantiates the formal object of sadness is to say that one has reasons for responding as one does, that one sees the object as possessing sadness-relevant features. But when one responds 'reflexively' to another's happy-look by feeling happy there are no similar reasons which justify one's feeling happy. One might argue that the other has a happy look and not a sad look, but one has no reasons of the kind that justify an emotional-object-directed-response. 'Why, when you do not believe that he feels happy, does his happy look make you feel happy?' is inappropriate in a way that 'Why, when you do not believe that he feels happy, are you annoyed by his happy look?' is not. The first question does not require an answer whereas the second does.

However, the fact that emotion-characteristics in appearances do not supply emotional-objects for the typical emotional responses that they evoke does *not* mean that just any response to an emotion-characteristic will be appropriate. Already we have suggested that the only appropriate response here is the emotion that mirrors the emotion-characteristic displayed in the appearance. One argues for the appropriateness of the response of felt-sadness to something that is sad-looking by arguing that that thing is sad-looking. To show that an appearance wears the emotion-characteristic which is mirrored in one's emotional response is to demonstrate the appropriateness of that response. The appropriateness of the mirroring emotional response to the emotion-characteristic worn by an appearance consists in the fact that no other, non-mirroring, emotional-objectless response would be accepted in the same unquestioning manner as equally fitting. Because the same appearance may be seen as wearing more than one emotion-characteristic, different emotional responses to the same appearance could be equally appropriate because more than one mirroring emotional response is possible. But an emotional response which does not mirror an emotion-characteristic that can be seen in the appearance (and which does not take an emotional-object) would be rejected as an inappropriate response.

Can we find a parallel between the listener's emotional response to the expressiveness heard in a musical work and an emotional response to an emotion-characteristic in an appearance to support the claim that music wears its expressiveness just as a person's

appearance may wear an emotion-characteristic? Apparently we
can. There is little doubt for instance, that the typical emotional
response to the emotion heard in a musical work is the feeling of
the emotion heard presented in the music. It is strange that this
is rarely remarked upon for, in this respect, responses to music
differ markedly from responses to other's felt-emotions or to the
represented content of a painting, where the emotional response
rarely mirrors the emotion being expressed or represented. The
question 'I know the music is sad but why does it make you feel
sad?', like 'Why does his happy look make you feel happy?' is
pointless. The arguments employed in justifying the aptness of a
mirroring emotional response to a musical work take the form of
showing that the music presents the emotion that our response
mirrors and not some other emotion. And lastly, although we
cannot justify our response by showing that the music's expressiveness instantiates the formal object of our feeling, it is not
the case that any other equally objectless, non-mirroring response
would 'do' as well.

An aesthetic response can be taken as an index of the responder's
understanding of the work of art to which he is responding; an
aesthetic response can be justified by reference to features of the
work of art *qua* work of art. From this it appears, paradoxically,
as if an emotional response to a musical work could never be an
aesthetic response, for such responses obviously do not take the
musical work as their emotional-object. The listener does not
believe that the musical expressiveness instantiates the formal
object of the emotion that he feels. Nor, since music is non-
representational (see R. Scruton, 'Representation in Music',
Philosophy, vol. 51 (1976), pp. 273–287) and does not therefore
provide any represented putative emotional-objects for the
listener's responding emotion, could the listener entertain without
belief thoughts about a musical work which could, at the same
time, make the work the emotional-object of his response and aim
at understanding the musical work. If emotional responses to
musical expressiveness are non-emotional-object-directed then
how could they be subject to justification and therefore aesthetic?

The theory that we are proposing solves this apparent paradox.
Although non-emotional-object-directed responses are not subject
to justification in the way in which emotional-object-directed
responses are, some such responses, namely the typical response
to an emotion-characteristic in an appearance (and to musical

expressiveness), are subject to criteria of appropriateness. This has been established in the above. Thus we can explain why an emotional response to a musical work can be both aesthetic and non-emotional-object-directed. The fact that our theory allows us to remove this counter-intuitive paradox counts very strongly in favour of the theory. Furthermore, our dissolution of the paradox cannot be robbed of its significance by the claim that emotional responses to the expressiveness heard in musical works are unique and strange in being both non-emotional-object-directed and subject to justification. By arguing that emotional responses to musical works are like emotional responses to the emotion-characteristics displayed in human appearances we have preserved the required connection between aesthetic responses to works of art and responses to 'human' situations.

In the above we have been guilty of implying that emotional responses to musical works are much simpler than they are in fact. The appropriateness of the typical, mirroring response to the expressiveness of a musical work can often be questioned, but this fact, we hope to make clear, does not undermine the points made above. Consider the following example: We have a musical work in which a prolonged sad section follows a brief, frenzied, gay section. We might rightly feel that a person who responded to this work by feeling happy and then sad displayed a lack of sensitivity and missed the significance of the first section, the function of which was to heighten the poignancy of the second section. Here we might argue that the appropriate response to the first section is not a feeling of gayness (nor need it be of sadness either) and we could provide reasons to support such a view. That is, the mirroring response may not, *in the full context of the work*, be appropriate, for the work may provide reasons for over-ruling the mirroring response. Similarly, if a section can be heard as presenting the aspects of several different emotion-character-istics, the subsequent course of the music may provide reasons why we should hear the section as presenting one rather than the other emotion-characteristic and therefore why one of the possible mirroring emotional responses is inappropriate. In the unusual case in which an emotional state such as hope is expressed in the music as a part of the natural progression of a sequence of emotions most of which are presented in the 'appearance' of the music, some thought may be required to appreciate that hope is being expressed in the music. If it is impossible to understand the music without recognising that hope is expressed in it and if, as one would expect, this recognition depends on reflection and consideration, then the mirroring response is unlikely to be an understanding one. The more sensitive, sophisticated response may, in the kinds of cases that we have described, over-rule a mirroring response which fails to take account of the full context provided by the complete musical work. The crucial point though is this: However sophisticated an aesthetic response to the expressiveness of a musical work may be, the mirroring response is ontologically prior to the more sensitive and sophisticated response and to be disregarded it must be over-ruled. And, sometimes at least, the typical, 'reflexive' response will be an understanding response. By contrast, an aesthetic response to a representational painting is necessarily sophisticated in that it must be thought-founded. There can be no ontologically prior 'reflexive' response which must be over-ruled to a representational painting; or, rather, the response to a representational painting as if it were non-representational would be itself a sophistication on the ontologically prior response to it as representational.

Further confirmation of our theory is afforded by a consideration of the way in which the listener's emotional response to a musical work is identified (by others) as an instance of, say, sadness. Another's emotions are often revealed to us by his behaviour; his behaviour may identify the emotional-object of his emotion, or it may indicate the desires that he holds towards the emotional-object, or it may betray or express the nature of his emotion. Now, if a listener to a musical work is delighted and intrigued by the ingenuity of the work's construction then his response takes the musical work as its emotional-object and may be identified in the usual way. But how can we identify his emotional response to the work's expressiveness as one of sadness, say? Music is non-representational, it represents no subject which could be the emotional-object of his emotional response and about which he could entertain the appropriate desires. Because his response has no emotional-object nor any entertained emotion-appropriate desires, the listener's response is only identifiable by the behaviour which is naturally expressive of the emotion that he feels. Sometimes, at least, he looks and acts as if he feels, say, sad, and from this behaviour we can identify the emotion that he feels. This is all very well in the case of sadness which has a characteristic mode of behavioural expression, but what of emotional states which lack such distinctive natural expressions in behaviour? How would one recognise that another's response to a musical work was a feeling of hope in the *music*? The answer is, I think, that one cannot and that, therefore, such emotional states are not felt as aesthetic responses to musical works. If a person avows he feels hope when listening to the music he must be able to supply an emotional-object for his feeling and, since no candidate for this object is given in the music, in doing so he makes obvious that his response is not an aesthetic one. He can only make his response identifiable as one of hope by indicating how the response is not a response to anything heard in the music. Again, there is an obvious contrast with responses to representational paintings. The subjects represented in paintings may be taken by the observer as emotional-objects for his response. He may knowingly entertain desires about them. The emotions that he feels or entertains may be identified by others by their emotional-objects and his entertained desires, whilst remaining obviously aesthetic responses. Thus, a wider range of aesthetic emotional responses are available to the observer of a representational painting than are available to the listener of a musical work.

The range of aesthetic emotional responses that may be made to musical works corresponds to the range of emotions that may be mirrored by emotion-characteristics in appearances. Only those emotions which may be naturally expressed in behaviour can be mirrored by emotion-characteristics in appearances, and only these same emotions can be aesthetic emotional responses to the emotions expressed in music. This agreement was predictable from our theory and its independent confirmation through a consideration of how emotional responses to the emotions expressed in music are identified therefore supports our theory. Previously we noted that the typical response to an emotion-characteristic in an appearance is a mirroring response and that the ontologically prior response to the expressiveness heard in music takes this mirroring form. The fact that no equally non-emotion-object-directed response to an emotion-characteristic in an appearance would be accepted as an appropriate response suggests that the available range of non-emotion-object-directed emotional responses to emotion-characteristics in appearances is restricted to what we have called the typical, mirroring response.

The fact that the range of aesthetic emotional responses to the emotions expressed in music is similarly restricted supports strongly our claim that the emotions expressed in music are best analysed as emotion-characteristics presented in sound.

Finally, let us consider whether our theory is able to account for the importance and value that we attach to the expressiveness heard in music. On our account music conveys to us what an emotion-characteristic 'sounds' like. To say merely that music may enrich our experience, understanding and appreciation of the emotion-characteristics in (human) appearances is to make a claim which is perhaps too feeble to justify the importance that we attach to the expressiveness of music. However, we can strengthen our claim in the following way: The emotions heard in music are powerfully evocative of emotional responses in the listener. The listener who feels a response which mirrors the emotion-characteristic presented in the music experiences an emotion which is uncluttered by the motives, desires and the need to act on his feeling which accompany the more usual occurrences of that emotion. He can reflect on his feeling of, say, sadness in a way that he could not normally do. Because his emotion is divorced from the sort of contexts in which it usually occurs he may come to a new understanding of it. The power of music lies in the way in which it works upon our feelings rather than in the way that it works upon our thoughts. Our theory quite rightly locates the value and importance that music has for us in what it makes us feel.

LEGAL MORALISM AND FREEFLOATING EVILS

BY

JOEL FEINBERG

I. Introduction

IT is always a good reason in support of penal legislation that it is necessary to prevent harm to persons other than the actor. That rather vague and innocuous statement has been called the "harm-to-others principle," or the "harm principle" for short, and as it stands (before the task of interpretation begins) it is beyond controversy. It neither claims that the need to prevent harm is a necessary condition for justified prohibitions nor a sufficient condition. Not necessary because it says nothing to exclude the possibility that there are reasons of wholly different kinds that support prohibitions; not sufficient, because for relatively trivial sorts of harm, it may not be worth the high practical costs of law enforcement to prevent them. Still the need for harm prevention *is* the sort of consideration that can lend moral legitimacy to coercive legislation, whether it succeeds in justifying it or not. Nobody denies that.

Most but by no means all writers are agreed that a second kind of reason can support the legitimacy of criminal prohibitions even when the harm principle does not apply. It is always a good reason in support of a proposed prohibition, they say, that it is necessary to prevent serious *offense* (as opposed to harm or injury) to persons other than the actor. This second statement of a class of qualified reasons has been called "the offense principle," and it can be used to support statutes against "open lewdness," "indecent exposure," solicitation, and other such offenses even when they do not directly cause or threaten harm to anyone.

Now what I shall call "liberalism" with respect to this question is the view that the harm and offense principles, duly clarified and qualified, between them exhaust the class of relevant reasons for criminal prohibitions. The liberal view denies in particular that the necessity to protect a free and informed actor from the harmful consequences of his *own* voluntary conduct is ever a good reason for restricting his liberty. That is to say that "liberalism," as I am using the term, rejects the legitimizing principle called "legal paternalism." But the liberal view also denies that the need to prevent any class of evils other than harms and offenses can ever be a good reason for criminal prohibitions. An alternative to the liberal view, then, can be put in the following very general way: "It can be morally legitimate for the state, by means of the criminal law, to prohibit certain types of action that cause neither harm nor offense to anyone, on the grounds that such actions constitute or cause evils of other kinds." This straightforward but vague denial of liberalism we can call "legal moralism in the broad sense."

More commonly "legal moralism" is defined in a narrower way that specifies the class of evils, other than harms and offenses, that can warrant preventive interference by the state, namely those "immoralities" or "sins" that are committed discreetly in private. "It can be morally legitimate," according to legal moralism in this strict and narrow sense, "to prohibit conduct on the ground that it is inherently immoral, even though it causes neither harm nor offense to the actor or to others." Harmless and inoffensive (indeed unobserved) actions that are nevertheless immoral (if there be such) would be a subclass of the wider genus of acts that produce certain "evils" other than harms and offenses. I will try to show that this wider class of impersonal or freefloating evils contains a variety of specimens other than conventional "immoralities," some of which, at least, are as theoretically interesting and important as the immoralities themselves. For that reason I shall be referring to the broader conception when I use the phrase "legal moralism" throughout this essay.

How might a liberal argue against legal moralism? Most liberals are content to put legal moralism on the defensive.[1] That is, they examine the writings of philosophers in the other camp to find out what arguments they give *for* legal moralism and then find flaws in those arguments. That of course does not prove the liberal's case, but the liberal can say that the burden of proof is on the shoulders of whoever advocates legal coercion. The notion of a "burden of proof," however, is a vague idea when employed outside rule-governed forensic contests, debates, trials, and the like. Outside of such contexts, the expression usually suggests only that there exists a set of "background considerations" that tend to support, or are reasons in favor of, or make a case for, one side or the other, not a case that is known in advance to be conclusive, but rather one that is in principle rebuttable. After a certain number of unsuccessful efforts at rebuttal we can think of the presumptive case as greatly strengthened, and even endorse it tentatively as correct until or unless it is overturned. So what we mean, probably, when we agree that the burden of proof is on him who advocates legal prohibition is that there is a standing *prima facie* case for liberty. That a given law would diminish liberty is a reason against having the law.

But maybe there is a similar, equally plausible, presumptive case *for* legal moralism. Perhaps it is even weightier than the presumptive case on the other side. That would shift the burden the other way without of course settling the matter conclusively one way or the other. (All of this is like deciding what score a "handicapped" baseball game is to have at the moment it begins as well as which team is to bat first.) What would such a case look like? Let me suggest that it would take as its general principle that it is always right, other things being equal, to prevent evils; that the need to prevent evils of any description is a good kind of reason in support of a legal prohibition. That appears at first sight to be at least as plausible a principle as that which makes the need to prevent one particular kind of evil, namely the loss of liberty, a presumptively good reason *against* legal coercion. If we then add to the legal moralist's case the proposition that there are kinds of evils that are neither harms in themselves nor the causes of harm or offense, his presumptive case is complete, and "the score of the game before it starts" is even, unless or until it can be shown that one of the conflicting presumptive cases is a great deal stronger than the other.

2. Harms and Offenses

Before looking at various purported "freefloating evils," let us briefly consider the concepts of harm and offense for the purpose of illuminating by contrast. Just what are we ruling out when we say that a given evil is neither a harm nor an offense? First of all, I should like to distinguish three concepts of harm. The first sense of "harm" is a derivative or extended one, and I mention it only to dismisss it, but its dismissal is important. I refer to the sense in which we can say that any kind of thing at all can be "harmed." By smashing windows, vandals are said to harm people's property; neglect can harm one's garden; frost does harm to crops. Quite clearly this is harm in a transferred sense; we don't feel aggrieved on behalf of the windows or the tomatoes, nor are they the objects of our sympathies. Rather our reference to their "harm" is elliptical for the harm done to those who have interests in the buildings or the crops, those who have in a manner of speaking "invested" some of their own well-being in the maintenance or development of some condition of those objects. By breaking windows, the vandals have done direct harm to the interests of the building's owner; they have harmed *windows* only in a derivative and extended sense.

The second sense of "harm" is that from which the transferred sense derives, namely harm conceived as the thwarting, setting back, or defeating of an interest. A person has an interest in something—a house, a garden, a corporation in which he owns stock, his own health, his career, the well-being of a loved one, or some kind of issue of events—when he has a *stake* in that thing, that is when he stands to gain or lose depending on the nature or condition of that thing.[2] One's interests, then, taken as a miscellaneous collection, consist of all those things in which one has a stake, whereas one's interest in the singular, one's personal interest or self-interest, consists in the harmonious advancement of all one's interests in the plural. These interests, or perhaps more accurately, the things these interests are *in*, are distinguishable components of a person's well-being: he flourishes or languishes as they flourish or languish. What promotes them is to his advantage or *in his interest*; what thwarts them is to his detriment, or *against his interest*. They can be blocked or defeated by events in impersonal nature or by plain bad luck. But they can only be "invaded" (to use the legal expression) by human beings, either by oneself acting negligently or perversely, or by others, singly or in groups and organizations. It is only when an interest is so *invaded* that its possessor is harmed in the legal sense (though obviously an earthquake or a plague can cause enormous harm in the ordinary sense). One person harms another in the present sense, then, by invading, and thereby thwarting or setting back, his interest. The test, in turn, of whether such an invasion has in fact set back an interest is *whether that interest is in a worse condition than it would otherwise have been in had the invasion not occurred at all.*

It is important to distinguish harm in the present sense from mere disappointment or frustration of desire. The relation of wants or desires to interests is too intricate a subject to be done justice here, but a few essential points can be made. A mere "passing desire," however genuine or intense, does not establish an interest. A sudden craving for an ice cream cone on a hot summer day, when plenty of cold water is available, does not itself make it true that ice cream is "in one's interest" at that time. A person is not harmed if he has to settle for the cold water.

though of course he may well be disappointed. Frustration of an immediate want sets back one's interest only when what one wants is either a means to, or a necessary condition for, the promotion of more ulterior ends in which one has an interest. These goals, to which immediate wants may or may not be linked, can themselves be arranged in an ascending order of ulteriority. At a lower level are those vitally necessary interests a person has in maintaining at least a minimal level of physical and mental health, material resources, economic assets, and political liberty, interests that are indispensably necessary to the achievement of his higher good or well-being as determined by his still more ulterior goals. In one way these "welfare interests" are the most important ones any person has and cry out for protection. When they are blocked or damaged, a person is very seriously harmed indeed, for in that case his more ultimate aspirations are defeated too; whereas setbacks to a higher goal (e.g. writing a book, or building a dream house) do not to the same degree inflict damage on the whole network of his interests. But in another way the objects of welfare interests are relatively trivial goods, necessary but grossly insufficient for a good life. They are, in Nicholas Rescher's words, the "basic requisite of a man's well-being,"[3] but by no means the whole of that well-being itself.

The desires that create our more ulterior interests are to be contrasted with the merely passing wants that are not linked to ulterior goals, and also to those instrumental wants which aim only at advancing our welfare interests. These are the desires we call ambitions or aspirations. When they are defeated we are not merely disappointed; rather in virture of our putting a stake in them, we are harmed when we lose that stake. All such investment is a risk; so to have interests at all is to be vulnerable. Ulterior interests are based on strong, stable, durable desires; these desires must be genuine wants and not mere idle wishes; they must value their objects at least partly as ends in themselves and not only as means to other things; they must be capable of promotion by one's own efforts, for they are not merely wants, but personal goals or objectives. Some of our most intense wants are not of the appropriate kind to ground interests since they are either not goals that one can pursue (e.g. wanting your college football team to win the championship) or they are not linked to ulterior interests (e.g. seeking an ice cream cone), or they are insufficiently ulterior, stable, and durable to represent any investment of a stake. When such desires are frustrated, our complex web of interests might shake but every strand holds. Our psyches are sturdy; we can take a certain amount of disappointment without our interests being affected, that is, without suffering harm.

The third sense of harm, while closely related to the second, is in fact a distinct notion that can often be at variance with it. This is a kind of normative sense of the word which it must bear in any plausible formulation of "the harm principle." To say that A has harmed B in this sense is to say much the same thing as that A has wronged B, or treated him unjustly. One person *wrongs* another when his indefensible (unjustifiable and inexcusable) conduct violates the other's right, and in all but certain very special cases such conduct will also invade the other's interest and thus be harmful in the sense already explained. Even in those exceptional cases in which a wrong is not a harm on balance to interests, it is likely to be a harm to some extent even if outbalanced by various benefits. For example, so-called "harmless trespass" on another's land violates the landowner's property rights and thereby "wrongs" him even though it does not harm the land, and even might incidentally improve it. But the law does recognize a proprietary interest in the exclusive possession and enjoyment of one's land, and for whatever it is worth, the trespass did invade *that* interest. It is "harmless" only in the sense that it doesn't harm any *other* interests, and certainly no interest of a "tangible and material kind." Another hard example is the wrongly broken promise that redounds, by a fluke, to the promisee's advantage. This wrong violates a kind of interest of the "victim's" in liberty, that is, an interest in himself tying down the future in a certain respect and determining through his own choice what is to happen. Insofar as *that* interest was invaded, he was *harmed* (as well as wronged), but in the example, no other interest of his is harmed and some are actually promoted, so that on balance, he actually benefits. All such apparent examples of wrongs that are not harms to interests can be interpreted in this way. There *can* be wrongs that are not harms *on balance*, but there are few if any wrongs that are not *to some extent harms.* Even in the most persuasive counterexamples, the wrong will usually be an invasion of the interest in liberty.

Though virtually all harms in the special narrow sense (wrongs) are also harms in the more general sense (invasions of interest), not all invasions of interest are wrongs, since some actions invade another's interests excusably or justifiably, or invade interests that the other has no right to have respected. The interests of different persons are constantly and unavoidably in conflict, so that any legal system determined to "minimize harm" must incorporate judgments of the comparative importance of interests of different kinds so that it can pronounce "unjustified" the invasion of one person's interest of high priority done to protect another person's interest of low priority. Legal wrongs then will be invasions of interests which violate established priority rankings. Invasions that are justified by the priority rules are not legal wrongs though they might well inflict harm in the non-normative sense of simple invasion of interest.

One class of harms (in the sense of invaded interests) must certainly be excluded from those that are properly called wrongs, namely those to which the victim has consented. These include harms voluntarily inflicted by the actor upon himself, or the risk of which the actor freely assumed, and harms inflicted upon him by the actions of others to which he has freely consented. I have not wronged you if I persuade you, without coercion, exploitation, or fraud to engage in a fair wager with me, and you lose, though of course the transaction will set back your pecuniary interest and thus harm you in that sense. The harm principle will not justify the prohibition of consensual activities even when they are likely to harm the interests of the consenting parties; its aim is to prevent only those harms which are wrongs. That is why the harm principle needs to be supplemented by an elaborate set of mediating maxims, interest-rankings, principles of justice, and the like, before it can be applied to real legislative problems.

I come now to the second class of evils that are suffered by individual persons and are often acknowledged by liberals to be the proper concern of the criminal law, those unpleasant but harmless experiences that some persons wrongly impose on others. Not everything that we dislike or resent, and wish to avoid, is harmful to us. Eating a poorly cooked dish may be unpleasant, but if the food is unspoiled, the experience is not likely to be harmful. So it is with a large variety of other experiences, from watching a badly performed play to receiving a rude comment. These experiences can distress, offend, or irritate us, without harming any of our interests. They come to us, are suffered for a time, and then go, leaving us as whole and undamaged as we were before. The unhappy mental states they produce are so diverse that they probably have nothing important in common except their unpleasantness. We can, however, distinguish two main species and a third left-over or miscellaneous subclass. The first species contains hurts, both physical and mental: pangs, twinges, aches, and stabs, and very roughly analogous forms of mental suffering, "wounded" feelings, bitterness, grief, "heartache," despair. These experiences are certainly evils, but unless they are intense and prolonged enough to distract or incapacitate and thereby set back an interest, they are not harms. Secondly, we can distinguish unpleasant physical sensations that do not in the strict sense *hurt*, for example, nausea, itches, dizziness, weakness, chill, and their rough mental analogues, states of mind that are not forms of suffering, but are nevertheless universally disliked—disgust, anxiety, boredom, irritation. Third, we can list experiences which, when caused by the obtrusive behavior of others, are offended states of mind in a stricter sense. These include affronts to the senses (grating noises, evil smells); disgust and revulsion; shock to moral, religious, or patriotic sensibilities; shame and embarrassment (including the vicarious kind); annoyance and "aggressive boredom"; resentment, humiliation, and anger (as from insults, mockery, flaunting, and taunting). One can undergo experiences of all these kinds without being harmed in the slightest; still these episodes are un-pleasant inconveniences which are often greatly resented, and from which we might well seek protection from the law, when they are avoidable in no other way. They are, in a word (the best word), *nuisances*, making it difficult for one to enjoy one's work or leisure in a locality that one cannot reasonably be expected to leave in the circumstances. In extreme cases (but still below the threshold of harm), the offending conduct commandeers one's attention, forcing one to relinquish control of one's inner states, and drop what one was doing or thinking in order to cope with distracting racket, irksome tediousness, embarrassment, shame, repugnance, or anger, when it is a great bother to have to do so. Our complaints about these episodes will not be tempered by the allowance that we *can* cope successfully and that our interests have emerged unscathed, for the suffering of harm is not the nub of our grievance.

3.   Harmless Exploitative Injustices

Apart from harms and offensive nuisances what other kinds of preventable evils might there be? There are some kinds of actions which *if general* would be harm-ful, and whose prohibition is justified on that ground alone by the harm principle, but which can be perfectly harmless in some individual instances nonetheless. I have in mind cases of "free-loading" and similar examples of cheating. In a famil-iar sense these examples are all instances of exploitative injustices, even when they injure the interests of no one. In various cooperative undertakings, each per-son must do his own share if all are to gain, but it is possible for a person to cheat, not do his share, and thus take his benefit as "free" only because the others are doing *their* shares. By cheating, the freeloader *exploits* the others' cooperativeness to his own benefit. He "takes advantage of them," as we say. If many of his partners did the same, then the result would be harm to the interests of everyone in the group. But when no others do the same, the harmful effects of one free-rider may be so trivial and dilute as to count for nothing. When one rider (only) avoids paying his train fare, the others' shares of the costs of the railroad, reflected in the owner's adjusted prices, may go up only a tiny fraction of a penny because of his nonpayment. But the others have voluntarily foregone the benefits he got in expectation that he would forego them too. Their grievance is not that their interests were harmed, and surely not that they were morally offended by what he did. (They were offended because of the perceived wrong done them; the basis of the wrong was not simply that they were offended.) Their grievance is simply that he took unfair advantage of their trust and profited *only* because of their forebearance.

Perhaps the most apt and familiar example of this kind is drawn from one of the largest of all the collective activities of our time, the cooperative movement of automobiles in all directions through a modern nation's highway system. Suppose that there is a restricted lane reserved for emergency vehicles on the right shoulder of a multilaned road. We are all creeping along bumper to bumper in heavy traffic returning from a well-attended football game. You look in your rearview mirror and see a car pull into that forbidden lane and accelerate rapidly by the line of cars jammed in the permitted lanes. Generously you infer that there is some extreme emergency that has impelled this motorist to so desperate a course. But as he passes on your right you note that his car is packed with spirited revelers; there are pennants flying from all the windows, and lusty voices are singing the college fight song. The rest of us have all stayed out of the restricted lane and because —only because—of our obedience, the disobedient motorist profits. He has exploited our good faith for his own benefit.[4]

And so we must add another category of evils to our general classification, namely those *exploitative injustices* that consist of benefits that are gained without causing harm to others only because others have voluntarily refrained from doing the same. This new category, however, does not require a new legislative principle. Since the wrongful conduct would be harmful if very widely practiced, and since there is no reason to exempt free-riders from the general duties of participants in the cooperative scheme, the harm principle will justify prohibitions of actions that can produce this third kind of evil. Moreover unfair exploitations, while distinguishable from harms and nuisances, share one very important central feature with them. All three types of evil are grounds of personal grievances. People may rightly protest that they have been *wronged* (taken advantage of) even while admitting that their interests have not been invaded. The question we must now raise is whether there are still other classes of evils that wrong no one in particular and thus cannot be voiced as grievances. Insofar as they are detached from individual needs, interests, deserts, claims, and rights, such evils could be characterized as "free-floating."

4. A Taxonomy of Evils

Let us mean by an evil, in the most generic sense, any occurrence or state of affairs that is rather seriously to be regretted. To say of such an event or condition that it is an evil is to say that it would be better (in some objective sense) if it did not exist or had never come to exist, that the universe would be a better place without it. This *summum genus* then can be divided exhaustively into two subordinate genera, which we can label "Legislative Evils" (or evils of legislative interest) and "Theological Evils" (or evils of theological interest) respectively. The former class contains all the evils that are reasonably foreseeable or preventable consequences of the actions or omissions of human beings. The latter class contains all those natural disasters that law books have traditionally called "Acts of God" and other regrettable occurrences and circumstances (for example the continued existence of killer diseases despite reasonable and even heroic human efforts to stamp them out) that are not imputable to human misconduct, indifference, or error. Such things of course *are* evils in the generic sense. Some of them are the data for "the problem of evil" in natural theology. Our concern here, however, is with the evil people do, for only that kind of evil could be the concern of rational coercive (criminal) legislation.

The legislative evils subdivide further into two species, the "Grievance Evils" and the "Freefloating Evils." The former, which contains the familiar harms, offensive nuisances, and exploitative unfairnesses, consists of all the legislative evils that can be grounds of personal grievances. The latter are evils that are imputable to human beings, but which do not give rist to personal grievances.

Bernard Gert has defended a thesis that would undermine the above classification. He has claimed that "evil" and "harm" are virtual synonyms, so that it is impossible to think of a harm that is not an evil or an evil that is not a harm. He may well have been led to this hasty identification by his concentration on evils that can be *inflicted* upon persons, for example as punishments.[5] As we shall see, however, there are other putative evils that could not in any usual sense be "inflicted" upon individual persons. To give Gert his due, most generic evils, or the most important generic evils, may well be harms, and indeed all harms, as such, are evils, at least to some degree "to be regretted." But if (as appears to be the case) there are free-floating evils, then not all evils are harms, and indeed some genuine evils are neither harms, offensive nuisances, nor exploitative injustices.

5. *Candidates for Free-Floating Evils*

Not everyone will agree that all or even most of the items on the following list are genuine evils. I don't even make the claim myself, but I submit (a) that everyone will acknowledge that at least one of them is plausibly held to be an evil in the legislative genus, and (b) that it will be very difficult to claim sincerely of any given item so acknowledged to be an evil that it is also a personal harm, offense, or "exploitation."

i. *Violations of taboos.* It has been said that all known human societies, primitive and advanced, have incest rules. In characterizing these rules as taboos, anthropologists mean that they are absolutely unconditional prohibitions applying without exception, whose violation not only cannot be justified, but cannot be excused either by any of the normal exculpating appeals (mistake, duress, etc.). A taboo is a prohibition whose form "puts the demand for reason out of place";[7] it is thought to be inviolate and sacrosanct and such that anyone who feels bound by it will think of it as underived from reasons, in any usual way, but rather something as basic and underivative as the process of giving reasons itself. Not that a given taboo cannot be supported by reasons. An isolated instance of brother-sister incest could lead to genetic abnormalities; isolated instances of parent-child incest would be clear cases of the sexual exploitation of children and likely to cause severe emotional damage to the victim; widespread violation of the rules would undermine, for better or worse, traditional social institutions, like the nuclear family. But the incest rules do not function simply to prevent injustices or inutilities. They have a powerful grip on us even when such reasons do not apply. After all, contraceptives and sterilization can prevent genetic disasters; intercourse in private can prevent offense and contagious example; and incestuous relations between consenting adults might bypass the objection based on exploitation. In the words of Graham Hughes: "It is hard to see what reason there is to declare it a heinous crime for a thirty-five-year-old man and his thirty-year-old sister to decide to go to bed together."[8] One reason why Hughes is right about this (though it is not his reason) is that criminal sanctions are hardly *necessary* to enforce a genuine taboo; crime statistics do not show a rash of brother-sister incest crimes. But leaving the question of criminal enforcement aside, how many of us can calmly consider, without flinching, the example of a contraceptively protected, privately performed, and genuinely consensual sexual act between a thirty-eight-year-old father and a twenty-year-old daughter, or (even more unthinkable) a thirty-eight-year-old mother and a twenty-year-old son? If such discreet and private acts are "evils," it cannot be because they harm or offend.

ii. *Conventional "immoralities" when discreet and harmless.* I have in mind here the usual list of so-called morals offenses when performed in private between consenting adults. They include all extramarital and homosexual intercourse, and perhaps solitary masturbation as well. Not many sophisticated persons will regard all these forms of conduct as "evils," but it is worth pointing out nonetheless that if they are evils they are often harmless and (since unobserved) inoffensive ones. It is more difficult to think of examples under this heading that do not pertain to sexual conduct, but the following contrived one might do. Imagine that a death in a family occasions not the usual public funeral and period of mourning but rather a secret family banquet at which the body of the deceased, hacked into pieces and baked in a garlic and mushroom sauce, is consumed by the survivors, having earlier secured the consent of the deceased while he was still alive. Our prevailing morality would certainly condemn such conduct, even though no interests were harmed or endangered by it, and no sensibilities offended.

iii. *Religiously tabooed practices.* Other dietary restrictions tend to be ascribed to religious codes instead of moral ones, or if to the moral ones, then only on the ground that they are religiously forbidden. Similarly, religious rules enforcing sabbatarian abstentions or prescribing somber modes of dress do not make violators (at least in our pluralistic society) "immoral"; violators cannot be "good Chassidic Jews" or "good Mennonite Christians," or the like, but they can be good persons, for all that. Even the religiously loyal subjects of the rules are likely to think of them as forbidding conduct that is *malum prohibitum* rather than *malum in se*. But then any kind of *malum* is an evil. I have in mind under this heading not widespread and public deviance, which could be thought to be a threat to the norm itself or to the religious way of life it helps define, but rather isolated and private violations—wolfing down an illicit pork chop in the privacy of one's chambers, or sipping the forbidden juice of the grape in one's desert tent. It is interesting to note in passing that we think of such conduct as evil (when we do) only because it violates religious norms, whereas the sexual prohibitions are thought to be moral rules quite independently of religious sanction.

iv. *Moral corruption of another (or of oneself)*. It is surely an evil to make a person a worse person than he would otherwise be, to change his virtues into flaws, to encourage his follies, and play to his weaknesses. Usually to corrupt a person is indirectly to harm his interests, since most moral virtues are useful possessions which, by contributing to one's popularity and reputation for trustworthiness, help one to make one's way in the world. Even if it should not harm the person who is made worse by the evil actions of another, his corrupted character is likely to produce more harm in the long run for those he deals with. It is at least conceivable, however, that circumstances nullify these indirect sources of harm, so that the corrupt person prospers from his moral flaws and others are largely unaffected by them. In that case the evil acts of his corruptor cause harm only to his character; it becomes a worse character than it would otherwise have been. But unless a person has an interest in having a good character, *he* is not harmed by the "harm" done to it, and his character itself is "harmed" only in the transferred sense, discussed and dismissed above. You do not harm me by "harming" my bicycle after I have thrown it away and abandoned all interest in it. And if *nobody* has an interest in the bicycle, you cause no genuine harm at all even if you smash it to bits. In the primary sense of harm, only beings with interests can be harmed, and that account excludes mere things, artifacts, lower animals, and even such valuable possessions as one's body, one's reputation, or one's character. Nevertheless, it seems obvious that a bad or worsened character is, in itself, an evil thing.

v. *Evil thoughts*. We are all proud of the Anglo-American law for its traditional reluctance to punish evil thoughts, but legal commentators themselves, when explaining this reluctance, eagerly pass the whole subject off to the moralists who have always attached great importance to it. *Evil intentions*, in particular, have long been thought to be the primary thing for which persons can be blamed, so that a person can be thought to be evil just insofar as his intentions are evil, even though those intentions, through lack of opportunity or change of mind, never issue in action, or because of lack of control, issue in actions more benign than those envisaged by the actor when he undertook them. Abelard identified sinning with evil intending and insisted that sin consists not merely in having evil desires but in consenting to them, that is resolving to act on them.[9] That may well be a plausible account of sin, but it won't do for what I have called "evil in the generic sense." Surely an evil desire is itself an evil state of affairs, and so are evil attitudes and emotional responses. The presence of an intention is hardly necessary to the evil of other kinds of mental states. Imagine, for example, a person of impeccable rectitude, who would never ever intend to do anything but her duty, as she and Immanuel Kant understand it, yet whose empirical nature is so corrupt that she welcomes and celebrates harm to others though she would never herself intend to cause it, the wife of an invalid who does her duty to the end but then kicks up her heels and dances with malicious joy at the thought of her husband's agonized and painful death.

vi. *Impure thoughts*. Moralists who use this expression have in mind lust mainly, or the entertaining of sexual fantasies. Abelard found nothing sinful in such thoughts as such, provided they remained idle and ungeared either to specific evil intention or to the kind of desiring he called "covetousness."[10] Still, other things being equal, I suppose he would think it a bad thing that such fantasies occur at all, even though no one is to blame for them. Moralists have been preoccupied with sexual impurity, but surely there is no conceptual reason why any type of forbidden conduct should not have its own corresponding type of "impure thought." One might classify under this heading, for example, the newly converted Moslem, "lusting" in his fantasies after pork or wine, or the pious youth dreaming of playing baseball on the sabbath.

vii. *False beliefs.* Consider beliefs we have, for example, about the distant past: about the conduct of the Peloponnesian War or about the character of Emperor Nero. Some of these beliefs (of course I know not which of them) are probably dead wrong, the result of early errors of observation or transmission, now beyond all correction. It would seem an evil state of affairs for *all* of us to believe something about an ancient figure that is in fact not only untrue of him but unfair to him as well. All the more so for that false belief to be enshrined indelibly in the history books as the official record of our civilization. The universe would be a better place (in that quaint phrase of the English intuitionists) if only beliefs that are at least approximately true and just were so certified. The point has a certain vividness when confined to beliefs about actual persons and their works, though a purist might well insist that "the universe would also be a better place" without false beliefs about continental drift, or the origins of planets, or the existence of God.

viii. *The Parfit case.* A famous example of Derek Parfit's,[11] designed to make another point in another context, can be used to show the possibility of a very narrow and specific class of evils that are without question both free-floating and *thoroughly* evil. Parfit's own purpose was to show that a plausible version of utilitarianism must condemn not only harms to specific persons but also evils of a more impersonal kind. Imagine, if you can, a woman who is warned by her doctor to take a certain medicine and abstain from sexual intercourse for a month until she is cured of a condition which would cause any child she conceives to be born with a physical abnormality (say a withered arm). Nevertheless, either through willful perversity or negligence, she ignores the doctor's orders and consequently conceives a child who is born with the abnormality. At this point, Parfit asks us to make the reasonable assumption that the inherited disability of the child, while of course a bad thing, is not so severe as to render his life not worth living. He never ever regrets that he was born, but only that he was born with a withered arm. Now if the child, grown older, complains to his mother that her outrageous behavior harmed him, or wronged him, or was unjust to him, she can undermine his grievance by replying in the following way: "I had two options in respect to your birth. One was to do what I did which led to your being born with a withered arm. The other was to obey the doctor which would have led to your never having existed at all. You admit that you are glad to have been born. Therefore you ought to be pleased (if not exactly grateful) that I did what I did." I submit that the mother's reply, while not relieving her of blame, does show that her child was not harmed by her wrongful conduct, for to be harmed one must be put in a worse state than one would otherwise have been in, and in this case, that condition is not fulfilled. The child's arm is a handicap to him, and its withered condition an indubitably evil state of affairs. But the child has no personal grievance against anyone. The wrongdoer in the example must be blamed for wantonly introducing a certain evil into the world, not for inflicting harm on a person.

ix. *The wanton, capricious squashing of a beetle (frog, worm, spider, wild flower) in the wild.* Small wriggling creatures often cause harm and/or offense to people who find them in city homes and apartments, but in the wilderness they bother no one. Still, while it might be harmful indirectly to many *other* animals, including human beings, to slaughter beetles by the thousands, no one, surely, will be harmed by the loss of just one. Perhaps the beetle itself is harmed by the taking of its life. Human beings and some of the higher animals do have an interest in staying alive which is harmed by their premature deaths. If a beetle has any interests at all, as opposed to mere instinctual urges and propensities, then no doubt an interest in staying alive is one them, but it is implausible, I think, to ascribe desires, goals, projects, or aspirations to a creature whose cognitive capacities (if any at all) are so primitive. So I doubt whether one harms such a being by painlessly killing it. Still the blotting out of any vital force, however rudimentary, when done for no reason at all, might strike many of us as an evil, much to be rued.[12]

x. *The extinction of a species.* There are only forty odd whooping cranes left, and our government, with the full support of the people, has poured hundreds of thousands of dollars into an effort to increase their numbers and allay the spectre of extinction. Perhaps the effort is meant to prevent indirect harm to human interests, since the loss of any species is likely to have profound effects on the whole eco-system of which we are a dependent part. But that cannot be the whole of the evil we perceive in such a loss, and environmental harm does not follow necessarily when a species disappears anyway. Consider the Colorado cave fish who have existed almost unchanged for millions of years in the dark isolation of their shallow cavern pools. The tiny ecosystem of which they are a part has no effect whatever on that of the rest of nature; yet the courts have recently enjoined engineering projects that would cause their extinction. In any case, to return to the example of the whooping cranes, the serious environmental harm caused by their decline must have been caused by the reduction of their numbers, in only a few decades, from (say) four hundred thousand to forty. Compared to that, the further reduction from forty to zero would be a trifle. Those of us who would be crushed in disappointment by the loss of the final forty, if we examined the grounds of our feelings, would find that we believe that the world would somehow be diminished in value by the loss of the whopping cranes, that the human beings who allow it to happen under their stewardship after all these millions of years of natural evolution would be (collectively) as wasteful and wanton as the squasher of the beetle, indeed much more so, for the avoidable loss of a whole species is a greater evil in "the eyes of the universe" than the loss of any single animal, indeed an evil of a different order of magnitude.[13]

xi. *The extinction of a national or cultural group.* One way of destroying an ethnic group is to commit mass murder or genocide, to destroy the group by killing all of its members, the method, in fact, by which human beings have destroyed whole biological species. That would be to cause enormous amounts of harm, directly to the victims and indirectly to many others, so it is not a good example of a "harmless evil." A more humane mechanism is that of cultural assimilation. In the first millenium A.D. the Jewish community of China was "killed by kindness." Welcomed by their Chinese hosts with warmth and friendliness and treated with unaccustomed equality, the Chinese Jews intermarried and disappeared with hardly a trace. The assimilative process sometimes takes place in a spontaneous, almost "voluntary" way as a group neglects its ancestral language and customs, apes those of its neighbors, and gradually ceases to be the group it once was, even though no individuals are directly harmed in the process. The Sumerians, Carthaginians, and Incas were conquered by force and then suffered the imposition of an alien language, religion, and culture, but the Welsh, the Bretons, and the Louisiana Cajuns might yet leave the stage of history in a quieter, less "harmful" manner. It is not only the present members of those groups who think of that possibility as an evil to be averted.

It is important to contrast the "evils" of cultural assimilation (if that's what they are) with the evils of cultural disintegration of which Lord Devlin has warned us. Devlin apparently has in mind a literal scattering of the individuals who once formed a group as their communal bonds break, or their military conquest by foreign powers made possible by the weakening of their moral fiber and group loyalty, or "the breakdown of law and order, something approaching anarchy"[14] as individuals having come to doubt some parts of their seamless morality quickly chuck all the rest of it. These kinds of disintegration are of course extremely harmful to the individuals who are violently torn away from one another, but the extinction of cultural identity through a kind of accelerated evolution need harm no one at all.

This point is worth making for a double reason, not only to illustrate the possibility of a category of free-floating evils, but also to counter typical efforts of legal moralists to seek reenforcement for their views from the harm principle. Very often we hear that pornography, aberrant sex, and the like, do great public harm by undermining valuable social institutions, for example by "harming the family." Even if the family as we now know it should in time become extinct, however, and even if that would be an evil, it doesn't follow that any given individual would be wrongfully harmed in the transitional process. The analogy to the extinction of species and cultural groups is helpful here. There is, after all, a morally crucial distinction between "destroying" a species by permitting it to evolve naturally over the centuries into some new and different species, and destroying it by shooting all its members. The family, like all social institutions, is always evolving in new directions. Where each link in the chain of change is voluntary, then there is no unconsented-to harm and no personal grievance, even though witnesses may understandably shed a prospectively nostalgic tear over the departure of the old way and its distinctive values. There is yet another useful application of this point. Suppose that in an ethnically pluralistic society higher birth rates permit some ethnic and religious subgroups to grow faster than others, so that over a century or so they greatly increase their relative size and their cultural influence in the society. The process in time may lead to drastic changes in the make-up of a whole people and its common culture, and that change may seem to some to be objectively regrettable. But who is harmed? Who can voice a personal grievance?

xii. *Drastic change in the moral and aesthetic climate, or in the prevailing style or "way of life."* Changes in habits, customs, and practices; in the way businesses concentrate or disperse in neighborhoods; in the way buildings are decorated and maintained; in the way people dress, speak, joke, find their entertainment, express their feelings, observe or ignore their religions, engage in courtship rituals and child-bearing practices—these and other cultural changes occur constantly and rapidly in twentieth century societies unless strongly braked by moral and legal constraints. When they proceed too rapidly, the older members of a community will sometimes come to feel like strangers in their own neighborhoods, aliens in their own country, isolated, lonely, out of the mainstream. The general social environment, the ambience of day to day living, the "tone" of social life, can change so drastically in one generation that individuals may think of their community as essentially different from what it once was, as a pair of blue silk stockings constantly darned with red wool patches may eventually become a different pair of stockings, made of a different kind of stuff and showing a very different color. This too is a kind of cultural extinction.

More commonly people think of their communities as unchanged in essential identity but what is vaguely called their "way of life" as radically transformed. The New England Protestant community still exists, but the law against blasphemy is no longer enforced, and profanity is in the very air that everyone breathes, originally no doubt a stench in the nostrils of the pious, but now hardly noticed. Miscegenation is no longer a crime in the South and interracial couples can now be seen in public throughout the land. Here and there coercive laws have been advocated or adopted to "preserve the traditional Welsh Sunday,"[15] to ban hog-raising or non-kosher food; to slow down the trend toward nudity which has already moved from Bermuda shorts to bikinis to see-through dresses; even to ban modern dancing, modern art, and jazz.[16] The Equal Rights Amendment has run into strong resistance, in bible-belt states especially, from persons who rightly sense that changing sex roles presage wholesale alterations in every department of the prevailing way of life. What is called a "moral code" is only a small and I think untypical part of a way of life, but it too is subject to the same forces of cultural change, as when premarital liaisons, for example, become common and eventually even accepted by prevailing standards. Not all changes in a way of life are to be regretted by any means, and indeed a case can be made that most changes reflect genuine personal and interpersonal needs. But it would be sanguine, I think, to suppose that all such changes must be for the better, and when they are for the worse, we can think of them as evils even before we know whether they harm anyone or not.

xiii. *Lower standards of manners and the spread of morally graceless conduct.* Every world traveler knows that standards of public manners vary widely from country to country. New York, London, and Tokyo are dynamic crowded centers of comparable size, but citizens of London and Tokyo, in their quite distinct ways, are elaborately polite and apologetic in their public encounters, whereas equally good-hearted New Yorkers tend to be more aggressive and gruffly blunt. There should be room for a great deal of relativity in the judgments we make about the customary responses of people in different cultures. Rules of manners are a great deal like rules of the road. The important thing is that there *be* rules and that they be understood and followed in similar ways by everyone. There is no reason why widely different sorts of standard manners might not work equally well in different places. The Londoner may find New York to be a jungle, but the New Yorker, knowing what to expect from his fellows, gets along just fine. It is possible, moreover, for a society to be too mannered. A certain natural bluntness is often to be preferred to highly ritualized circumlocutions. Perhaps that too is, in large degree, a matter of taste. But when all relativity has been paid its due, it must be acknowledged that certain critical judgments about standards of manners have the ring of truth to them. A society that respects its aged, for example, is much to be preferred to one in which the infirmities of advanced age are objects of mockery, even though there may be no more suffering on balance in the latter because the attitudes in question are traditional, easily anticipated, and adjusted to. And there might well be some golden mean—or at least some acceptable range—between overly mannered and overly aggressive styles. It is possible, I think, to imagine gradual changes in our standards of manners in objectively undesirable directions —changes that threaten to take the grace and civility out of our encounters with strangers. If such changes were neither little noted nor long regretted, people would take them in stride, and develop immunity to any harm from them. Nevertheless, the change would be regrettable.

xiv. *General ugliness, depressing drabness, and the like.* How pleasing things look may be a matter of taste, but tastes too are sometimes subject to objective standards of criticism. Negative judgments about the look of the south Bronx are not like expressions of dislike for the taste of Brussels sprouts. The "tone" or "ambience" of a neighborhood is not only a function of the design, decoration, and condition of its buildings, but also of such factors as the neatness and cleanliness of its streets, the freshness of its air, its spaciousness or crowdedness, its coherence or jumbledness, its smells and noises, the visible character of the people on its streets and their conspicuous enterprises, its signs and symbols, its color, verve, and mood. Some communities, blessed with a pleasing look and tone, protect the attractiveness of their neighborhoods with zoning restrictions: only buildings in the traditional style can be constructed in Nantucket. If the pleasing look of that lovely isle were to be replaced by the familiar commercial tawdriness of most tourist havens, that would be a "loss," even if it were no one's loss in particular.

6. Focus on Social Change Evils: The Conservative Thesis

It will repay our attention at this point to focus more sharply on the "social-change evils" (11-14), for when the legal moralist rests his case on the need to prevent these evils, he is defending what H. L. A. Hart calls "the conservative thesis,"[17] a very special variant of the general moralistic position and perhaps that version with the greatest intuitive plausibility. Often the conservative thesis, so-called, is confused, even by its advocates, with appeals to other grounds for "enforcing morality." The *psychic aggression thesis* and the *social disintegration thesis* differ from it, for example, in that they are at least covert appeals to the harm principle. The former rests on the dubious empirical premise that deviations from conventional morality even in private are threats to the mental health of others; the latter rests on the even more dubious sociological premise that conventional immoralities threaten every individual with the disintegration of his society and ensuing anarchy. Psychic wounds of sufficient severity are personal harms, and so are conditions of anarchy, so any liberal who accepts the empirical premises stating that such harm follows indirectly from private immoralities can respect-fully consider the claim that the immoralities ought to be forbidden by the criminal law.

A third way of arguing for the legal enforcement of morals is to invoke explicit-ly or tacitly the *offense principle*, and argue that legal impunity for discreetly private immoralities will be directly offensive in any case. As the immoralities spread, it is claimed, their presence will inevitably be felt in subtle but persuasive ways that shock or disgust the ordinary person. If ten percent of the population have homosexual tendencies, a permissive law allowing their private (and only private) indulgence will be like the houseekeeper who sweeps so much dirt under the rug that it causes large crinkles, mounds and bulges, as offensive to the unwill-ing observer as the dirt itself would be (or almost so). There are empirical presup-positions behind this version of the argument too which if true would require the liberal to admit at least the relevance of the reasoning.

A fourth way of arguing has a quite different character. It conceals no empirical premises and can tempt the liberal in no way. According to this way of arguing, which we can call "pure moralism," certain types of immoralities, even when private and harmless, are such evident and odious evils that they should be forbid-den on that ground alone. The argument has a perfect simplicity: single premise and single conclusion. James Fitzjames Stephen gave the most eloquent expression of pure moralism when he wrote his much quoted line: "There are acts of wicked-ness so gross and outrageous that . . . [protection of others apart], they must be prevented at any cost to the offender and punished if they occur with exemplary severity."[18] Stephen's view is easy to confuse with the "conservative thesis" but it is really quite distinct from it. The pure moralist argues that such and such activi-ties are inherently immoral; ergo they should be prohibited even when private and harmless to individuals. According to the conservative, it is social change (for the worse) that is the relevant freefloating evil and it is a common "way of life," not the interests and sensibilities of individual citizens, that requires protection from the criminal law.

It bears repetition that a group's moral code is only part of its "way of life," and by no means the only part that the conservative wishes to preserve. The conserva-tive argument would apply just as well to whatever other elements are equally central to a way of life. It might seem that no other elements could be as central as the shared moral convictions of a group and that the priority of a moral code is true almost by definition, or at least that its truth follows from a clear understand-ing of what the morality of a group is. This objection can be forestalled, I think, by a distinction made by Hart and various others between a "moral minimum," namely "those restraints and prohibitions that are essential to the existence of any society of human beings whatever"[19] and rules that are not essential to all societies but are distinctive of the society in question. The moral minimum includes rules against violence, homicide, mendacity, and fraud, and it goes without question that these rules are central to *any* group's way of life. The moral-minimum rules, however, are all derived from the harm principle, and no one has ever seriously suggested that they do not warrant legal enforcement. Controversy arises only over the moral residuum, those rules that hold their place in a society's moral code whether or not they are thought to prevent individual harms.

Another distinction in terms of "centrality" can be made among the rules of the moral residuum itself. Some of these are, and some are not, part of a society's "central core of rules or principles which constitute its pervasive and distinctive style of life."[20] These rules, Hart adds, "do not include every jot and tittle" of a society's code. Among rules in our "central core" that need not even be in the code of every conceivable society are the rules defining and protecting the institution of monogamous marriage which, according to Hart, "is at the heart of our conception of family life" and whose "disappearance would carry with it vast changes throughout society so that without exaggeration we might say that it had changed its essential character."[21] No doubt the moral rules Hart has in mind, including perhaps the prohibition of polygamy, polyandry, and adultery, are indeed among the central parts of the moral code of our society, but they are probably joined in that central core by prohibitions of sexual conduct that cannot be thought to threaten monogamous marriage at all, for example bestiality, masturbation (until recently), and nonpromiscuous cohabitation as a kind of trial marriage. There are, moreover, rules, standards, and ideals in the central core that cannot be thought of as "moral" at all: standards of dress and decorum, religious rites, rituals, and festivals, use of a particular common language, patriotic observances, and the like. A "way of life" is a vague notion in the extreme, but it was once thought clear enough to support the inclusion of baseball and apple pie near the top of the list of items that constitute the "American way of life."

Such conservative writers as Walter Berns[22] and Alexander Bickel[23] argue for the legal enforcement of moral norms not because they think that sin should be punished and immorality diminished as ends in themselves (à la Stephen), but because they think legal force is needed to counter threats to the "moral environment" for our traditional way of life. Their targets are such things as dirty words, pornographic books, and live sex shows to consenting audiences. But the form of their arguments is that which has been used in the past to argue for the prohibition of alcoholic beverages, gambling, soft drugs, even dancing, modern art, and jazz. The temperance movement that succeeded in imposing prohibition on the country was only partly concerned to prevent the harms caused by excessive drinking, and the forms of its arguments were not typically paternalistic. One of its primary targets was the spreading influence of life-styles that deviated from the traditional norms the movement represented, on the one hand the free-wheeling style of the sophisticated cocktail-swigging urban or suburban middle classes, on the other the ethnic customs of immigrant workers of Catholic and Lutheran backgrounds in which the social drinking of whiskey or beer played a large role. Joseph Gusfield writes that:

the issue of drinking . . . became a politically significant focus for the conflicts between Protestant and Catholic, rural and urban, native and immigrant, middle and lower class. . . . The demand for prohibition laws arises when drinkers have social and political powers as a group, and in their customary habits and beliefs deny the validity of [the] abstinence norms [that form a central part of the way of life of the earlier dominant majority]. By the 1840's the tavern and beer parlor had a leading [and unquestioned] place in the leisure of Germans and Irish. . . . There was no tradition [among them] of temperance norms to appeal effectively to a sense of sin. By the 1850's the issue of drinking reflected a general clash over cultural values and the temperance movement found political allies among the nativist movements. . . . Prohibition came as the culmination of the movement to reform the immigrant cultures and at the height of the immigrant influx into the U.S. . . . *The process of deviance designation in drinking must be seen in terms of the cultural dominance rather than as reflecting necessities of social control.*[24] [emphasis added.]

It may be thought that the norm against drinking in Bible-belt communities was a *moral* norm, and I confess that I find the distinction between moral and non-moral norms very difficult to grasp, especially when the norms in question are at most part of the moral residuum. (Within the class of norms constituting the "moral minimum" there is no difficulty. "Thou shall not kill" and "Thou shall not cheat" are prototypically moral rules.) But if the norm against drinking is border-line "moral," many of the other norms for which the prohibitionists sought legal sanction were not: "During the 1920's the prohibition organizations included . . . among other non-alcohol problems to which they gave attention, . . . obscene literature, modern dancing, and jazz."[25] And who has not heard fulminations against neighborhood crap games, interracial courtships, sabbatarian violations, rhythm and blues (what used to be called "racial music"), TV cop shows, comic books, and more, and the advocacy of coercive legislation against them in order to prevent cultural erosion and similar evils?

Moral and non-moral norms that do not prevent harms so much as preserve a traditional way of life are not themselves threatened by every kind of non-conforming action. Gusfield tells us that the repentant deviant who never doubts the legitimacy of the norm but breaks it in a morally weak moment is no threat to the existence of the norm he violates. Nor is the so-called sick deviant who is thought to be unable to help himself. Even the cynical deviant who is self-seeking, amoral, and unrepentant is no real threat to the norm. He doesn't denounce the norms he violates and brandish alternative ones which he deems superior. On the contrary he owes allegiance to no norms but self-serving ones, and he is an un-appealing model for imitation. The real threat to the norm itself, according to Gusfield, is the "enemy deviant": "he accepts his own behavior as proper and derogates the public norm as illegitimate. Such an attitude is particularly apparent in instances of 'business crimes'—gambling, prostitution, drug use—where the very acceptance of such action as legitimate supports the presence of buyers on an economic market."[26] Middle-class housewives who hear from their cleaning women about winnings and losses in the numbers game will learn that betting is as much a part of the distinctive black subculture, and as natural and accepted by its members, as gospel singing and soul food. And one is not likely to encounter much guilt about marijuana smoking in the youthful subculture where it prevails. When deviant conduct becomes respectable in this way it is perceived as a real threat to the existence of the norm itself and not merely a deviation from it. Cultural conflict is in the offing and the traditional norm might lose, and with its loss will come a drastic change in a way of life. That is the point at which the demand for legal enforcement becomes most insistent.

Despite the familiarity of the conservative style of argument and its common employment in editorials, sermons, and "letters to the editor," both its friends and enemies among academic writers tend to get it not quite right when they para-phrase it in their learned articles. A case in point: Ronald Dworkin attributes to Lord Devlin the view that the enforcement of morals (that is the prohibition of "immoral acts" even when harmless and private) derives its justification from "the majority's right to follow its own moral convictions in defending its social environment from changes it opposes."[27] He then argues quite effectively that the opinions held by the majority about certain deviant sexual practices, most notably about homosexuality, are not genuine moral convictions at all, but only prejudices, emotional allergies, feeble rationalizations, mere parrotings of alleged moral authorities, and the like. If they *were* genuine moral convictions based on reasons and consistent with widely shared general principles, then Dworkin suggests that he would have little objection to their legal enforcement even when unnecessary to prevent harm and offense. "What is shocking and wrong is not Devlin's idea that the community's morality counts, but his idea of what counts as the community's morality."[28] Dworkin himself is in theory a kind of legal moralist: that an act is of a sort deemed wrong by the consensus of genuine moral conviction in a community is itself a good and relevant reason, on his view, for banning it, even when it is harmless and inoffensive. The occurrence even in private of such acts must, on Dworkin's view, be a kind of freefloating evil that the state is entitled to prevent. This view resembles pure moralism more than it resembles the conservative thesis, but unlike Stephen's view that an act's objective wickedness is a sufficient ground for prohibiting it, Dworkin requires only that there be a consensus of sincere and genuinely moral conviction that it is wicked, a condition that might be somewhat easier to satisfy.

But in any case, neither Dworkin's position nor the one he ascribes to Devlin are forms of the conservative thesis as commonly defended. The conservative is not directly affronted by what he cannot see, nor does he believe that anyone is harmed by (say) consensual acts between adults. But he insists that deviant conduct changes "his" society in essential ways and makes him an alien in his own community. The people with whom he comes in contact every day may, for all he knows, have different attitudes and opinions from those he used to be able to count on. Now he cannot be as free and easy with them as before. They may in turn suspect that he is not really one of them, and turn either a cold shoulder or a resentful or patronizing countenance on him. In any case one will have to be more careful than before when there is no knowing whether one's associates are discreet homosexuals or sexual perverts, or (even worse) respecters and defenders of such deviants. There may be no garish public displays of their deviance if the law employs an offense principle, but still one can see them pouring out of theaters whose marquees (discreetly of course) advertise x-rated films, and one can notice the proliferation of books with sexual themes in bookstores and libraries. Inevitably there is a concomitant change in the way people—especially younger people —talk. Offensive words lose their offensiveness to most of one's fellow citizens, and subjects rarely talked about in public are now routine topics of general conversation. The air one breathes is a different air, and one is impelled quite naturally to think of metaphors about cultural littering and moral pollution. Perhaps most discouragingly of all, one feels one's influence over one's own children slipping, and one's efforts to transmit traditional values to them undermined. The latter lament is expressed poignantly by Walter Berns:

. . . unfortunately, in the present intellectual climate, education in this area is almost impossible. Consider the case of the parent who wants to convince his children of the impropriety of the use of the four-letter verb meaning to copulate. At the present time the task confronting him is only slightly less formidable than that faced by the parent who would teach his children that the world is flat. Just as the latter will have to overcome a body of scientific evidence to the contrary, the former will have to overcome the power of common usage and the idea of propriety it implies. . . . Now, to a quickly increasing extent, the four letter verb—more "honest" in the opinion of its devotees—is being used openly and therefore without impropriety. The parent will fail in his effort to educate because he will be on his own, trying to teach a lesson his society no longer wants taught—by the law, by the language, or by the schools.[29]

So in the end, the aging conservative feels that he is not only an alien in his own land, but a stranger in his own family.

It will be little comfort to him to show, in the manner of Ronald Dworkin, that his attitudes are not genuine moral convictions. He may be happy to admit that there are, or could be, other communities whose customs, practices, and traditions, whose norms of conduct and standards of manners, while greatly different from those of the community he treasures, may be equally rational, or if you will, "moral." This is not the point. Our own traditions, he might reply, have been built up by many generations of our ancestors; it would be a waste and a betrayal to let them wither away, to be eroded like the pillars of ancient temples in the sandstorms. Once the radical new changes have taken place, the old way is gone forever, and this, he might add, is an evil of the same sort as the extinction of a biological species.

Then, the final note of bitterness. "All this happened without anyone consulting me," he might complain. "What vote did *I* have about whether the old ways were to continue or not? What choice, in fact, did anyone have? An overwhelming majority of us, helpless to use the law in our defense, simply watched the changes take place, with growing resentment or passive resignation." "It is not a sufficient answer," says the conservative philosopher, "that social practices will not change unless the majority willingly participates in the change. Social corruption works through media and forces quite beyond the control of any conscious design at all." Deep changes in the moral environment, then, are thought to be not simply evil, but also *unfair,* the violation of the "rights of the majority to defend its social environment from changes it opposes." In this way the conservative thesis borrows support from a new source, an appeal to a kind of moral majoritarianism. It may well be that certain social changes are free-floating evils, but be that as it may, *that* is not why the state has a right to resist them by using the criminal law. Rather it is because these changes are contrary to the will of the majority, and therefore illicit in their origins. Raymond Gastil puts the majoritarian case for "the enforcement of morals" succinctly. Likening the moral environment to a public park, he writes: "Since everyone's likes and dislikes cannot be accommodated in the same square, the obvious basis of decision as to regulation becomes the desire of the majority of its users."[30] Many conservatives, I think, would settle for less. Thinking of attitudes that were once virtually unanimous but now dwindled and threatened, they may claim legal protection only for those central core moral standards to which not merely a simple majority, but the overwhelming consensus of citizens, have always paid allegiance.

7. *Arguments for the Conservative Thesis Based on Fairness*

There are, then, two forms of the conservative argument for the enforcement of morals, or if you will, two parts or stages of the argument. One is an appeal to the rights of an overwhelming majority, as such, to prevent unwanted changes in its traditional way of life. This form of the argument is essentially based on fairness, for it concludes that it is unfair to alter the moral environment of a community without the consent of a majority (or at least a quite substantial minority) of its members. The other form of the argument gets along without an appeal to fairness or to majority rights, invoking instead what I have called "the principle of legal moralism in the broad sense," that the prevention of certain freefloating evils is a good reason for legal coercion. Extreme and unwelcome changes in a group's traditional way of life are then held to be among the sorts of freefloating evils that the state has a right to prevent by criminal legislation.

How should we respond to these arguments? The argument from fairness, I think, is not only defective in its own terms; it can be used to justify far more coercion than even the conservative presumably would welcome, and in the end it can be turned back against the conservative thesis itself. First of all, Gastil's "public square" analogy will not long survive scrutiny. You cannot have a band concert, transcendental meditation sessions, carnivals, six-day bicycle races, automobile traffic, and public promenades all at the same time in the same small public square, and which activities should be permitted under these crowded circumstances admittedly is a question of public policy, to be settled in a democracy (within certain constitutional limits) by majoritarian procedures. But there is plenty of room, even in a small public park, for an unlimited variety of thoughts, beliefs, and attitudes. Catholics take up no more room than Protestants, Republicans no more than Democrats, blacks no more than whites. And if we find it easy to accommodate religious, political, and ethnic pluralism, indeed pluralism of every *other* kind, why not moral pluralism too? Why is a vote required to decide whether to let in homosexuals as well as heterosexuals, voluptuaries as well as virgins, secret readers of pornography, pot-smokers, and numbers-players, as well as bible students, pipe-smokers, and chess players? (Remember that offensive displays, solicitations, and the like *can* be prohibited on liberal principles.) Walter Barnett chides proponents of the conservative position for uncritically assuming "that two or more moralities cannot exist in mutual toleration in the same society,"[31] even while they are willing to concede, however grudgingly, that the whole spectrum of religious differences can easily be accommodated, not to mention the political, ideological, ethnic, aesthetic, and linguistic contrasts. Barnett pounces in particular on Devlin's insistence that every society must choose between monogamy and polygamy. Why could they not live side by side in the same society? he asks, and finds it impossible to "see any inherent incompatibility between them."[32] There would simply be "two marital regimes in a society to choose from,"[33] instead of one.

If we remind ourselves, as we constantly must in this discussion, that we are not thinking of offensive public displays or obtrusive nuisances forced on the attention of disgusted captive observers, but only practices and preferences freely exercised in private or in reserved public places before willing observers, our initial doubts about the plausibility of moral pluralism quickly vanish. A neighborhood can be harmonious and attractive for anyone to live in even though it contains Liberal and Fundamentalist Protestants, Roman and Greek Catholics, Reform and Orthodox Jews, Moslems, Atheists, and indifferents. Any one of these may disapprove of the religious practices of the others and resent it if they were constantly obtruded upon his attention. But what the others do in their own churches, he will admit, is their business and no barrier to friendly neighborliness with them. How is the case any different when we consider homosexuals and "perverts," crapshooters and drinkers? We would be offended if we could escape being captive witnesses of their disapproved activities only at great inconvenience to ourselves, but what goes on in the privacy of their bedrooms and public meeting places need not sever the bonds of community between us. Our metaphorical public park is not as crowded as Gastil assumes.

But even if we were to grant (as we should not) the aptness of the "public square" analogy, it would not follow in any automatic way that majority rule would be the only morally legitimate procedure for deciding who is to have access to the park. The park commission composed of officials elected in free elections would surely have a right to decide on general policy grounds to exclude military bands, motorcycles, or even bicycles, or as the case may be, to reserve a place and time for band concerts and bicycles, but ban horseback riding, ball games, and unleashed dogs. But when antecedently recognized *rights* enter the picture, there the majoritarian procedures find their limit. The park commissioners could hardly settle their problem by restricting the park to either males or females, old or young, black or white, socialists or economic conservatives. Neither a majority nor its representatives can be permitted to make its decision in that fashion. How then could a majority rightly make its decision on the equally irrelevant ground of sex preferences, or private reading tastes?

Finally, the majoritarian argument backfires against its proponents in another way. If we are going to use the political analogy at all, we should take it seriously. Democratic theory endorses the moral propriety of majority rule only when minorities have been left free to try to become majorities if they can. Gastil himself observes that "The right to try to form new majorities is the basic right given to individuals in both the majority and the minority that makes meaningful the rights of either."[34] Trying to become a majority presumably requires efforts to *persuade* one's fellows to join one's cause, but that opportunity is hardly open to the person whose favored activities are deemed criminal and banned on pain of punishment. When the minute vegetarian party loses an election and is thus shown to be a very tiny minority indeed, this is not followed by the legal prohibition of vegetarianism and the jailing of the party's leaders. How then does the analogy extend to (say) homosexuality? (Actually the analogy is not only inconsistently applied by conservatives, it is flawed from the beginning in any case. "Moral minorities" do not necessarily even wish to persuade a majority to their styles of life, but only to persuade the majority to leave them in peace.)

Whatever principle of fairness the moral conservative uses to justify the legal prohibition of unestablished minority styles of life, he will be hard put to explain why the principle doesn't establish with equal cogency the fairness of sweeping totalitarian restrictions. In particular, if it's fair to enforce moral conformity on conservative grounds why is it not fair to enforce religious conformity in religiously homogeneous communities on the same grounds? Surely the moral heterodoxies of today's swingers are no more odious to moral conservatives than were the damnable heresies and sacrileges of rival religious sects to true believers in days gone by. And when we subtract from the sum total of our moral code that rather substantial part of it that coincides with the universal moral minimum (that is, its prohibitions against force, violence and fraud) what is left can hardly be deemed more essential to the identity of our community than religious fidelity was to the homogeneously pious communities of our ancestors. So the argument from the need to preserve a way of life would apply *a fortiori* to religious nonconformity. And indeed a precisely parallel argument for the legal prohibition of religious unorthodoxy was abandoned historically only after a couple of centuries of indecisive warfare between mutually intolerant sects.

It would be impossible, moreover, for the conservative argument to stop short of crossing the line between the prohibition of a disapproved sort of conduct and the prohibition of speech advocating that conduct, or even speech advocating the permissibility or the legalizing of that kind of conduct. If speech is to be left free while conventional immoralities are to be prohibited, the case for the prohibition must be based on other than conservative grounds. One newspaper article advocating the legalization of marijuana could do more to weaken the barrier to the spread of pot smoking than a hundred youths who smoke in the public park or a thousand youths who smoke unobserved in their private quarters. One article by a respected psychoanalyst or anthropologist defending the reasonableness in some circumstances of adultery could do more to weaken the norm against that practice than a thousand circumspect liaisons.

Once more, how is the conservative argument to stop short of justifying, again on grounds of "fairness," the enforced regulation of forms of hair dress, the wearing of long beards, the styles of clothing of those who advertise themselves as nonconformists? Do not these *visible* deviations from the standards that define our social environment weaken those norms as much as the existence of deviant attitudes, tastes, sex lives, reading and entertainment preferences when the only manifestations of the latter are in private?

Considerations of fairness, when they do have a bearing on these issues, seem to oppose rather than reenforce the conservative argument. If we assume, as seems natural, that human nature comes in different sizes and shapes, so to speak, that there are deep and morally significant differences among normal people in respect to basic temperament and emotional needs, then to insist that only some of these types of character, even if they are the most common ones, are entitled to their satisfaction, would seem to be unfair to the others, a form of discrimination as arbitrary as racial prejudice. Suppose most people wore a size nine shoe. If making shoes in any other size were forbidden by law, wouldn't that be unfair to those who happen to have unusually large or small feet? Mill's case for "experiments in living" was only partly based on utilitarian considerations, his own protests notwithstanding. It is not *fair* to a young person not to let him try on a large variety of life-styles in his search to find one that best fits his inherited propensities and distinctive needs.

The shoe-size analogy is not wholly apt. I must admit that not all is relativity in this area. There are certain kinds of human character and modes of life that I would hate to see triumphant in the Darwinian struggle that a liberal state would permit. I do not view with equanimity the prospect of a community whose majority is primarily devoted to lotus-eating, or to the exclusive reading of pornography, and the like. But I don't understand why conservatives who share these particular attitudes of mine pessimistically assume that in a fair fight the better values would inevitably be at a disadvantage, so that only the values they believe to be superior need the added help of the state's iron fist. Do they really believe that pornography seriously threatens to make the human race forget Shakespeare, or that many, most, or even all people would prefer a steady diet of mass produced stories generated by some simple formula to Saul Bellow's novels or Henry Kissinger's memoirs? (When did a publisher ever give a pornographer a two million dollar advance?)

I would hate to see us become a nation of pornography readers for the same reason I deplore the widespread consumption of bad literature of any kind (I mean literature that is bad on certain *literary* grounds). People who enjoy trite and obvious novels written by formula—potboilers, "good guy–bad guy" Westerns, sentimental tear-jerkers, gothic romances—tend to lack discrimination and independent judgment in real life. They will be as easily manipulated by advertisers and politicians as they are by hack writers, for their responses to stock stimuli in art and life are unthinking knee-jerks. They are as likely to be incapable of discriminating nuances of feeling in their dealings with others as the pornography-addict is incapable of meeting the challenge of a genuine love affair. Requiring courses in good literature in our schools receives its primary justification from the power of literature to enlarge our insight, through vicarious identifications with plausible characters, into "the varieties of human ideals, outlooks, . . . and experiences."[35] Stereotyped pseudo-literature has the very opposite effect. So if the bad effects on feeling and judgment of a habitual preference for pornography are the grounds for prohibiting it, then they equally justify the criminal prohibition of all cynically hack-written pseudo-literature. Proper education in the feelings should be compulsory, but for children only. For adults it is never too late for education, but much too late for compulsion.

But to get back to fairness, when *is* the "fight" between contending lifestyles a fair one? No parliamentary body legislates these things; we have no "moral constitution" specifying the permissible means of persuasion; there are no written rules of procedure analogous to those governing judicial proceedings. But if the idea of fairness is to have any application to the processes of cultural change, I should think that it would rule out all influences on the outcome but the perceived merits and demerits of the alternatives. He who would reform our moral environment by fair means should be prepared openly and forthrightly to express his dissent, and attempt to argue, persuade, and offer reasons, while continuing to live in his own preferred way with persuasive quiet and dignity, neither harming others nor offering counterpersuasive offense to tender sensibilities. On the other hand, a citizen uses illegitimate means of social change when he abandons argument and example for indoctrination and propaganda, force and fraud. If the latter are the things that make the contest unfair, then it is surely unfair to use the power of the state to affect moral belief *one way or the other*. (Again, the example of religious doctrines and observances in a religiously pluralistic society makes a good model.) A contest is fair when neither contender has an unfair advantage; it can hardly be fair when the referee forcibly sides with one of the contenders.

8. *Arguments for the Conservative Thesis Based on the Need to Prevent Freefloating Social Change Evils*

It would seem then that cultural change in a democratic society is at most a freefloating evil. Impersonal evils, however, cannot be personal grievances, or violations of individual rights. In some cases, of course, one person is justified in using force against a second to prevent the second from harming a third. One need not, therefore, have a personal grievance of one's own in order to have a moral justification for coercion, provided that one acts to protect the rights of another. But *no one at all* needs "protection" from the occurrence of a freefloating evil or can claim the prevention of the evil as *his* due. So invasions of the interest that persons are presumed to have in their own liberty, if done in order to arrest cultural change, cannot be justified on the grounds that individuals must be protected from harm, nuisance or exploitation, but rather on the quite distinct *kind* of ground that certain alleged freefloating evils must be prevented.

There are three lines of liberal response to this conservative mode of justification. First of all the cultural changes in question may not be evil at all. Not all changes are changes for the worse. It is often enough clear in retrospect that severe changes in a traditional way of life have been all for the better. How many of us now regret the passing of theocratic puritanism, or strict racial segregation? Yet those changes were as deep and revolutionary in their time as any now foreseen by the gloomiest conservative. The characteristic conservative argument, however, as we have noted, is not that any given way of life is uniquely rational, but rather that any severe change in a traditional culture is evil *as such*, even though it might seem on other grounds to be an improvement. Lord Devlin clearly held the view that *any* change in the essential norms of a society is a change for the worse. That too was the view, at least in respect to religious dissenters seeking legal rights, of Lord Thurlow, a nineteenth-century English Lord Chancellor, who said to a group of dissenters: "I'm against you by God, sir. I'm in favor of the established church; and, if you'll get your damn religion established, I'll be in favor of that."[36] Quite explicitly it was the *establishment* as such that Lord Thurlow was "in favor of," not any particular set of religious doctrines. The same sorts of preferences are expressed about other cultural norms by Ernest van den Haag in a paradigmatic statement of the conservative thesis:

Every community has a right to protect what it regards as its important shared values. In India, I would vote for the prohibition against the slaughtering of cows. In Israel, I would vote for the prohibition against the raising of pigs for slaughter. In the United States, where a certain amount of sexual reticence has been a central value of traditional culture, I would vote for the rights of communities to protect their sexual reticence.[37]

With the generosity of one who enjoys the benefits of historical hindsight, I can grant the conservative a small part of his thesis, if only for the sake of the argument that can be employed against him. Let it be allowed then that there is some loss (cost, "evil") involved in *any* drastic cultural change as such. Nevertheless a given drastic change might yet be a great improvement *on balance* even when one takes account of the cost. Other things being equal, it was perhaps a regrettable thing that the Puritan way of life ceased being our dominant style, or that the ante-

and post-bellum Southern ways of life had to go with the wind, or that Victorian double standards were finally purged from the cultural body. But "other things" were not equal. Repression, exploitation, and hypocrisy were great component evils, and their reduction was a gain that far outweighed the losses we can grant in charity to the conservative. In the case of looming changes that are now the subject of controversy, neither side has the benefit (yet) of hindsight, and both must concede that only time will tell. But the verdict of history may never be uttered if all change is forcibly blocked by the criminal law.

The second line of liberal criticism is that legal enforcement is hardly required to preserve some parts of the status quo whose change would be on balance evil. The entrenched majority has great advantages in the free competition of life-styles even without the help of the state. Merely social pressures to conform to those traditional norms that are thought to be indispensable by the great majority will be difficult to resist and the norms themselves highly immune to erosion. The most sacred of the norms, those that function as unqualified taboos, for example those forbidding mother-son incest, are not likely to fall in an epidemic of contagious violation. Criminal enforcement is ludicrously redundant in their case.

The third liberal line is perhaps the most important theoretically. Even if a given social change would be an evil on balance, and even if it were necessary to use the criminal law to prevent it, it would be morally illegitimate to do so anyway. Legal enforcement would be illegitimate in almost all conceivable cases, not only on the grounds of unfairness presented in the previous section, but on the very general ground that the need to prevent freefloating evils, while always a relevant reasons for action, is not the kind of reason that can have enough weight to justify invasions of the interests (the interest in liberty, among others) of specific, particular, flesh and blood human beings. That is not to say that reasons in the freefloating category never have *any* weight. Preventing a freefloating evil is not simply morally irrelevant, neither here nor there, totally beside the point. On the contrary it does have some weight as a reason for coercion (the Parfit example alone shows this) and must be rebutted or outbalanced by reasons on the other side. But the reasons on the other side, as we have seen, are reasons of another *kind*, reasons of a sort that are generally more weighty. The need to prevent an impersonal evil that no one "suffers" is usually not as weighty a reason as the standing presumption in favor of liberty, and the general case against invading the interests of specific real persons. That is very much like saying that males as a group are heavier than females as a group, though in a given unusual case, one of the heavier females might weigh more than one of the lighter males. I think it is even more like saying that human beings tend to weigh more than mice, even though in an extremely rare case a given bloated mouse may weigh more than a premature infant human. At any rate, even though some freefloating evils are real evils and even great evils, it remains true that insofar as an evil is freefloating, that subtracts from its weight on the scale of reasons.

When a person has been harmed in one of his vital interests or even when he has been seriously inconvenienced to his great annoyance, a *wrong* has been done to him; he is *entitled to complain;* he has a *grievance* to voice; he is the *victim* of an *injustice;* he can demand *protection* against recurrences; he may deserve *compensation* for *his* losses. But no individual person is entitled to complain in the same way when a free-floating evil is produced by another's action. Who is wronged when the adult brother and sister discreetly go to bed together? Where is the injustice when a grown man in the privacy of his chambers enjoys impure thoughts over his pornographic magazine? Who is the victim when a religious person omits one of his required observances or when a person of rectitude experiences feelings of vindictive satisfaction at the sufferings of another? Who needs protection against widespread false beliefs about some ancient emperor? Who should be compensated if the Colorado cave fish become extinct? On the other side, all of us are harmed by criminal prohibitions to whatever extent they invade our "interest in liberty," and certain identifiable individuals are especially harmed by coercive interference in their lives, and even by criminal punishment. To justify such palpable harms on the ground that they are necessary to prevent even greater free-floating evils is to imply that the evils inflicted on persons are less serious evils than states of affairs that harm no one, being only regrettable subtractions from the net value of the universe—a judgment, it seems to me, that could only rarely be correct, and in its application to the "enforcement of morals controversies," one that is downright perverse.

There is a special offensiveness in the invocation of the evils of social change to justify the infliction of harms on individual persons. Moral arguments of that kind fly in the face of our understanding of personal autonomy. If I am forbade on pain of criminal punishment and public humiliation from acting as I prefer in ways that harm no one and in places where I offend no one, on the ground that in so doing I woud be subtly changing the moral environment of my fellow citizens, I am being asked to acquiesce in an argument that utterly demeans my autonomy. Surely a person's autonomy, whatever else it may consist in, excludes his thinking of his activities, practices, beliefs, and preferences as no more than part of others' "environments." How can I have any personal autonomy if my neighbors can claim a *right* to have me think, feel, and privately behave only in ways they approve? There is nothing offensive to autonomy in the practice of limiting some people's liberty for the sake of other people's interests; using persons as "means to an end" is inoffensive when the "end" is the protection of *other* persons, but morally odious when the "end" is anything else.

There are still two lines of defense open to the conservative who relies on the prevention of severe social change as such in his defense of the legal enforcement of morals: he can deny that the social changes that he thinks evil would be exactly *free-floating* after all, or he can admit that they are free-floating but insist that they are such great evils that the necessity to prevent them has even greater weight on the scales than the presumptive case for liberty. To take the first line would not necessarily be to abandon legal moralism for the harm and offense principles, for the conservative might wish to claim that one can have a personal grievance at the conduct of others on grounds other than that the conduct harms, offends, or exploits anyone. The child with the withered arm, in the Parfit case, might have a grievance against his mother, for example, even though he admits that he wasn't harmed by her objectionable conduct. I confess that I cannot see how a person whose interests have not been invaded, and who is still able to live a good life, can have any personal grievance at the people who constitute his social environment when the latter discreetly live their own lives and form their own views in ways that he finds regrettable. He might protest that a way of life is about to become extinct to our discredit or to the universe's disvalue, but that is a complaint, not a grievance. And if he presses the analogy to the abrupt extinction of a biological species he is on shaky ground. The more obvious biological analogy, as we have seen, would be to the evolution of new traits in a species rather than to the destruction of all its members, and who is wronged or harmed in any way by that?

A more plausible way of arguing for a grievance even without a harm is to argue that persons brought up in a traditional way of life often design their own lives in all good faith in reliance on the old ways being continued. Emotionally unprepared, then, for drastic changes, they are left high and dry in their declining years, not only disappointed but righteously embittered by changes which are in their eyes betrayals.

The sense of grievance in these cases is understandable, even where the aggrieved party can show no genuine harm to his interests or rude affronts to his sensibility. Understandable, perhaps, but justifiable? I think not. No one ever signed a "social contract" with such people, or made a solemn vow, or even an informal promise, to keep things unchanged. If aggrieved parties believe otherwise on ideological grounds, then they are victims, in a way, of their own conservatism.

Still another ground for fancied grievance without harm or offense has a certain superficial plausibility about it until it is subjected to critical scrutiny. Imagine a conservative who reasons as follows: I concede that immoralities done discreetly in private by individuals or consenting adult groups do not cause me personal harm, and since I am not a direct witness to such goings on, they do not cause me offense in a way that the offense principle could be expected to take into account. What I am worried about is the offense that will be caused me *in the future* if the conduct in question becomes more and more widespread and increasingly tolerated by the general public. I am protected by the offense principle now, but as more and more people are converted to the deviant conduct, or to tolerance of it and even respect for it, the conditions for the application of the offense principle to the conduct in question will no longer be satisfied. In particular the standard of universality will not be met, as it will no longer be true that shock and disgust will be "the reactions that could reasonably be expected from almost any person chosen at random."[38] Then the deviant minority will go public with impunity, and people like me, though still technically in the majority, will be the captive witnesses of scenes that offend and dismay us. Homosexuals will walk arm in arm down public streets and kiss and pet on public park benches; pornography sections will be in every drug store and supermarket; visible and audible reminders of the offensive changes will keep us constantly irritated and harrassed. At that point, it won't do to talk about "freefloating evils"; our offense will be personal enough, but we will no longer qualify for the protection from the offense principle. In those circumstances, when we complain that our "moral environment" has been polluted, we will not mean simply that regrettable things are occurring in secret behind locked doors, but rather that disgusting changes are taking place (no doubt at an accelerated rate) in the world of common perception.

The first response to this lament should be an attempt to offer comfort and reassurance. Not everything that is tolerated and respected when done in private can be witnessed even by those who morally accept it without causing offense. All of us are sometimes naked in our bathrooms and bedrooms, but we still do not tolerate nakedness in public. Married sexual intercourse is not considered immoral by anyone but it is still not accepted on the public streets. If liberty prevails, homosexuals may indeed become increasingly bold. Homosexual couples may behave in public in ways similar to those now permitted their heterosexual counterparts. But what reason is there to think that they will be able to go beyond the limits we now impose on heterosexuals without causing near-universal offense? And permission to operate bordellos, pornographic cinemas, dirty book stores, and the like, does not imply license to litter, to solicit by personal confrontation, to advertise in garish or tasteless ways, to convert pleasant neighborhoods into ugly, noisy, tawdry ones while immune to the possibility of control by zoning restrictions. Still, when all of that is said and done, one must concede to the worried conservative that there is no assurance that the changes he fears will not produce visible effects that will offend him. We can worry, for example, that standards of "tastelessness," "ugliness," "garishness," and "tawdriness" will themselves be eroded.

So the best way to reply to this conservative's "grievance" is to grant him that his fears have some substance, but urge him to use methods short of the criminal law to support his own tastes and standards. There is indeed something odd about his lament when one thinks of it as an *argument* for criminalization, even an argument with true empirical premises. For if he begins by accepting the harm and offense principles as mediated by the various supplementary maxims and standards argued for in Part II above, then he cannot very well demand exemption later, as a kind of afterthought, when he realizes how those standards may affect him. What he is arguing for now is the (or a) principle of legal moralism, and he is arguing for it on the grounds that the offense principle as properly mediated does not give his sensibility sufficient protection. He can hardly do this after having granted the cogency of the reasons that support the various restrictions mediating the offense principle's application. That is uncomfortably similar to accepting the rules of baseball as useful and fair, and then having a "second thought" about them upon realizing that against teams with a certain kind of strength the rules might permit one's own team to lose. Closer to home, it is like accepting the harm principle, but then having second thoughts when one realizes that a certain kind of behavior now prohibited because it is harmful may one day cease to be harmful, so that it may eventually have to be permitted. That is the exact analogy to the present conservative argument, for its advocate accepts the offense principle until he realizes that one day a certain kind of public activity now prohibited because it is offensive may cease to be sufficiently offensive to warrant prohibition. The reply to that is that if the conduct does cease to be sufficiently offensive, why then prohibit it? The conservative's answer can only be that even though the conduct is not sufficiently offensive to warrant prohibition, on principled grounds, it will nevertheless be very offensive to *him*.

The final argument for the conservative position is its most formidable one. It is available to the conservative who has accepted all my conclusions up to this point (unlikely fellow!). He can agree that the majoritarian arguments for the legal enforcement of morals fail, and that other arguments based on fairness do no better. He can agree, therefore, that voluntary private immoralities that cause no harm are at most free-floating evils, and further that the need to prevent evils in that category is in general a reason of an inferior kind to the need to satisfy genuine individual grievances. He can agree, finally, that free-floating evils cannot be the ground of personal grievances. His last stand must be that some (admittedly uncharacteristic) free-floating evils are such great evils that the need to prevent them *as such* is a weightier reason than the case for individual liberty on the other side of the scales. All the conservative can do at this point is present relevant examples in a vivid and convincing way; the relative "weight" of acknowledged reasons is not otherwise amenable to proof. More exactly he offers *counterexamples* to the liberal thesis that personally harmless transactions between consenting adults in private cannot be evils of sufficient magnitude to justify preventive coercion.

Let us begin with the standard liberal example of the pornographic film or the nude stage show. Imagine that the advertising for these entertainments is perfectly honest and straightforward. On the one hand, it does not itself luridly pander to lusts in a way that would offend passersby; on the other hand it does not conceal the true nature of the shows in a way that would mislead customers into expecting something that is not pornographic. Imagine further that children are not permitted entrance. Since neither compulsion nor deception is used to dragnet audiences, every person who witnesses the show does so voluntarily knowing full well what he is in for. No one then can complain that he has been harmed or offended by what he sees. The shows therefore can be banned only on the ground that the erotic experiences in the minds of the spectators are inherent evils of a free-floating kind.

The playfully skeptical conservative can now begin to alter the facts in these hypothetical paradigms until his liberal adversary begins to squirm. He asks us to suppose, for example, that the voluntary audience is thrilled to watch the explicit portrayal on the stage of sexual intercourse, or even "sodomy and other sexual aberrations." Imagine live actors and actresses performing live sex for the delectation of live voyeurs. Well, surely this would be degrading and dehumanizing for the actors, protests the liberal. In that case, the state has a right to make sure that the actors too, and not only the audience, are voluntary participants. But why shouldn't some contracts between producers and actors be capable of passing the test of voluntariness? No doubt the actors' work would be unpleasant, but let us suppose that it is well paid. People have been known to put up, quite voluntarily, with great discomforts for the sake of earning money. Could sexual exhibitionism be that much worse than coal mining? Maybe it could. But shouldn't it be up to the free choice of the actor to decide whether a certain amount of public degradation is worth ten thousand dollars a week? It would be paternalistic to prevent him from doing what he wants to do on the ground that we know better than he what is good for him. Liberal principles, then, offer no grounds to justify legal prohibition of such diversions. That may not embarrass the liberal (very much), but other conservative counterexamples lie in wait for him.

Imagine a really kinky live sex show primarily for those voluntary spectators who prefer their sex with sado-masochistic seasonings. William Buckley eagerly takes up the argument from here:

Does an individual have the right to submit to sadistic treatment? To judge from the flotsam that sifts up in the magazine racks, there is a considerable appetite for this sort of thing. Let us hypothesize an off-Broadway show featuring an SM production in which the heroine is flailed—real whips, real woman, real blood—for the delectation of the depraved. One assumes that the ACLU would defend the right of the producers to get on with it, trotting out the argument that no one has the right to interfere with the means by which others take their pleasure.

The opposing argument is that the community has the right first to define, then to suppress, depravity. Moreover, the community legitimately concerns itself over the coarsening effect of depravity.[39]

That the community has the right to define and suppress depravity as an inherent evil is, of course, the conservative thesis here at issue. That the community can be concerned with "coarsening effects," on the other hand, is the sort of consideration a proponent of the harm principle might invoke if he thought on empirical grounds that people with coarsened characters tend to cause harm to unwitting victims, so it is a consideration that can be put aside here.

Vicarious sexual pleasures of a "depraved" sort are not the only examples of private enjoyments found repugnant by some moralists. Professional boxing matches are another case in point. Here some of the liberals themselves are among the most dennunciatory. The *New York Times* published an editorial demanding the abolition of professional boxing altogether shortly after the bloody first Frazier-Ali fight.[40] One of the many indignant letters to the editor that followed denounced the *New York Times,* in turn, on familiar liberal principles:

. . . Ali and Frazier fought of their own free choice. Neither of them has complained that he was forced to submit to brutal and dehumanizing treatment. Those who paid money to see the fight did so willingly and most of them thought they got their money's worth. . . . [W]hat was immoral about this fight? No rights were transgressed. Those who disapprove of professional boxing were not forced to watch.

. . . The parallel to declining civilizations of the past referred to in your editorial is without any basis in fact. The contestants in the cruel sports that were practiced in the dying days of the Roman Empire, for example, were not free men with free choice. . . .[41]

The liberal author of that letter is set up for the last of the ingenious conservative counterexamples to be considered here. Irving Kristol has us consider the possibility of gladiatorial contests in Yankee Stadium before consenting adult audiences, of course, and between well-paid gladiators who are willing to risk life or limb for huge stakes. The example is not at all far-fetched. We can imagine that, with closed circuit TV, the promoter could offer twenty million dollars to the winners and ten million to the estates of the losers. How could we advocate legal prohibition without abandoning the liberal position that only the harm and offense principles can provide reasons of sufficient strength to override the case for liberty? Kristol has no doubts that the liberal is stuck with his huge free-floating evil and can urge prohibition only at the cost of hypocrisy:

I might also have [used the word] . . . "hypocritical." For the plain fact is that none of us is a complete civil libertarian. We all believe that there is some point at which the public authorities ought to step in to limit the "self-expression" of an individual or a group even where this might be seriously intended as a form of artistic expression, and even where the artistic transaction is between consenting adults. A playwright or theatrical director might, in this crazy world of ours, find someone willing to commit suicide on the stage, as called for by the script. We would not allow that—any more than we would permit scenes of real physical torture on the stage, even if the victim were a willing masochist. And I know of no one, no matter how free in spirit, who argues that we ought to permit gladiatorial contests in Yankee Stadium, similar to those once performed in the Colosseum of Rome—even if only consenting adults were involved.[42]

Kristol's trap will catch only the most rigid and dogmatic liberal. From those who are more sensitive to moral perplexities his examples will elicit at least three types of reply. First, Kristol is entirely too complacent about the problem of determining genuine "willingness" and "voluntary consent." The higher the risk of harm involved, the stricter must be the standards, one would think, for voluntariness. When it is a person's very life that is at issue the standards would have to be at their very strictest. Perhaps the state would have a right on liberal principles to require such things as psychiatric interviews, multiple witnessing, cooling-off periods, and the like, before accepting a proffered consent as fully voluntary. Kristol talks glibly of finding "willing" public suicides in "this crazy world of ours," not noticing that an agreement is hardly consensual if one of the parties is "crazy." To exploit a crazy man in the way he describes is not distinguishable from murder and equally condemned by the harm principle. Admittedly a self-confident and powerful gladiator need not be "crazy" to agree to risk his life before the howling mobs for twenty million dollars. But there is a presumption that such a person doesn't fully understand what he is doing, or is not fully free of neurotic influences on his choice, a presumption that is rebuttable in principle, though it could be difficult and expensive to rebut in fact. The methods for establishing genuine consent, in fact, could be so time consuming and costly, and so fallible in the end, that it might be the wisest course, on liberal grounds, for the law to treat the presumption of nonvoluntariness as nonrebuttable.

The second point to make about Kristol's examples is that the coercion-justifying evil they portray so vividly is not the one cited in the conservative argument we have been considering. Getting one's pleasure from watching others torture or kill themselves or others in theaters or arenas is a definite free-floating evil, a blotch on "the universe's moral record," even if it wrongs no one. Moral corruption of the witnesses through reenforcement of their appetite for gore and the weakening of restraints is another inherent evil even when it leads to no harm. But neither of these evils that Kristol makes so much of is the freefloating evil the conservative evokes. *That* evil is the erosion of the social norms that create and preserve a community consensus of "shared values." The conservative's favorite freefloating evil is drastic cultural change as such. If that is the evil the prevention of which justifies legal force, then the law comes too late in Kristol's gladiatorial example. If seventy thousand people fill Yankee Stadium and enough attend closed television showings in theaters to permit the producer to pay thirty million dollars (my example) to the gladiators and still make a profit for himself, then we are as a people already morally corrupted according to the old shared standards, and legal coercion, at best, can only treat the symptoms.

But the final point in rejoinder is the most pertinent one. The gladiatorial contests and "voluntary" submission to torture cases are the most extreme hypothetical examples of freefloating evils that the conservative's imagination can conjure. They are so extreme that it is not even clear that they are possible instances of genuinely voluntary conduct. There seems little likelihood that they will ever be attempted at least in the foreseeable future. Yet there is no denying that they are convincing examples of very great evils. A liberal might treat them as the limiting case of the "bloated mouse" that has more weight than the skinny human being. The need to prevent them would be, in his view, the very weightiest reason for coercion that one could plausibly imagine from the category of (merely) free-floating evils. He could then concede that the question of whether they could legitimately be prevented by state coercion is a difficult and close one, and admit this without hypocrisy or inconsistency. He would still hesitate to resort to legal coercion even to prevent the greatest of freefloating evils, simply because he cannot say who is *wronged* by the evils. But at any rate, he can concede that the case is close.

But the actual examples that people quarrel over: pornographic films, bawdy houses, obscene books, homosexuality and other deviant sexual preferences, prostitution, private gambling, drinking, soft drugs, and the like, are at most very minor freefloating evils, and at the least, not intuitively obvious evils at all. The liberal can continue to oppose legal prohibitions of them, while acknowledging that the wildly improbable evils in the hypothetical examples of Bernes, Buckley, and Kristol are other kettles of fish. The liberal position least vulnerable to charges of inconsistency and hypocrisy is the view that the need to prevent free-floating evils, while always a relevant reason for coercion, is nevertheless a reason in a generally inferior category, capable of being weighed on the same scale as the presumptive case for liberty only in its most extreme—and thus far only hypothetical—forms.

University of Arizona
Tucson, Arizona

NOTES

[1] See for example Ronald Dworkin, "Lord Devlin and the Enforcement of Morals," *Yale Law Journal*, Vol. LXXV (1966), reprinted as Chapter 10 in Dworkin's *Taking Rights Seriously* (Cambridge, Mass.: Harvard University Press, 1977), and H. L. A. Hart, "Immorality and Treason," *The Listener* (July 30, 1959), reprinted in R. A. Wasserstrom (ed.), *Morality and the Law* (Belmont, Cal.: Wadsworth, 1971), pp. 49–54.

[2] See my "Harm and Self-Interest," in *Law, Morality, and Society: Essays in Honour of H. L. A. Hart*, ed. by P. M. S. Hacker and J. Raz (Oxford: Clarendon Press, 1977), pp. 345 ff.

[3] Nicholas Rescher, *Welfare, The Social Issue in Philosophical Perspective* (Pittsburgh: University of Pittsburgh Press, 1972), p. 6.

[4] This paragraph was taken from my "Civil Disobedience in the Modern World," *Humanities in Society*, Vol. 2, No. 1 (Winter, 1980).

[5] Bernard Gert, *The Moral Rules* (New York: Harper & Row Torchbooks, 1973), pp. 55 ff.

[6] See Jerome Neu, "What is Wrong With Incest?", *Inquiry*, Vol. 19 (1975).

[7] *Ibid.*, p. 32.

[8] Graham Hughes, *The Conscience of the Courts: Law and Morals in American Life* (Garden City, N.Y.: Anchor Press/Doubleday, 1975), p. 29.

[9] *Abelard's Ethics*, trans. J. Ramsay McCallum (Oxford: Basil Blackwell, 1935), Chapter III.

[10] *Ibid.*

[11] See Jonathan Glover, *Causing Death and Saving Lives* (Harmondsworth, Middlesex: Penguin Books, 1977), pp. 67–69.

[12] For a development of this point, among others, see A. M. MacIver, "Ethics and the Beetle," *Analysis*, Vol. 8 (1948). Reprinted in *Ethics*, ed. by Judith J. Thomson and Gerald Dworkin (New York: Harper & Row, 1968).

[13] See my "Human Duties and Animal Rights" in *On The Fifth Day*, ed. by R. K. Morris and M. W. Fox (Washington, D.C.: Acropolis Books, Ltd., 1978), pp. 67–68.

[14] The quoted words are from Walter Barnett's excellent "Corruption of Morals: The Underlying Issue of the Pornography Commission Report," *Arizona State University Law Journal*, Vol. 1971, no.

2 (1971), p. 212. In my opinion Barnett's article is one of the best in the extensive journal literature on legal moralism. See also his *Sexual Freedom and the Constitution* (Albuquerque: University of New Mexico Press, 1973).

[15] Basil Mitchell, *Law, Morality, and Religion in a Secular Society* (London: Oxford University Press, 1970), pp. 34–35.

[16] See Joseph R. Gusfield, "On Legislating Morals: The Symbolic Process of Designating Deviance," *California Law Review*, Vol. LVI (1968), p. 69.

[17] H. L. A. Hart, "Social Solidarity and the Enforcement of Morality," *University of Chicago Law Review*, Vol. 35 (1967), p. 2.

[18] James Fitzjames Stephen, *Liberty, Equality, Fraternity* (Cambridge: Cambridge University Press, 1967), p. 162.

[19] H. L. A. Hart, "Social Solidarity and the Enforcement of Morality," *op. cit.*, p. 9.

[20] *Ibid.*, p. 10.

[21] *Loc. cit.*

[22] Walter Berns, "The Case for Censorship," *The Public Interest*, Vol. 22 (1971), pp. 3–24.

[23] Alexander Bickel, "Dissenting and Concurring Opinions," *The Public Interest*, Vol. 22 (1971), pp. 25–44.

[24] Joseph R. Gusfield, *op. cit.*, pp. 59, 64–65, 66.

[25] *Ibid.*, p. 69.

[26] Loc. cit.

[27] Dworkin, *op. cit.* (footnote 1) in *Taking Rights Seriously*, p. 242.

[28] *Ibid.*, p. 255.

[29] Berns, *op. cit.*, pp. 19–20.

[30] Raymond D. Gastil, "The Moral Right of the Majority to Restrict Obscenity and Pornography Through Law," *Ethics*, Vol. 86 (1976), p. 237.

[31] Walter Barnett, *op. cit.*, p. 215.

[32] *Ibid.*, p. 216.

[33] *Loc. cit.*

[34] Raymond Gastil, *op. cit.*, p. 232.

[35] C. J. Ducasse, *Art, The Critics, and You* (New York: Hafner, 1948), p. 143. See also I. A. Richards on "stock responses" in Chap. 25, "Badness in Poetry," of his *Principles of Literary Criticism*, third edit. (New York: Harcourt, Brace, 1949), pp. 201–06.

[36] As quoted by Graham Hughes, *The Consicence of the Courts: Law and Morals in American Life* (Garden City, N.Y.: Anchor Press/Doubleday, 1975), pp. 46–47.

[37] Ernest van den Haag in *The New York Times*, Sunday, November 21, 1976, Section Two, p. 26.

[38] Joel Feinberg, " 'Harmless Immoralities' and Offensive Nuisances," in Norman S. Care and Thomas K. Trelogan, *Issues in Law and Morality* (Cleveland and London: Case Western Reserve University, 1973), p. 83. See also the trenchant criticisms of that article by Michael D. Bayles and my Reply to Bayles, both in the same volume, and Donald Vandeveer, "Coercive Restraint of Offensive Actions," *Philosophy and Public Affairs*, Vol. 8 (1979), pp. 175–193.

[39] William F. Buckley, Jr., "Death For Gilmore?", *New York Post Magazine*, December, 1976, p. 32.

[40] *The New York Times*, editorial page, March 10, 1971.

[41] Gurdip S. Sidhu, M.D., Letter to the Editor, *New York Times*, March 17, 1971.

[42] Irving Kristol, "Pornography, Obscenity, and the Case for Censorship," *The New York Times Magazine*, March 28, 1971.

PETER HYLTON

RUSSELL'S SUBSTITUTIONAL THEORY*

The work in which the basis of *Principia Mathematica* was first presented (Russell, 1908) contains one peculiarly baffling passage. After setting up a hierachy of propositions. Russell says:

> In practice, a hierachy of *functions* is more convenient than one of propositions. Functions of various orders may be obtained from propositions by the method of *substitution*.
>
> (Russell, 1908, p. 77)

In what immediately follows, however, Russell seems to put forward not a method of obtaining functions but rather a method of eliminating them, replacing them by what he calls "matrices":

> If *p* is a proposition, and *a* a constituent of *p*, let "*p/a*;*x*" denote the proposition which results from substituting *x* for *a* wherever *a* occurs in *p*. Then *p/a*, which we will call a *matrix*, may take the place of a function; its value for the argument *x* is *p/a*;*x*, and its value for the argument *a* is *p*.... *In this way we can avoid apparent [i.e. bound] variables other than individuals and propositions....*
>
> Although it is *possible* to replace functions by matrices, and although the procedure introduces a certain simplicity into the explanation of types, it is technically inconvenient. Technically it is convenient to replace the prototype *p* by Φ*a*, and to replace *p/a*;*x* by Φ*x*; thus where, if matrices were being employed, *p* and *a* would appear as apparent variables, we now have Φ as an apparent variable.
>
> (*loc. cit*; long emphasis mine)

Russell is here alluding to a theory which he developed around 1906, and called "the substitutional theory". This theory should not be confused with what is today called "the substitutional theory of quantification". The modern theory has essentially to do with the substitution of names for one another within sentences or other linguistic objects; in Russell's theory, as we shall see, neither propositions nor the entities substituted within them are linguistic. (Russell's other name for the theory is also, in retrospect, unfortunate. He calls it "the no-classes theory", but this is a term which he applies equally to the type theory of *Principia*. Since this name is ambiguous in this way I shall avoid it.) The purpose of this paper is to explain Russell's substitutional theory and, more especially, to explain why he developed it and why he subsequently discarded it. An account of the philosophical pressures which led to the substitutional theory is an indispensable part of a general understanding of the philosophical context of *Principia Mathematica*: I hope to provide such an account. The substitutional theory turned out to be a blind alley, but an understanding of Russell's motives in exploring it will help to show the general direction in which he wished to proceed.

I

My aim in this section is to sketch enough of Russell's philosophy of the relevant period to make clear the constraints within which he hoped to be able to avoid the paradox which bears his name. I shall show that the need to escape from the paradox conflicts with Russell's most fundamental philosophical assumptions, giving rise to a tension within his thought. This enables us to understand the attraction which the substitutional theory had for Russell: it seemed to offer a way of avoiding the paradox without threatening his philosophy. As will become apparent in section III, however, the substitutional theory turned out to lack the advantages which Russell first attributed to it, so that in the end he abandoned it as "technically inconvenient". The tension in Russell's thought thus remains unresolved, and survives in *Principia*, where it tends to distort Russell's account of type theory, adding confusion to matters which would in any case not be straightforward.

My discussion in this section draws largely upon Russell's *Principles of Mathematics*. While his views changed between the publication of that book (1903) and the period which is our concern (say, 1905–7), these changes must, I believe, be understood as modifications of the basic framework of *Principles*.

(i) *The Universality of Logic*

The truths of logic, as Russell saw the matter, embody the correct principles of reasoning. This idea may seem uncontroversial, even obvious, but in fact it marks a crucial difference between Russell's conception of logic and that of the modern logician (post-Gödel, say). According to Russell's understanding of logic, all reasoning employs logic and is subject to logic. Logic can, therefore, have no meta-theory: we cannot reason about logic from the outside, for all reasoning is, *ipso facto*, within logic. We can of course set up different formalisms, and study their metatheories; but nothing that we can treat in this way is *logic*. It is in this spirit that Russell denies the possibility of (the usual kind of) independence proofs for the axioms of logic:

[I]t should be observed that the method of supposing an axiom false, and deducing the consequences of this assumption, which has been found admirable in such cases as the axiom of parallels, is here not universally available. For all our axioms are principles of deduction; and if they are true, the consequences which appear to follow from the employment of an opposite principle will not really follow....

(Russell, 1903, p. 15)

One cannot deny an axiom of logic and see what follows, for the axioms of logic are the principles of correct reasoning, and the notion of one thing following from another is lost if one of these axioms is denied. If an axiom of logic is denied, reasoning itself becomes impossible.

This conception of logic, as embodying the correct principles of reasoning, and thus as universal, is quite different from the modern view of the subject. A central concept of modern logic is that of truth in an interpretation, where an interpretation will include the specification of a set as the universe of discourse, i.e. what the variables are to be interpreted as ranging over. The notion of an interpretation is a metatheoretic one, and one that is consequently foreign to Russell's thought. Russell's logic is not a formalism which awaits interpretation to give a meaning to its formulae. Rather, these formulae already have meaning, and the range of the variables in them is not some independently specified universe of discourse but, simply, *the* universe. A universal quantification thus makes a claim about all objects, and the question of its truth or falsity for a given interpretation does not arise: either the claim is true of all objects that there are or it is not. (Similar remarks are true also about Frege's conception of logic. Frege, like Russell, thinks of logic as universal, and thus as not subject to interpretation; hence his insistence that his logic, unlike Boole's, expresses a content, e.g. Frege 1882, pp. 90–91. See also van Heijenoort, 1967(b).)

An understanding of the way in which Russell thinks of logic enables us to explain features of his work which, from a modern point of view, appear as oddities or as trivial mistakes. One such feature is the fact that Russell can give no coherent account of the notion of a rule of inference. This is because the notion is an essentially meta-theoretic one. If the rule of inference is just one more statement within the theory, then we require another rule of inference to show that the conclusion follows from the premisses together with this statement; and the new rule is in turn subject to just the same argument (see Carroll, 1895). Rules of inference are thus a source of difficulty for Russell. He speaks of "a respect in which formalism breaks down" (Russell, 1903, p. 41), and retreats to the view that the validity of an inference cannot in the end be a matter of rules but rather "must be simply perceived, and is not guaranteed by any formal deduction" (loc. cit.). It is to be noted that this same view of rules of inference holds sway also in *Principia*, although Russell is there somewhat less frank about its difficulties. The rules are, again, simply counted as among the primitive propositions of logic, and the consequence, again, is that no clear account of their use emerges (Whitehead and Russell, 1910, e.g. pp. 94, 98, 106; this view of rules of inference is, I believe, a partial explanation of the notorious fact that *Principia* contains no explicit rule of substitution).

The universality of logic, as I have tried to indicate, follows directly from the conception of logic as embodying the correct principles of reasoning. This is a conception which Russell everywhere presupposes, but nowhere articulates; he does not seem to have been aware of it as an assumption, to which there might be alternatives. We cannot, therefore, explore Russell's arguments for the conception. What we can do, however, is to see how crucial a role it played in Russell's thought at this period. In particular, I shall argue that Russell's overarching project of reducing mathematics to logic gets its purpose—in Russell's eyes, at least—from this conception of logic.

If one thinks of the reduction of mathematics to logic as being simply the construction of a mapping, subject to certain constraints, between two uninterpreted formalisms, then it is clear that the philosophical interest of this achievement requires explanation. The obvious form of such an explanation is that the one formalism, considered either as uninterpreted or as subject to its natural inter-pretation, has some philosophically significant property, and that the reduction shows that, contrary to what would otherwise be supposed, the other formalism also has this property. Thus the logical positivists

claimed that the logic of *Principia* was analytic, and that the reduction of mathematics to this logic showed that mathematics also is
analytic. But this motive cannot be imputed to Russell, for he did *not*
think that logic is analytic; he seems to take the reduction of mathematics to logic as showing that, since mathematics is synthetic a
priori, logic must be so too (Russell, 1903, p. 457; 1912, pp. 82–90).
Nor can it be claimed that it is any epistemological characteristic–
certainty, for example–which Russell ascribed to logic and hoped to
transfer, via the reduction, to mathematics; Russell's paradox, and the
difficulty of its solution, made it impossible to suppose that logic is
more certain than mathematics. Russell even went so far as to claim
that a part of our evidence for the axioms of logic comes from the
fact that they enable us to derive the independently known truths of
mathematics (Russell, 1906(c), p. 194; see also Whitehead and Russell,
1910, p. 37).

Russell's reason for the reduction of mathematics to logic, therefore, cannot be to show mathematics to be analytic, or to increase the
certainty of our knowledge of it. Russell's motive in this, his
dominant intellectual project for nearly ten years, can only be understood in terms of the conception of logic that I have sketched. If logic
consists of the correct principles of inference, and mathematics is
reducible to logic, then mathematics is thereby shown to involve no
assumptions which are not already involved in any thinking or
reasoning at all. In particular–and this, I believe, takes us to the heart
of the matter–mathematics is thereby shown not to depend upon any
facts about the forms of our intuition of space and of time, and so the
Kantian theory is refuted:

There was, until very lately, a special difficulty in the principles of
mathematics.... Not only the Aristotelian syllogistic theory, but also the modern
doctrines of Symbolic Logic, were either theoretically inadequate to mathematical
reasoning, or at any rate required such artifical forms of statement that they could not
be practically applied. *In this fact lay the strength of the Kantian view....* Thanks to
the progress of Symbolic Logic.. this part to the Kantian philosophy is capable of a
final and irrevocable refutation.

(Russell, 1903, p. 4; my emphasis. See also p. 457.)

What I wish to emphasise, then, is not just that Russell held the
conception of logic which I have described, but that this conception
was a fundamental part of his philosophy: without appealing to this
conception we are unable to explain the importance of what was most

central to Russell's thought in this period, namely the reduction of mathematics to logic[1]. (Frege's motives in undertaking the logistic reduction must, I believe, be explained similarly, i.e. in terms of his conception of logic as universal. Frege spoke of logic as "analytic", but this word did not play the same explanatory role in his philosophy as it did in, say, Carnap's.)

(ii) *Terms, Concepts, and Propositions*

In this sub-section I shall explain other aspects of Russell's underlying philosophy, especially his views about the nature of propositions and the status of their constituents. I begin with the notion of a *term*, as it occurs in *Principles*. The word "term" is, according to Russell, "the widest word in the philosophical vocabulary" (Russell, 1903, p. 43)[2]. Anything you can think of or talk about is a term; hence, as Russell says, "to deny that such and such a thing is a term must always be false" (loc. cit.). Ordinary concrete objects, abstract objects, and putative but non-actual objects are all terms; Russell's own examples include a man, a moment, a relation, a chimera, and the Homeric Gods (Russell, 1903, pp. 43, 449). Terms are not the words which name these things, but are the things themselves. Thus not every term *exists*, in the ordinary sense of being in space and time; but every term *is*, or subsists, or has Being. In *Principles* Russell clearly believes that every name we can use succeeds in naming some term; but, as we shall see in section II, the possibility of a different view was already implicit in his philosophy.

Russellian terms unite to form Russellian propositions. Propositions are thus not linguistic entities, except when they are about words. Russell is, at this time, never interested in words for their own sake. When he mentions them at all, it is usually only to say that they are *not* his concern, as here:

> *Words* all have meaning, in the simple sense that they are symbols which stand for something other than themselves. But a proposition, unless it happens to be linguistic [i.e. about words] does not itself contain words: it contains the entities indicated by words. Thus meaning, in the sense in which words have meaning is irrelevant to logic.
> (Russell, 1903, p. 47)

The term, or terms, which forms the subject-matter of a proposition will in the normal case be one of the terms *occuring* in the proposition, or, equivalently, one of the *constituents* of the proposition.

Thus when Russel speaks of Socrates occuring in (say) the proposition that Socrates is human, this means exactly what it says: it is Socrates, the man himself, who is a constituent of the proposition (Russell, 1903, e.g. p. 43)[3]. The general rule is that the terms which are the subject-matter of the proposition are also among its constituents. The only exceptions to this rule are provided by those propositions which contain denoting concepts. A denoting concept, such as *all numbers*, is a single term which stands in the rather mysterious relation of denoting to some other term or terms. The denoting concept *all numbers* stands in this relation to all the numbers. Denoting concepts differ from other terms in that when a denoting concept occurs in a proposition the subject matter of the proposition is not that denoting concept itself, but is rather the term or terms which it denotes. Thus the proposition that Socrates is human both *contains* Socrates and is *about* Socrates, but the proposition that all numbers are prime contains the single denoting concept *all numbers*, but is about all the numbers. Russell introduced denoting as a mechanism whereby a proposition might be about infinitely many objects – as is the proposition that all numbers are prime – without containing infinitely many objects (Russell, 1903, e.g. p. 73); but once introduced the notion came, as we shall see, to be used in other ways and to other ends.

Terms unite to form propositions, but not just any combination of terms forms a proposition. We can attribute mortality to Socrates, but we cannot attribute Socrates to mortality. This is the basis of a distinction which Russell makes among terms. Those terms which can only occur in a proposition as subject, never as what is attributed to the subject, he calls "things". All other terms are called "concepts", and Russell holds that they can occur in propositions either as subject or as what is attributed to the subject (Russell, 1903, pp. 44–45). This, for our purposes, is the crucial point. Unlike Frege's distinction between *Gegenstände* and *Begriffe*, Russell's distinction between things and concepts is not a distinction between what can occur only as subject and what can occur only attributively. "Every term", Russell says, "is a logical subject: it is, for example, the subject of the proposition that itself is one." (Russell, 1903, p. 44). Some logical subjects can appear *only* as logical subjects, while others can appear both as logical subjects and attributively:

Socrates is a thing, because Socrates can never occur otherwise than as a term [i.e. as subject] in a proposition: Socrates is not capable of the curious twofold use which is involved in *human* and *humanity*.

(Russell, 1903, p. 45)

One confusing piece of terminology should be noted here. Although everything is a term, Russell speaks of something occuring as a term in a proposition only if it is a subject of that proposition; similarly he speaks of the terms of a proposition, meaning its logical subjects (Russell 1903, e.g. p. 45). The reason for this is that one of the things that Russell means by "term" is logical subject; everything is a term because everything can be a logical subject, but in a given proposition only some among its constituents occur as terms, i.e. as logical subjects.

Russell does not simply assume that the distinction he draws among terms is the correct one. He explicitly considers the view, analogous to Frege's, that what can occur attributively cannot also occur as subject, i.e., as he puts it, that

a distinction ought to be made between a concept as such and a concept used as a term, between e.g. such pairs as *is* and *being*, *human* and *humanity*, one in such a proposition as "this is one" and 1 in "1 is a number".

(Russell, 1903, p. 45)

Russell rejects this view, and his reasons for doing so are of the first importance. The basis for the rejection is that the view cannot be stated without presupposing its own falsehood. Consider the proposition that *human* is, and *humanity* is not, capable of occuring as a logical subject. In this proposition, *humanity* occurs as a logical subject; but this is just what the proposition says is impossible. So the fact that there is such a proposition shows that it cannot be true. It is worth quoting Russell at some length on this point:

... suppose that *one* as adjective differed from 1 as term. In this statement, *one* as an adjective has been made into a term; hence either it has become 1, in which case the supposition is self-contradictory; or there is some other difference between *one* and 1 in addition to the fact that the first denotes a concept which is a term. But in this latter hypothesis there must be propositions concerning *one* as term, and we shall still have to maintain propositions concerning *one* as adjective ... yet all such propositions must be false, since a proposition about *one* as adjective makes *one* the subject, and is therefore really about *one* as a term .... This state of things is self-contradictory.

(Russell, 1903, p. 46)

This argument presupposes that the statement that *one* as adjective differs from 1 as a term is subject to the same rules as are the statements we make using *one* as an adjective. The argument, that is, could be defeated by the claim that when we say that *one* is an adjective we are talking in the metatheory about a language in which *one* can only occur as an adjective; the fact that it occured as a term in the metatheory would then not be damaging. But we have already seen that the universality of logic would, in Russell's eyes, rule out the possibility of any such appeal to a metalanguage not subject to the rules of logic. If this argument of Russell's is successful, it shows more than may at first sight appear. It does not in fact depend upon its being the same term which appears now as subject, now as adjective. All that is crucial to it is that a term will appear as subject in any proposition about it, e.g. that it cannot appear as logical subject, that it is a term, that it occurs in a proposition. So any proposition which says of anything that it is not a logical subject must be false: everything is a logical subject.

We can attain a different perspective on this argument by comparing it to the difficulty that Frege found himself in concerning the concept *horse*. As we have already seen, Russell's position is that everything can be a logical subject, whereas Frege's is that some things—*Begriffe*—cannot be. Russell takes as contradictory what Frege simply calls "an awkwardness of language" (Frege, 1892, p. 46), namely that the concept *horse* is not a concept. Since a Fregean concept can never occupy the subject place in a proposition, the phrase "the concept *horse*", which does occupy subject position, cannot refer to a concept. Thus for Frege the two phrases "the concept *horse*" and "...is a horse" do not refer to the same thing: as Russell might put it, the concept taken as predicate is for Frege different from the concept taken as subject (this mode of expression is not, of course, Fege's). How, then, can Frege say, as he does, that "the concept...is predicative" (Frege, 1892, p. 43)? The expression "the concept" in this sentence, since it occupies subject position, refers to a concept taken as subject, not as predicate (as Russell might put it). But then the sentence, taken literally, is false. If Frege's theory is true, then, there is no way in which we can say that a concept is essentially predicative in nature, and so no way in which we can state Frege's theory itself.[4] For Russell this is enough to show that Frege's theory cannot be true: the theory consists of propositions which according to that theory itself cannot be propositions at all, and if they are not propositions, they certainly cannot be true.

Now it might be thought that these difficulties arise for Frege only because we take too naive a view of the matter. Russell argues that there cannot be entities which are incapable of becoming logical subjects, but this, it might be held, need not rule out a view like Frege's. Such a view requires a hierachy of levels of concepts. Call the kind of concept that can be attributed to Socrates (whether truly or falsely) a "first-level" concept. Then first-level concepts *can* be logical subjects; we cannot attribute other first-level concepts to them, but there are second-level concepts which can be attributed to them, and third-level concepts which can be attributed to second-level concepts, and so on. Thus there is nothing which cannot, at some level and in some sense, be a logical subject, nothing that we cannot talk about; yet no concept can have a first-level concept attributed to it. This view is, however, subject to the same objection as was the more naive view, although the objection naturally takes a more sophisticated form. The naive view was self-defeating because the attempt to say that a given concept could not be a logical subject involved making that concept a logical subject. The more sophisticated view is self-defeating in a parallel, if more devious, fashion.

Consider the statement that only first-level concepts can be attributed to Socrates. If this statement is to do what we want, it must imply that second-level concepts (and concepts of every higher level) can *not* be attributed to Socrates. But now consider the concept "...can be attributed to Socrates". Assuming the universality of logic, this concept itself must occupy a determinate position in the hierachy of concepts; but it cannot do so. The concept is true of first-level concepts, and so should be a second level concept; but it is false of second-level concepts (and of concepts at every higher level), and so should be a third-level concept (and also a fourth-level concept, and so on). So it turns out that we cannot establish a hierachy of concepts, because the statements by means of which we attempt to do so must be nonsensical if the hierachy is correct.

Russell does not discuss Frege's hierachy of concepts, but he does employ an argument with the same structure as the above. Considering the view that variables only range over some given universe of discourse, not over all objects, he says:

We might say that a given function ϕx will always have a certain *range of significance* which will be either *individuals*, or *classes*, or .... The difficulty of this view lies in the proposition (say) 'ϕx is only significant when x is a class'. This proposition must not be restricted, as to its range, to the case when x is a class; for we want it to imply 'ϕx is not significant when x is not a class'. We thus find that we are brought back after all the variables with an unrestricted range.

(Russell, 1906 (c) pp. 204–5)

What makes this of particular interest is that the theory of types is vulnerable to the same argument. *Principia* employs the notion ". . . is of the same type as . . ." not only in its expository prose but also in its numbered sentences: *9.14, for example, is a primitive proposition which states "if 'ϕx' is significant, then if x is of the same type as a, 'ϕa' is significant, and vice versa." (Whitehead and Russell, 1910, p. 133). Now ". . . is of the same type as a", where a is some individual, is a concept which is true of individuals. If the type restrictions are to be effective it must also be false, and thus significant, of non-individuals. But by the vice versa clause of *9.14, if a concept is significant as applied to two entities, the two must be of the same type. So if there is such a concept as ". . . is the same type as . . .", then there is only one type; but if there is no such concept then we cannot establish the type-hierachy[5].

(iii) *The Paradox*

The considerations thus far advanced were taken by Russell to establish two doctrines. The first is that concepts–the objective correlates of the predicates of sentences–are logical subjects or terms; given the universality of logic, the attempt to say of a particular concept that it is not a logical subject must presuppose that it *is* a logical subject. The second doctrine is that there can be no distinctions of type among logical subjects, i.e. that all terms are intersubstitutable *salva significationem*; again the crucial point is the universality of logic, which makes distinctions of type impossible, since the statement of such a distinction would itself violate the distinction.

These two doctrines together yield a contradiction–a version of Russell's paradox with predication substituted for class membership, and concepts or propositional functions for classes[6]. It was in fact in this form that Russell first stated the paradox in his letter to Frege, of the 16th June 1902:

Let w be the predicate, being a predicate which cannot be predicated of itself. Can w be predicated of itself? From either answer the opposite follows.

(Russell, 1902, p. 125)

Frege simply ignores this version of the paradox, and concentrates on the statement in terms of classes, because his hierachy of concepts prevents the paradox for *Begriffe*. This is why the source of the contradiction in Frege's system is most naturally thought of as being the notorious axiom V of *Grundgesetze*, which states that the *Wertverläufe* (value-ranges) of two concepts are identical just in case the two concepts are co-extensive. Given that *Wertverläufe* are objects, this allows us to derive the contradiction. Each *Wertverlauf* must either fall under or fail to fall under any given concept – including that concept with which it is associated. So there is a concept expressed by "... is a *Wertverlauf* which does not fall under the concept with which it is associated"; and there is a *Wertverlauf* associated with this concept. Now we have only to ask whether this *Wertverlauf* falls under the concept with which it is associated, and the paradox results. In Frege's system the paradox thus stems from the assumption that there is an object associated with every concept, together with the identity-conditions for those objects. But for Russell the paradox arises without the use of any special assumption. For Russell there is no question whether concepts are *associated* with things that can play the role of logical subjects; concepts themselves must be capable of playing this role. The arguments which I have explored earlier in this section seem to prove that this must be so; yet if it is so, paradox seems to result.

There is thus a fundamental tension between, on the one hand, Russell's doctrine of the universality of logic, and, on the other hand, the need to avoid the paradox. The substitutional theory was an attempt to resolve this tension, and to avoid the paradox by means consistent with the universality of logic. The arguments we have examined show, or at least were taken by Russell to show, that concepts must capable of being used as logical subjects, and that there can be no distinctions of type among logical subjects. Given that there *are* concepts, the contradiction follows immediately: but, equally, our conclusions appear quite harmless if we deny that there are concepts. The argument that concepts must be capable of occuring as logical subjects did not show that there are any concepts, and would be quite consistent with this denial. A theory which did not assume that there are any concepts (or propositional functions) would therefore seem to offer Russell a way out of his dilemma: and this was the attraction of the substitutional theory.

II

In this section I shall, very briefly, explain the substitutional theory, and show how it exploits the notion of an incomplete symbol to attain an expressive power which one might suppose impossible without the assumption of classes, or concepts. I shall not, however, attempt any rigourous development of the theory, much less a proof that it is, as Russell thought it to be, adequate to encode mathematics[7].

It follows from what has already been said that the substitutional theory is to avoid the assumption that there are concepts. We are no longer to analyse propositions into a subject (or subjects) and what is said about the subject. Instead of this, the theory treats propositions as unanalysable. We still speak of propositions as containing entities, and we can substitute one entity for another in a proposition to obtain a possibly different proposition. But what is abandoned is the idea that p can be analysed into two elements, a and the property which p asserts to hold of a[8]. Writing at a time before he was fully committed to the substitutional theory, Russell put it like this:

> ... if we make statements of the form $F!x$ about a number of different values of x, we cannot pick out an entity F which is the common *form* of all these statements, or is the property assigned to x when we state $F!x$.
>
> (Russell, 1906 (a), p. 137)

The language here is the language of propositional functions, but it is, strictly speaking, superfluous. If we recognise propositional functions as entities which differ in type from objects, then we must *say* that they are of different type: and we have seen the trouble to which this leads. But a theory which does not recognise propositional functions as among the entities of the world is not committed to saying anything about them. Such a theory can be explained by talking only of propositions, and of substitutions of one entity for another within propositions. (The situation is perhaps a little more complicated than this way of putting it would suggest; this will emerge when I discuss the role of the idea of an incomplete symbol.)

The substitutional theory, then, assumes an ontology of entities, some of which are propositions, and the notion of substitution. The expression "$p/a;b$" is to mean "the result of substituting a for b in p". Strictly speaking, this notation is defined only in the context "$p/a;b!q$", which means "q results from substituting b for a in p", but Russell frequently uses the shorter notation as either a name or an assertion of the q such that $p/a;b!q$. I shall follow Russell's usage on this point.

The notion of substitution is meant to apply to more than one entity at once, i.e. we want to be able to substitute b for a and b' for a', and so on. Now we could say that "$p/(a, a');(b, b')$" is to mean "$(\exists r)$ $(p/a;b!r \ \& \ r/a';b'!q)$", and so on. But this would not be satisfactory. We want q to contain b' in just those places where p contains a'; but if a is a constituent of a', then $p/a;b$ will not contain a' at all. To define the sort of multiple substitution that we want we first define various notions:

$$a \ \mathrm{ex} \ p = \mathrm{df.} \ (\forall x)(p/a;x!p)$$

This is read "a does not occur in P", and simply means that a is not a constituent of p. The negation of this we abbreviate as "a in p". If two entities have no constituents on common, they are said to be independent of one another:

$$p \ \mathrm{ind} \ q = \mathrm{df.} \ (\forall x)\sim(x \ \mathrm{in} \ p \ \& \ x \ \mathrm{in} \ q)$$

(See Russell 1906(b), p. 169 for these definitions.) Now we can define simultaneous substitution for two entities. Suppose we want to substitute c and d for a and b in p. If b is in a, choose an entity a' which is not in p, and which is independent of b and of d. First substitute a' for a, then d for b, then c for a'. If b is not in a, choose an entity b' which is not in p, and which is independent of a and of c. First substitute b' for b, then c for a, then d for b'. By this technique of choosing neutral entities, we can define simultaneous substitution for any given number of entities.

The power of the substitutional theory comes from the way in which it exploits the notion of an incomplete symbol. This notion, although not this name, first appears in 'On denoting' (Russell 1905 (b); I shall abbreviate this article as O.D.), but the concentration on definite descriptions there makes the matter hard to grasp in its full generality. It seems to be widely believed that the main point of O.D. is to show that sentences such as "The King of France is bald" or "The round square does not exist" can be meaningful without our having to assume that there is (in some sense) such a thing as the round square or the King of France. Ayer certainly holds this view (Ayer, 1972, pp. 49–51), and Sainsbury seems to have this idea in mind when he says "The theory of descriptions offered a release from the supposed need for nonexistent beings" (Sainsbury, 1979, p. 17). This idea is, however, quite mistaken, and it prevents us from achieving a clear view of exactly what change in Russell's philosophy is effected by O.D.. We have seen that when a proposition is expressed by a sentence including a denoting phrase then, according to the view in *Principles*, the proposition is *about* what is denoted but *contains* the denoting concept. Thus, while the proposition that Socrates is mortal contains the man that it is about, the proposition that the Queen of England is mortal does not contain the woman that it is about, but rather contains the denoting concept *the Queen of England*. But then the proposition that the Queen of England is mortal does not require that there *be* a Queen of England in any sense, merely that there be a denoting concept that purports to denote her. It thus appears that the mechanism of denoting–i.e. the theory which Russell held before O.D.–can be employed to do away with the need to recognise the King of France or the round square. Russell did not employ the theory of denoting in this way in *Principles*, but he came to do so before he wrote O.D.:

'The present king of England' is a complex concept denoting an individual; 'The present king of France' is a similar concept denoting nothing. The phrase intends to point out an individual, but fails to do so: it does not point out an unreal individual, but no individual at all. The same explanation applies to mythical personages, Apollo, Priam, etc. These words have a *meaning* . . . but they have not a denotation: there is no entity, real or imagined, which they point out.

(Russell, 1905 (a), p. 100)

Since this pre-O.D. theory enables Russell to avoid the view that there must be such an entity as the King of France, we cannot think of O.D. as designed to achieve this result.

The decisive move in O.D., then, is not the rejection of the view that denoting phrases must actually denote something if they are to have a use–for this was a view that Russell had already rejected, on a quite different basis. The decisive move is, rather, the rejection of the idea that denoting phrases function as logical units. According to the *Principles* view, a phrase such as "the F" in a sentence corresponds to an entity, the denoting concept *the F*, in the propositions which correspond to the whole sentence. According to the theory of O.D., by contrast, there is no entity in a proposition which corresponds to the phrase "the F". If the sentence is, say, "G (the F)" (i.e. "The F is G") then the form of the corresponding proposition is more accurately given by the sentence

$$(\exists x)(Fx \ \& \ (\forall y)(Fy \equiv y = x) \ \& \ Gx)$$

In this sentence there is no occurrence of the phrase "the F"; and similarly, according to O.D., there is in the corresponding proposition no entity corresponding to the phrase "the F". This is why Russell calls such phrases "incomplete symbols": by itself such a phrase does not stand for anything and thus, in Russell's terminology, has no meaning; but certain longer expressions, containing such phrases, do have meaning if taken as wholes. An incomplete symbol is thus a symbol which has been defined in certain contexts, but which does not itself stand for anything. We have already seen that there are pressures in Russell's thought which lead towards the view that expressions which stand for entities are everywhere intersubstitutable *salva significationem*, and this enables us to make a sharp contrast between these expressions and incomplete symbols, for the latter will make sense only in contexts for which they have been defined, and from which they are eliminable. This is why Russell says that an incomplete symbol is a phrase which "by itself has no meaning at all, but by the addition of other symbols or words becomes part of a symbol or phrase which has meaning, i.e., is the name of something." (Russell, 1906(b), p. 69).

The importance of this move is concealed rather than revealed by focusing on phrases of the form "the F". There are two connected reasons for this. The first, and more important, is that although phrases of the form "the F" are only defined contextually, it turns out that they are in fact defined for *all* contexts in which we would naturally use a singular referring expression. Secondly, although a phrase such as "the F" does not stand for the F, still, if an ordinary sentence containing the phrase is true, there must be an object which is uniquely F. By speaking here of an "ordinary sentence", I mean to exclude both denials of existence ("There is no such thing as the F") and negations of wide scope ("It is not the case that: the F is G"). Excluding sentences of these kinds, i.e. considering only those which purport to affirm or deny something about the F, we can say that there must be a unique F if a sentence containing the phrase "the F" is to be true.

The power of the notion of an incomplete symbol, which is concealed by its application to definite descriptions, is clearly shown by the use that Russell makes of it in the substitutional theory. The most crucial incomplete symbol (in its simplest form) is "p/a". This symbol does not stand for an entity, though both "p" and "a" do, and there is no entity which is p/a, whatever p and a may be (whereas for some instances of F, there is an entity which is the F, even though "the F" does not stand for this entity). The symbol "p/a" is defined, but only in certain contexts. We have already seen the definition of "$p/a;b!q$", but in this context "p/a" does not even appear to name an entity– "the result of replacing a in p by" is clearly not the name of anything. The other contexts which are crucial for the theory are "$b \in p/a$" and "$p/a = q/b$". Both of these are defined, and in such a way that it is clear that there is no entity named by "p/a":

$$b \in p/a = \text{df. the } q \text{ such that } p/a;b!q \text{ is true}$$
$$p/a = q/b = \text{df. } (\forall x)(p/a;x \equiv q/b;x)$$

The definition of "$=$" between symbols of the form $p/a_1 \ldots a_n$ is a straightforward generalisation of the above:

$$p/a_1 \ldots a_n = q/b_1 \ldots b_n = \text{df.} (\forall x_1 \ldots x_n)$$
$$(p/(a_1 \ldots a_n);(x_1 \ldots x_n)$$
$$\equiv q/(b_1 \ldots b_n);(x_1 \ldots x_n)$$

The extension of "$\in$" is a little more complicated, and two cases should be treated differently. First:

$$b_1 \ldots b_n \in p/(a_1 \ldots a_n) = \text{df the } q \text{ such that } p/(a_1 \ldots a_n);$$
$$(b_1 \ldots b_n)!q \text{ is true}$$

Secondly:

$$q/(b_1 \ldots b_n) \in p/(a_1 \ldots a_{n+1}) = \text{df. } (\forall r,c_1 \ldots c_n)$$
$$\{(q/(b_1 \ldots b_n)) = (r/(c_1 \ldots c_n)) \supset \text{the } s \text{ such that}$$
$$p/(a_1 \ldots a_{n+1});(r,c_1 \ldots c_n)!s \text{ is true}\}$$

The symbol "p/a" or, more generally, symbols of the form "$p/a_1 \ldots a_n$", is thus defined for certain contexts. These are sentences in which symbols of this form appear to occupy subject-position and to be referring expressions. But the definitions show that these sentences are in fact only misleading ways of expressing propositions which are more accurately (though less briefly) expressed by sentences in which "$p/a_1 \ldots a_n$" does not occupy subject-position, or appear in any sense to refer to an entity. Thus the definitions show that some of these sentences may be true even though there is no such entity as p/a. Russell calls things such as p/a "matrices", and attempts to show that they can perform all the functions which classes must perform if we are to reduce mathematics to the theory of classes. Now there are no such things as matrices. Symbols of the form "p/a" enable us to talk, in certain contexts, as if there were; but these symbols get their significance not from standing for entities but simply because our definitions have given them a significance in those contexts. A symptom of this is that such expressions are eliminable wherever they are significant. It is natural to express this by saying, as Russell does, that a matrix is a mere symbol. Though Russell is certainly, by modern (or Fregean) standards, careless about use and mention, it would be a mistake to think that his use of this quite natural mode of expression indicates any real confusion. Still less should we take it as showing that Russell held matrices to be linguistic entities. This view makes nonsense of Russell's claim that "a matrix is not an entity" (Russell, 1906(b), p. 170), for one could hardly deny that the *expression* "p/a" is an entity. To put the matter beyond all doubt, he does occasionally spell out his position more rigourously: "When we say 'so-and-so is not an entity', the meaning is, properly speaking, "The *phrase* 'so-and-so' is not the name of an entity.' " (loc. cit.).

Russell did not, in O.D., cast doubt on the idea that only a genuine entity can be the subject of a proposition. On the contrary, he actually removed some of the qualifications with which he had previously held this view. What is new with O.D. is the idea that in many or most sentences the grammatical subject does not correspond to an entity. The decisive break with *Principles* is not the rejection of the view that only entities which *are* in some sense or having Being can occur in propositions; Russell continues to believe this. The decisive break is rather that the grammatical form of the sentence is no longer to be taken as the logical form of the proposition. Thus we can make sense of sentences which appear to be about matrices – and we can claim that some of these sentences are true – without having to assume that there *are* matrices.

This is important because we can now avoid the paradox while still admitting that entities are everywhere intersubstitutable *salve significationem*. As Russell puts it, reverting to the terminology of propositional functions:

... it is essential to an entity that it is a possible determination of x in any propositional function Fx; that is, if Fx is any propositional function, and a any entity, Fa must be a significant proposition.

(Russell, 1906(b), p. 171)

Now if p/a were an entity we should, according to this principle, have to admit that "$p/a \in p/a$" expresses a proposition; and thus the danger of paradox arises. But in fact "p/a" is only a symbol which our definitions allow us to eliminate from certain contexts. If we try to read "$p/a \in p/a$" in accordance with our definitions we get something like "the result of replacing a in p by the result of replacing a in p by"–and taken as a complete utterance this is clearly nonsense. What the matrix-notation allows us to do is to achieve the effects of a type-hierarchy while still maintaining that there are no distinctions of type among entities. The hierarchy is based on the impossibility of substituting more or fewer than n entities for n entities and still obtaining a proposition, i.e. on the fact that

$$p/(a_1 \ldots a_n);(b_1 \ldots b_m)!q$$

only makes sense if $n = m$. If we express all matrices in the form "$p/(a_1 \ldots a_n)$" and call n the *type* of the matrix, it follows that "$A \in B$" will not express a proposition unless *either* A is an entity and B is a type-1 matrix, *or* A is a type-n matrix and B is a type-$n + 1$ matrix. On the other hand, it follows from our definitions that if either of these conditions *is* satisfied then "$A \in B$" *will* express a proposition. We thus obtain a hierarchy of matrices which is entirely analogous to the hierarchy of classes (or propositional functions) in simple type theory. The crucial difference is that, because matrices are not entities, the restrictions on meaningfulness do not need to be stated. If we use our definitions to eliminate all uses of defined expressions, it will simply be evident whether or not the resulting sentence is significant. As Russell puts it:

When a formula contains matrices, the test of whether it is significant or not is very simple: it is significant if it can be stated wholly in terms of entities. Matrices are nothing but verbal or symbolic abbreviations; hence any statement in which they occur must, if it is to be a significant statement and not a mere jumble, be capable of being stated without matrices.

(Russell, 1906(b), p. 177)

The point here is simply that uses of matrix-expressions, except for their use in the original substitution context, "$p/a;b!q$", make sense only in virtue of our contextual definitions. So we ought to be able to eliminate all such uses to obtain a sentence which is "stated wholly in terms of entities", i.e., a sentence in which all apparent referring expressions refer to entities. If we cannot do this, because a matrix-expression occurs in a context from which our definitions do not enable us to eliminate it, then the sentence does not express a proposition.

Let us speak of the *basic language* of the substitutional theory as the language of the theory without any of the expressions introduced by contextual definitions; and of the *extended language* as the basic language with the expressions introduced in this manner. Then we can make the point of the above paragraph by saying that in the basic language of the theory there are no type-restrictions upon significance. Every apparent subject-expression is a genuine subject-expression, and these are interchangeable *salva significationem*. In the extended language there will be type-restrictions among apparent subject-expressions, i.e. among matrix-expressions, but these restrictions will follow from the way in which matrix-expressions are introduced by contextual definitions, and will not need to be stated *ad hoc*. Any putative sentence of the extended language which violates type-restrictions will contain expressions introduced by contextual definition in a context from which our definitions do not enable us to eliminate them; or else will contain such expressions in contexts from which they cannot be eliminated without our substituting more or fewer than n entities for n entities in some proposition. In either case the attempt to restate the sentence in the basic language will make the failing evident, without the need to appeal to type-restrictions. Because the type-restrictions only hold among incomplete symbols, and not among genuine entities, they are, strictly speaking, superfluous; we do not need to worry whether type restrictions of this Pickwickian kind are self-defeating, for our theory need never state them.

The substitutional theory thus allows us to simulate (some fragment of) the theory of classes without assuming that there are classes, or propositional functions; and since we avoid these assumptions we seem also to avoid the need for type-restrictions. Other means of simulating the theory of classes are restricted in power because they offer no means of expressing quantification over classes (e.g. Quine's theory of virtual classes; Quine, 1963, pp. 15–21); Russell's theory, however, allows us to do this. We cannot, of course, say "For all one-place matrices, $p/a, \ldots p/a \ldots$" or "For all matrices of one-place matrices, $p/(q/a), \ldots p(q/a) \ldots$", but we can achieve the effect of saying this. I assume we have the notion "a is a proposition".[9] Then we can say:

> $(\forall x, y)$(If x is a proposition & y in x then $\ldots x/y \ldots$)
>
> $(\forall x, y, z)$(If x is a proposition & y in x & z in x then $\ldots x/(y, z) \ldots$)
>
> $(\forall x, y, z)$(If x is a proposition & y is a proposition & y in x & z in y, then $\ldots x/(y/z) \ldots$)
>
> and so on.

Thus quantification over matrices is eliminable by means of quantification over propositions of the requisite degree of complexity and their constituents.

Some idea of the power of the theory may be gathered from the way in which it can handle the definition of the ancestral of (the analogue of) a relation. Suppose we have a two-place matrix, $p_1/(a_1, a_2)$ (p_1 might be, say $a_1 + 1 = a_2$, in which case $p_1/(a_1, a_2)$ is the analogue of the successor relation). We wish to find a matrix $q/(b_1, b_2)$ such that $q/(b_1, b_2);(x, y)$ is true just in case one of the following list of propositions is true:

> $p_1/(a_1, a_2);(x, y)$
>
> $(\exists z)(p_1/(a_1, a_2);(x, z)$ & $p_1/(a_1, a_2);(z, y))$
>
> $(\exists x, z')(p_1/(a_1, a_2);(x, z)$ & $p_1/(a_1, a_2);(z, z')$ & $p_1/(a_1, a_2);(z', y))$
>
> $(\exists z, z', z'')(p_1/(a_1, a_2);(x, z)$ & $\ldots$
>
> $\ldots$

In other words, we want $q/(b_1, b_2)$ to be the ancestral of $p_1/(a_1, a_2)$. Now consider the proposition:

> $(\forall x, y)\{(x$ is a proposition & y in x & $(\forall z, w)$
>
> $(x/y;z$ & $p_1/(a_1, a_2);(z, w) \supset x/y;w)$
>
> & $(\forall z)(p_1/(p_1/(a_1, a_2);(b_1, z) \supset x/y;z)) \supset x/y;b_2\}$

If now we call this proposition q, then $q/(b_1, b_2)$ is the matrix that we want. (This way of defining the ancestral of a given relation is directly analogous to that in Whitehead and Russell, 1910, pp. 543–544, except that we use matrices instead of classes.)

III

In this section I turn to the question of why Russell abandoned the substitutional theory. We have already seen that it is not because he finds the theory inadequate for mathematics: as late as 1908 he says that the theory is "possible ... although ... technically inconvenient" (Russell, 1908, p. 77; quoted in full, p. 1, above).[10] Nor is it plausible to suppose that the technical inconvenience of the theory would by itself deter Russell; we have seen that the reasons which drove him to develop the theory were fundamental to his philosophy, and we should expect to find that the theory was abandoned for reasons no less fundamental.

One such reason, which has been held to explain Russell's abandonment of the substitutional theory, stems from his concern with the concept of truth. In the *Principles of Mathematics*, and throughout the three or four years immediately following its publication, Russell accepted the concept of truth as indefinable, and the fact that all propositions are either true or false as inexplicable. He even went so far as to say that our preference for true propositions over false ones could only be explained as "an ultimate ethical proposition" (Russell, 1904, p. 76). Not surprisingly, he came to find this unsatisfactory, and sought to explain truth in terms of the correspondence of the constituents of a proposition with reality. This theory, as Russell developed it, had the immediate consequence that, while the constituents of a proposition are real, propositions themselves are not. Expressions which appear to refer to propositions are incomplete symbols which have meaning only in a context in which we assert the proposition, or suppose it, or deny it, etc. Russell, that is to say, came to deny that propositions have any reality independent of our acts of judgement. This view is incompatible with the substitutional theory, which demands the independent existence of propositions for, as we have seen, the theory makes essential use of quantification over propositions.

Russell's concern with the nature of truth thus provides a possible reason for his abandonment of the substitutional theory, and it has been claimed that it is *the* reason (see Grattan-Guinness, 1974, pp. 398–401). Closer consideration, however, suggests that this reason was at least not primary. One issue here is simply the timing of the two changes in Russell's views. Circumstances suggest that he abandoned the substitutional theory towards the end of 1906, or very early in 1907. The two articles of 1906 in which Russell advocates the theory are followed not by works in which he develops it further, but by a period during which he does not discuss such fundamental matters in print. The next time he does so, it is to put forward the type theory of *Principia Mathematica*, based not on substitution but on propositional functions (Russell, 1908). A paper which he read in March 1907 only alludes to these issues, but it is to propositional functions that it alludes, not to substitution (Russell, 1907(b)). But if Russell did abandon the substitutional theory this early, it was not because he no longer believed in the reality of propositions. In another paper of 1907 he declares himself undecided as to the existence of propositions (Russell, 1907(a), section III), and it is not until 1910 that he publicly rejects them (Russell, 1910, pp. 147–58). A second reason not to take the rejection of propositions as explaining the abandonment of the substitutional theory is that by doing so we overestimate Russell's concern with the consistency of his various theories. Given the importance of the issues at stake, it would have been unsurprising if Russell had both developed a logic relying upon quantification over propositions and explained the nature of truth in a way which implies that propositions do not exist, leaving the reconciling of these two positions as an open problem to be solved later. Indeed we may say not only that Russell *might* have done this but that he did do it for, as Grattan-Guinness points out, *Principia Mathematica* itself relies upon quantification over propositions (Whitehead and Russell, pp. 41–43; see Grattan-Guinness, 1974, p. 401).

Russell's abandonment of the substitutional theory is to be explained not in terms of a conflict between that theory and other parts of his philosophy, but rather in terms which are internal to the theory and to his reasons for adopting it. To put the matter very briefly, the substitutional theory as I have sketched it (the simple substitutional theory, as I shall call it) turns out to be vulnerable to paradoxes. These paradoxes are what we would call semantic rather than logical, but within the substitutional theory they arise without the use of any special assumptions. The theory can be modified so as to avoid these paradoxes, but, so modified, it lacks just those features which, I claimed, made it attractive to Russell. Given that the theory no longer possessed those features, we can understand why Russell might have abandoned it for reasons of technical convenience.

One example of the paradoxes to which the simple substitutional theory is vulnerable is the following. Some matrices have only propositions as members: p/a is such a matrix just in case $p/a;b$ is true only where b is a proposition. With each such matrix, p/a, we associate a proposition, p_a^*, which says that all the members of p/a are true, i.e. $(\forall x)(p/a;x \supset x$ is true$)$. Now let q be the following proposition:

$$(\exists p, a)(p_a^* = ((\forall x)(p/a;x \supset x \text{ is true})) \& \sim (p_a^* \in p/a)).$$

Then q/p_a^* is a matrix all of whose members are propositions. So we associate with it a proposition, $q_{p_a^*}^*$ which says that all the members of q/p_a^* are true. But now is $q_{p_a^*}^*$ a member of q/p_a^*? The members of q/p_a^* are those propositions which say of some matrix that all of its members are true, and which are not themselves members of the matrix of which they say this. $q_{p_a^*}^*$ satisfies the first of these conditions, so it is a member of q/p_a^* just in case it also satisfies the second condition by failing to be a member of the matrix all of whose members it asserts to be true. But since that matrix is q/p_a^* itself, we have a contradiction.

The semantic paradoxes are often taken as showing that the notion of truth should be excluded from logic. But in this case such a reaction would be inappropriate. First, the universality of logic means that we cannot exclude truth from our logic without rejecting the notion altogether, and this is something that Russell would certainly not have been prepared to do at this stage in his philosophical development. A second, more fundamental point, is that the substitutional theory demands that we employ the notion of truth. We cannot, for example, define membership in a matrix except by saying something equivalent to: "b is a member of p/a" is to mean "the q such that $p/a;b!q$ is true". This use of the notion of truth is sometimes disguised by Russell's habit of using sentences ambiguously, sometimes as names of propositions and sometimes as assertions of them; but this ambiguity itself makes an essential, if tacit, use of the notion of truth.

The simple substitutional theory presented in On the substitutional theory of classes and relations (Russell, 1906 (b)) is thus vulnerable to paradox, and this presumably explains the odd history of this paper, which Russell read to the London Mathematical Society in May 1906, but withdrew from publication in October of the same year. In the intervening months he not only realised the problem, but also found a solution. On 'insolubilia' and their solution by symbolic logic (Russell, 1906 (c), first published in September 1906) directly addresses the semantic paradoxes (Russell speaks of the *Epimenides* or liar paradox, but his solution applies quite generally), and proposes to avoid them by distinguishing types of proposition. The distinction is effected according to the number and type of bound variables which they contain. The lowest level propositions contain no bound variables. Then we have propositions containing one variable ranging over individuals, propositions containing two variables ranging over individuals, and so on. Propositions containing variables ranging over propositions form a distinct and higher order, whose lowest level consists of propositions containing one variable ranging over propositions containing one variable ranging over individuals (propositions containing no variables seem to be counted among individuals), and so on. Whatever we may say about a proposition of one type cannot be said with sense about a proposition of any other type: words such as "true" which appear to violate this requirement are deemed ambiguous (Russell, 1906 (c), p. 208). Thus the paradox which I explained above is blocked. Since p_a^* is $(\forall x)(p/a;x \supset x$ is true), p_a^* is of higher type than anything which can be substituted with sense for a in p, so $p_a^* \in p/a$ is nonsensical.

This version of the substitutional theory (ramified substitutional theory, as I shall call it) does not allow us to quantify over all propositions, but only over all propositions of a given type. As in the case of the analogous restriction on propositional functions in ramified type theory, this restriction threatens our ability to do mathematics. In particular, the law of mathematical induction becomes impossible to state (Russell, 1906 (c), p. 211). In ramified type theory the axiom of reducibility was introduced to avoid this difficulty, and here Russell makes an analogous move:

There is no objection, on the score of the *Epimenides* to the assumption that every statement containing x and a variable is *equivalent*, for all values of x, to some statement containing no apparent variable.

(Russell, 1906 (c), p. 212)

This assumption makes the ramified substitutional theory as powerful as the simple version for all mathematical purposes, while still preserving its freedom from semantic paradoxes.

To understand why Russell abandoned the ramified substitutional theory, we have to refer back to the reason which, I argued, explains why he first adopted the substitutional theory. If we make distinctions of type among the entities assumed by our logic, then we must be able to state the resulting type restrictions. But such statements themselves violate type restrictions. Thus any logic with the universality which Russell took as definitive of logic cannot be subject to type restrictions. The substitutional theory seemed to be able to accomodate this argument without paradox, because there are no distinctions of type among the entities which it assumes (matrices are not entities). But this crucial virtue belongs only to the simple substitutional theory, for in the ramified version we have to acknowledge distinctions of type among the propositions which the theory assumes to exist. Statements of the restrictions upon meaningfulness which arise from these distinctions will be subject to the kind of difficulty which I discussed in the case of concepts or propositional functions: they cannot be reconciled with the universality of logic. If my account of the attraction which the simple substitutional theory had for Russell is correct, then the ramified version would have no such attraction for him. There would, in fact, be no reason for him to work within this theory rather than to assume propositional functions; he might well switch from one theory to the other for reasons of technical convenience.

IV

Whether the reduction of mathematics to logic is possible depends, of course, upon what one understands by logic; this will also determine the philosophical interest which a successful reduction would have. The essential feature of logic as Russell saw it was, I argued, its universality. If logic consists of the principles of correct reasoning, then all reasoning must be subject to logic. Logic will thus be all-pervasive and inescapable. It is only in terms of this conception of logic, I claimed, that we can understand the philosophical significance which Russell attributed to the logistic reduction.

It does not immediately follow from the universality of logic that the assumption of the existence of concepts or propositional functions is an extra-logical assumption. This assumption, unlike that of the existence of sets, does not appear to introduce any special subject-matter, for concepts are, arguably, involved in all propositions and thus in all reasoning. The difficulty comes from the fact that the indiscriminate assumption of concepts leads to paradox, and more discriminating assumptions require statements which are incompatible with the universality of logic. It was this problem which, I claimed, led Russell to develop the substitutional theory, for that theory appeared to be a consistent logic powerful enough to encode mathematics, but which did not violate the universality of logic. But this appearance, as we have seen, proved to be illusory. The notions of substitution and truth, which allowed Russell the hope of reducing mathematics to a theory which assumed neither classes nor concepts, also proved powerful enough to yield paradoxes. As in the case of the indiscriminate assumption of propositional functions, the restrictions which restored consistency were incompatible with the universality of logic.

The conflict between the universality of logic and the need to avoid the paradox thus remains, unresolved, in Russell's work. Not surprisingly, it tends to distort Russell's own account of that work. In *Principia* he sometimes writes as if neither propositions nor concepts had to be assumed outright:

... we will use such letters as *a,b,c,x,y,z,w*, to denote objects which are neither propositions nor functions. Such objects we shall call *individuals*. Such objects will be constituents of propositions or functions, and they will be *genuine* constituents, in the sense that they do not disappear on analysis as (for example) classes do . . . .

(Whitehead and Russell, 1910, p. 51)

This seems to imply that only individuals (neither propositions nor propositional functions) are genuine constituents of propositions, constituents which do not "disappear on analysis". But this is wishful thinking on Russell's part. It is clear why Russell should want to think that his theory does not assume either propositions or concepts: what is at stake is not ontological economy for its own sake, but rather the coherence of the whole enterprise. It is equally clear, however, that *Principia* relies inescapably upon the assumption of the existence of propositional functions (and also, although less obtrusively, of propositions; see p. 47 above). This same unwillingness of Russell to acknowledge the implications of type theory shows up over the introduction and use of the circumflex notation, " ∧ ". This is used as an abstraction operator: if "*Fx*" is an open sentence, then "*Fx̂*" is the name of an entity, a propositional function. It is never acknowledged as a piece of basic notation, however, and the first numbered sentence in which it appears–*9.131–is a definition of some other notion, as if the circumflex notation had already been defined.

In relating the curious history of Russell's substitutional theory I have articulated and insisted upon a tension in Russell's thought. *Principia Mathematica* is, notoriously, a technical achievement which is marred by apparent inconsistencies and incoherences, such as those I mentioned in the previous paragraph. What I wish to suggest is that many of the confusions in *Principia* are to be seen not as resulting from more or less trivial errors but from a fundamental tension in Russell's philosophy.

University of California,
Santa Barbara.

NOTES

* I am indebted to Burton Dreben for helpful discussions and advice; and to Susan Neiman for criticism of the final draft of this paper.

[1] This claim is borne out by Jager, who neglects the conception of logic which I have emphasised, and seems to think that the only motive which the logistic reduction could have is that of showing mathematics to be analytic. Nonplussed by Russell's statement that logic is synthetic a priori, he fails to give any coherent account of Russell's motives. In particular, Jager denies that the reduction can be seen as in any way anti-Kantian, in spite of Russell's explicit statements that it is. See Jager, 1972, pp. 218–221.

I should emphasise that my discussion has glossed over several subtle issues, e.g. what Russell meant by "analytic" and by "synthetic a priori", and the role of the refutation of Kant's theory of mathematics within a more general attack upon Kant, as well as upon the idealist tradition which Russell saw as stemming from Kant.–These matters will be given fuller treatment in Hylton, forthcoming.

[2] Russell's use of the word "term" in *Principles* is closely related to Moore's use of the word "concept" in The nature of judgement. See Russell 1903, pp. xviii, 44; and Moore, 1899.

[3] This view is so counter-intuitive that it may be hard to believe that Russell meant it literally, but the evidence that he did so is overwhelming. Moore, 1899, does something to explain the reasons for this view. See Hylton, forthcoming, for a full discussion.

[4] This is at least one of the origins of the doctrine of Wittgenstein's *Tractatus*: that certain facts about language are unsayable.

[5] The point that the statement of type-restrictions must violate type restrictions was made by Max Black (Black, 1944). Black, however, made the point only as an argument against the idea that type restrictions should be imposed upon ordinary language. My claim is that the unstatability of type theory within type theory was a problem for

Russell in any case, and that this problem largely accounts for the difficulty he had in producing a theory which would avoid the paradox.

[6] Russell's reasons for taking propositional functions, rather than classes, as primitive in *Principia* seem to be twofold. First, propositional functions, unlike classes, are implicit in every proposition. This universality makes them good candidates for being logical entities, whereas classes, if assumed as primitive, would form a special subject-matter, the study of which would take us beyond logic. Secondly, Russell believed, or hoped, that type restrictions as applied to propositional functions had a naturalness that they would not have if applied directly to classes. Russell sometimes speaks as if it were the fact that classes are not assumed as primitive in *Principia* which enabled him to avoid the paradox (e.g. Russell, 1944, p. 14). A charitable exposition of Russell must understand this as a reference to the second of the above reasons, for if propositional functions are not subject to type-restrictions a contradiction directly analogous to the class paradox arises. See Russell 1906 (a), p. 154 fn.; Quine, 1966, pp. 660–61.

[7] Grattan-Guinness, 1974, goes further in some directions than I have done. Strictly speaking, a rigorous development of the theory is impossible, for Russell never presents the theory in rigourous form. His worknotes are full of attempts at an axiomatisation, but none seems to have satisfied him. The difficulties Russell encountered here are no doubt the "technical inconvenience" of Russell, 1908, p. 77.

[8] If Russell had worked out the implications of this view, his underlying philosophy would have changed very considerably. In 1900 Russell had written: "That all sound philosophy should begin with an analysis of propositions is a truth too evident, perhaps, to demand proof." (Russell, 1900, p. 8). Over the next decade the analysis of the proposition was his constant and central concern. The substitutional theory has the immediate consequence that propositions have to be accepted as basic, unanalysable entities.

[9] Russell changes his mind about whether this notion is to be assumed as primitive or not. In any case, we must either assume it or find a way of defining it.

[10] *Pace* Quine, who claims that Russell abandoned the hope that the substitutional theory would be adequate for mathematics soon after the paper of February 1906. Quine, 1967, pp. 150–51.

BIBLIOGRAPHY

Where two citations are given, the first is the original publication, while the second is that actually consulted. Pagination is therefore taken from the second citation.

Ayer, A. J., 1972, *Russell*, Viking, New York.
Black, M., 1944, Russell's philosophy of language, in Schilpp.
Carroll, L., 1895, What the tortoise said to Achilles, *Mind*.
Frege, G., 1882, Uber den Zweck der Begriffschrift, *Jenische Zeitschrift für Natur-wissenschaft*. Translated in Frege, 1972.
Frege, G., 1892, Uber Begriff und Gegenstand, *Vierteljahrschrift für wissenschaftliche Philosophie*. Translated in Frege, 1952.

Frege, G., 1952, *Translations from the Philosophical Writings of Gottlob Frege*, ed. P. Geach and M. Black, Blackwell, Oxford, 1952. Second edition, 1960.

Frege, G., 1972, *Conceptual Notation and Related Articles*, ed. T. W. Bynum, Clarendon Press, Oxford, 1972.

Grattan–Guinness, I., 1974, The Russell archives: Some new light on Russell's logicism, *Annals of Science.*

Hylton, P. W., forthcoming, *Russell and the Origins of Analytic Philosophy*, Oxford University Press.

Jager, R., 1972, *The Development of Bertrand Russell's Philosophy*, Allen & Unwin, London.

Moore, G. E., 1899, The nature of judgment, *Mind.*

Quine, W. V. O., 1963, *Set Theory and its Logic*, Harvard, Cambridge, Mass.

Quine, W. V. O., 1966, Russell's ontological development, *Journal of Philosophy.*

Quine, W. V. O., 1967, Introduction to Russell, 1908, in van Heijenoort, 1967a.

Russell, B. A. W., 1900, *The Philosophy of Leibniz*, Cambridge U.P., London. Allen and Unwin, London, 1937.

Russell, B. A. W., 1902, Letter to Frege, 16th June 1902, printed in van Heijenoort, 1967a.

Russell, B. A. W., 1903, *The Principles of Mathematics*, Cambridge U.P., London Allen and Unwin, London, 1937.

Russell, B. A. W., 1904, Meinong's theory of complexes and assumptions, *Mind.* Reprinted in Russell, 1973.

Russell, B. A. W., 1905a, The existential import of propositions, *Mind.* Reprinted in Russell, 1973.

Russell, B. A. W., 1905b, On denoting, *Mind*, 1905. Reprinted in Russell, 1973.

Russell, B. A. W., 1906a, On some difficulties in the theory of transfinite numbers and order types, *Proceedings of the London Mathematical Society.* Reprinted in Russell, 1973.

Russell, B. A. W., 1906b, On the substitutional theory of classes and relations, first published in Russell, 1973.

Russell, B. A. W., 1906c, Les paradoxes de la logique, *Revue de Metaphysique et de Morale.* Reprinted under the title On 'Insolubilia' and their solution by symbolic logic in Russell, 1973.

Russell, B. A. W., 1907a, On the nature of truth, *Proceedings of the Aristotelian Society.*

Russell, B. A. W., 1907b, The regressive method of discovering the premisses of mathematics, first printed in Russell, 1973.

Russell, B. A. W., 1908, Mathematical logic as based on the theory of types, *American Journal of Mathematics.* Reprinted in Russell, 1956.

Russell, B. A. W., 1910, *Philosophical Essays*, Longmans, London, 1910. Allen and Unwin, London, 1966.

Russell, B. A. W., 1912, *The Problems of Philosophy*, William and Norgate, London. Oxford U.P., London, 1959.

Russell, B. A. W., 1944, My mental development, in Schilpp, 1944.

Russell, B. A. W., 1956, *Logic and Knowledge*, ed. R. Marsh, Allen and Unwin, London, 1956.

Russell, B. A. W., 1973, *Essays in Analysis*, ed. D. Lackey, Braziller, New York.

Sainsbury, M., 1979, *Russell*, Routledge and Kegan Paul, London.

Schilpp, P. A., 1944, *The Philosophy of Bertrand Russell*, Northwestern, Chicago.

van Heijenoort, J., 1967a, *Sourcebook in Mathematical Logic*, Harvard, Cambridge, Mass., 1967.

van Heijenoort, J., 1967b, Logic as calculus and logic as language, *Synthese*.

Whitehead, A. N., and Russell, 1910, *Principia Mathematica*, vol. I, Cambridge U.P., London, 1910. Cambridge U.P., London, 1925.

A PRIORI KNOWLEDGE*

Philip Kitcher

I

" $\mathbf{A}$ priori" has been a popular term with philosophers at least since Kant distinguished between a priori and a posteriori knowledge. Yet, despite the frequency with which it has been used in twentieth century philosophy, there has been little discussion of the concept of apriority.[1] Some writers seem to take it for granted that there are propositions, such as the truths of logic and mathematics, which are a priori; others deny that there are any a priori propositions. In the absence of a clear characterization of the a priori/a posteriori distinction, it is by no means obvious what is being asserted or what is being denied.

"A priori" is an epistemological predicate. What is *primarily* a priori is an item of knowledge.[2] Of course, we can introduce a derivative use of "a priori" as a predicate of propositions:[3] a

* I am grateful to several members of the Department of Philosophy at the University of Michigan for their helpful comments on a previous version of this paper, and especially to Alvin Goldman and Jaegwon Kim for their constructive suggestions. I would also like to thank Paul Benacerraf, who first interested me in the problem of characterizing a priori knowledge, and prevented many errors in early analyses. Above all, I am indebted to Patricia Kitcher and George Sher, who have helped me to clarify my ideas on this topic. Patricia Kitcher's advice on issues in the philosophy of mind relevant to §V was particularly valuable.

[1] There are some exceptions. Passing attention to the problem of defining apriority is given in John Pollock, *Knowledge and Justification* (Princeton, 1974) Chapter 10; R. G. Swinburne "Analyticity, Necessity and Apriority," (*Mind*, LXXXIV, 1975, pp. 225–243), especially pp. 238–241; Edward Erwin "Are the Notions 'A Priori Truth' and 'Necessary Truth' Extensionally Equivalent?" (*Canadian Journal of Philosophy*, III, 1974, pp. 591–602), especially pp. 593–597. The inadequacy of much traditional thinking about apriority is forcefully presented in Saul Kripke's papers "Identity and Necessity" (in Milton K. Munitz (ed.), *Identity and Individuation*, New York, 1971, pp. 135–164), especially pp. 149–151, and "Naming and Necessity" (in D. Davidson and G. Harman (eds.), *Semantics of Natural Language*, D. Reidel, 1972, pp. 253–355, 763–769), especially pp. 260–264.

[2] See Kripke, loc. cit.

[3] For ease of reference, I take propositions to be the objects of belief and knowledge, and to be what declarative sentences express. I trust that my conclusions would survive any successful elimination of propositions in favor of some alternative approach to the objects of belief and knowledge.

priori propositions are those which we could know a priori. Somebody might protest that current practice is to define the notion of an a priori proposition outright, by taking the class of a priori propositions to consist of the truths of logic and mathematics (for example). But when philosophers allege that truths of logic and mathematics are a priori, they do not intend merely to recapitulate the definition of a priori propositions. Their aim is to advance a thesis about the epistemological status of logic and mathematics.

To understand the nature of such epistemological claims, we should return to Kant, who provided the most explicit characterization of a priori knowledge: "we shall understand by a priori knowledge, not knowledge which is independent of this or that experience, but knowledge absolutely independent of all experience."[4] While acknowledging that Kant's formulation sums up the classical notion of apriority, several recent writers who have discussed the topic have despaired of making sense of it.[5] I shall try to show that Kant's definition can be clarified, and that the concept of a priori knowledge can be embedded in a naturalistic epistemology.

II

Two questions naturally arise. What are we to understand by "experience"? And what is to be made of the idea of independence from experience? Apparently, there are easy answers. Count as a person's experience the stream of her sensory encounters with the world, where this includes both "outer experience," that is, sensory states caused by stimuli external to the body, and "inner experience," that is, those sensory states brought about by internal stimuli. Now we might propose that someone's knowledge is independent of her experience just in case she could have had that knowledge whatever experience she had had. To this obvious suggestion there is an equally obvious objection. The apriorist is not ipso facto a believer in innate knowledge: indeed, Kant emphasized the difference between the two types of knowledge. So we cannot accept an analysis which implies that a priori

---

[4] *Critique of Pure Reason* (B2–3).
[5] See Pollock, loc. cit., Swinburne, loc. cit., Erwin, loc. cit.

knowledge could have been obtained given minimal experiences.[6]

Many philosophers (Kant included) contend both that analytic truths can be known a priori and that some analytic truths involve concepts which could only be acquired if we were to have particular kinds of experience. If we are to defend their doctrines from immediate rejection, we must allow a minimal role to experience, even in a priori knowledge. Experience may be needed to provide some concepts. So we might modify our proposal: knowledge is independent of experience if any experience which would enable us to acquire the concepts involved would enable us to have the knowledge.

It is worth noting explicitly that we are concerned here with the *total* experience of the knower. Suppose that you acquire some knowledge empirically. Later you deduce some consequences of this empirical knowledge. We should reject the suggestion that your knowledge of those consequences is independent of experience because, at the time you perform the deduction, you are engaging in a process of reasoning which is independent of the sensations you are then having.[7] As Kant recognized,[8] your knowledge, in cases like this, is dependent on your total experience: different total sequences of sensations would not have given you the premises for your deductions.

Let us put together the points which have been made so far. A person's experience at a particular time will be identified with his sensory state at the time. (Such states are best regarded physicalistically in terms of stimulation of sensory receptors, but we should recognize that there are both "outer" and "inner" receptors.) The total sequence of experiences X has had up to time t is *X's life at t*. A life will be said to be *sufficient for X for p* just in

---

[6] Someone might be tempted to propose, conversely, that all innate knowledge is a priori (cf. Swinburne op. cit. p. 239). In "The Nativist's Dilemma," (*Philosophical Quarterly*, 28, 1978, pp. 1–16), I have argued that there may well be no innate knowledge and that, if there were any such knowledge, it would not have to be a priori.

[7] Pollock (op. cit. p. 301) claims that we can only resist the suggestion that this knowledge is independent of experience by complicating the notion of experience. For the reason given in the text, such desperate measures seem to me to be unnecessary.

[8] See the example of the man who undermines the foundations of his house, (*Critique of Pure Reason*, B3).

case X could have had that life and gained sufficient under-standing to believe that p. (I postpone, for the moment, questions about the nature of the modality involved here.) Our discussion above suggests the use of these notions in the analysis of a priori knowledge: X knows a priori that p if and only if X knows that p and, given any life sufficient for X for p, X could have had that life and still have known that p. Making temporal references explicit: at time t X knows a priori that p just in case, at time t, X knows that p and, given any life sufficient for X for p, X could have had that life at t and still have known, at t, that p. In subsequent discussions I shall usually leave the temporal ref-erences implicit.

Unfortunately, the proposed analysis will not do. A clear-headed apriorist should admit that people can have empirical knowledge of propositions which can be known a priori. How-ever, on the account I have given, if somebody knows that p and if it is possible for her to know a priori that p, then, apparently, given any sufficiently rich life she could know that p, so that she would meet the conditions for a priori knowledge that p. (This presupposes that modalities "collapse," but I don't think the problem can be solved simply by denying the presupposition.) Hence it seems that my account will not allow for empirical knowledge of propositions that can be known a priori.

We need to amend the analysis. We must differentiate situ-ations in which a person knows something empirically which could have been known a priori from situations of actual a priori knowledge. The remedy is obvious. What sets apart correspond-ing situations of the two types is a difference in the ways in which what is known is known. An analysis of a priori knowledge must probe the notion of knowledge more deeply than we have done so far.

III

We do not need a general analysis of knowledge, but we do need the *form* of such an analysis. I shall adopt an approach which extracts what is common to much recent work on knowl-edge, an approach which may appropriately be called "the psychologistic account of knowledge."[9] The root idea is that the question of whether a person's true belief counts as knowledge depends on whether the presence of that true belief can be explained in an appropriate fashion. The difference between an item of knowledge and mere true belief turns on the factors which produced the belief; thus the issue revolves around the way in which a particular mental state was generated. It is important to emphasize that, at different times, a person may have states of belief with the same content, and these states may be produced by different processes. The claim that a process produces a belief is to be understood as the assertion that the presence of the current state of belief is to be explained through a description of that process. Hence the account is not committed to supposing that the original formation of a belief is relevant to the epistemological status of later states of belief in the same proposition.[10]

The question of what conditions must be met if a belief is to be explained in an appropriate fashion is central to epistemology, but it need not concern us here. My thesis is that the distinction between knowledge and true belief depends on the characteristics of the process which generates the belief, and this thesis is independent of specific proposals about what characteristics are crucial. Introducing a useful term, let us say that some processes *warrant* the beliefs they produce, and that these processes are *warrants* for such beliefs. The general view of knowledge I have adopted can be recast as the thesis that X knows that p just in case X correctly believes that p and X's belief was produced by a

---

[9] Prominent exponents of this approach are Alvin Goldman, Gilbert Harman and David Armstrong. See: Alvin Goldman, "A Causal Theory of Knowing" (*Journal of Philosophy*, LXIV, 1967, pp. 357-372), "Innate Knowledge" (in Stephen P. Stich (ed.) *Innate Ideas* [Berkeley, 1975] pp. 111-120), "Discrimination and Perceptual Knowledge" (*Journal of Philosophy*, LXXII, 1976, pp. 771-791), "What is Justified Belief?" (in George S. Pappas (ed.) *Justification and Knowledge*, [D. Reidel, forthcoming]); Gilbert Harman, *Thought* (Princeton, 1973); David Armstrong, *Belief, Truth and Knowledge* (Cambridge, 1973).

[10] Psychologistic epistemologies are often accused of confusing the context of discovery with the context of justification. For a recent formulation of this type of objection, see Keith Lehrer, *Knowledge* (Oxford, 1974), pp. 123ff. I have tried to show that psychologistic epistemology is not committed to mistakes with which it is frequently associated in "Frege's Epistemology," (*Philosophical Review*, 88, 1979, pp. 235-62). I shall consider the possibility of an apsychologistic approach to apriority in §VII below.

process which is a warrant for it. Leaving the task of specifying the conditions on warrants to general epistemology, my aim is to distinguish a priori knowledge from a posteriori knowledge. We discovered above that the distinction requires us to consider the ways in which what is known is known. Hence I propose to reformulate the problem: let us say that X knows a priori that p just in case X has a true belief that p and that belief was produced by a process which is an *a priori warrant* for it. Now the crucial notion is that of an a priori warrant, and our task becomes that of specifying the conditions which distinguish a priori warrants from other warrants.

At this stage, some examples may help us to see how to draw the distinction. Perception is an obvious type of process which philosophers have supposed *not* to engender a priori knowledge. Putative a priori warrants are more controversial. I shall use Kant's notion of pure intuition as an example. This is not to endorse the claim that processes of pure intuition are a priori warrants, but only to see what features of such processes have prompted Kant (and others) to differentiate them from perceptual processes.

On Kant's theory, processes of pure intuition are supposed to yield a priori mathematical knowledge. Let us focus on a simple geometrical example. We are supposed to gain a priori knowledge of the elementary properties of triangles by using our grasp on the concept of triangle to construct a mental picture of a triangle and by inspecting this picture with the mind's eye.[11] What are the characteristics of this kind of process which make Kant want to say that it produces knowledge which is independent of experience? I believe that Kant's account implies that three conditions should be met. The same type of process must be *available* independently of experience. It must produce *warranted* belief independently of experience. And it must produce *true* belief independently of experience. Let us consider these conditions in turn.

According to the Kantian story, if our life were to enable us to acquire the appropriate concepts (the concept of a triangle and

---

[11] More details about Kant's theory of pure intuition can be found in my paper "Kant and the Foundations of Mathematics" (*Philosophical Review*, 84, 1975, pp. 23–50), especially pp. 28–33.

the other geometrical concepts involved) then the appropriate kind of pure intuition would be available to us. We could represent a triangle to ourselves, inspect it, and so reach the same beliefs. But, if the process is to generate *knowledge* independently of experience, Kant must require more of it. Given any sufficiently rich life, if we were to undergo the same type of process and gain the same beliefs, then those beliefs would be warranted by the process. Let us dramatize the point by imagining that experience is unkind. Suppose that we are presented with experiments which are cunningly contrived so as to make it appear that some of our basic geometrical beliefs are false. Kant's theory of geometrical knowledge presupposes that if, in the circumstances envisaged, a process of pure intuition were to produce geometrical belief then it would produce warranted belief, despite the background of misleading experience.

So far I have considered how a Kantian process of pure intuition might produce warranted belief independently of experience. But to generate *knowledge* independently of experience, a priori warrants must produce warranted *true* belief in counterfactual situations where experiences are different. This point does not emerge clearly in the Kantian case because the propositions which are alleged to be known a priori are taken to be necessary, so that the question of whether it would be possible to have an a priori warrant for a false belief does not arise. Plainly, we could ensure that a priori warrants produce warranted *true* belief independently of experience by declaring that a priori warrants only warrant necessary truths. But this proposal is unnecessarily strong. Our goal is to construe a priori knowledge as knowledge which is independent of experience, and this can be achieved, without closing the case against the contingent a priori, by supposing that, in a counterfactual situation in which an a priori warrant produces belief that p then p. On this account, a priori warrants are ultra-reliable; they never lead us astray.[12]

Summarizing the conditions that have been uncovered, I propose the following analysis of a priori knowledge.

(1) X knows a priori that p if and only if X knows that p and

---

[12] For further discussion of this requirement and the possibility of the contingent a priori, see §V below.

X's belief that p was produced by a process which is an
a priori warrant for it.
(2) α is an a priori warrant for X's belief that p if and only
    if α is a process such that, given any life e, sufficient
    for X for p, then
    (a) some process of the same type could produce in X
        a belief that p
    (b) if a process of the same type were to produce in X a
        belief that p then it would warrant X in believing
        that p
    (c) if a process of the same type were to produce in X a
        belief that p then p.

It should be clear that this analysis yields the desired result that,
if a person knows a priori that p then she could know that p whatever (sufficiently rich) experience she had had. But it goes beyond
the proposal of §II in spelling out the idea that the knowledge
be obtainable in the same way. Hence we can distinguish cases
of empirical knowledge of propositions which could be known a
priori from cases of actual a priori knowledge.

IV

In this section, I want to be more explicit about the notion of
"types of processes" which I have employed, and about the
modal and conditional notions which figure in my analysis. To
specify a process which produces a belief is to pick out some
terminal segment of the causal ancestry of the belief. I think
that, without loss of generality, we can restrict our attention to
those segments which consist solely of states and events internal
to the believer.[13] Tracing the causal ancestry of a belief beyond
the believer would identify processes which would not be available independently of experience, so that they would violate our
conditions on a priori warrants.

Given that we need only consider psychological processes, the
next question which arises is how we divide processes into types.
It may seem that the problem can be sidestepped: can't we

---

[13] For different reasons, Goldman proposes that an analysis of the general
notion of warrant (or, in his terms, justification) can focus on psychological
processes. See section 2 of "What is Justified Belief?"

simply propose that to defend the apriority of an item of knowledge is to claim that that knowledge was produced by a psychological process and that *that very process* would be available and would produce warranted true belief in counterfactual situations where experience is different? I think it is easy to see how to use this proposal to rewrite (2) in a way which avoids reference to "types of processes." I have not adopted this approach because I think that it shortcuts important questions about what makes a process the same in different counterfactual situations.

Our talk of processes which produce belief was originally introduced to articulate the idea that some items of knowledge are obtained in the same way while others are obtained in different ways. To return to our example, knowing a theorem on the basis of hearing a lecture and knowing the same theorem by following a proof count, intuitively, as different ways of knowing the theorem. Our intuitions about this example, and others, involve a number of different principles of classification, with different principles appearing in different cases. We seem to divide belief-forming processes into types by considering content of beliefs, inferential connections, causal connections, use of perceptual mechanisms and so forth. I suggest that these principles of classification probably do not give rise to one definite taxonomy, but that, by using them singly, or in combination, we obtain a number of different taxonomies which we can and do employ. Moreover, within each taxonomy, we can specify types of processes more or less narrowly.[14] Faced with such variety, what characterization should we pick?

There is probably no privileged way of dividing processes into types. This is not to say that our standard principles of classification will allow *anything* to count as a type. Somebody who proposed that the process of listening to a lecture (or the terminal segment of it which consists of psychological states and events) belongs to a type which consists of itself and instances of following

---

[14] Consider, for example, a Kantian process of pure intuition which begins with the construction of a triangle. Should we say that a process of the same type must begin with the construction of a triangle of the same size and shape, a triangle of the same shape, any triangle, or something even more general? Obviously there are many natural classifications here, and I think the best strategy is to suppose that an apriorist is entitled to pick any of them.

a proof, would flout *all* our principles for dividing processes into types. Hence, while we may have many admissible notions of types of belief-forming processes, corresponding to different principles of classification, some collections of processes contravene all such principles, and these cannot be admitted as genuine types.[15]

My analysis can be read as issuing a challenge to the apriorist. If someone wishes to claim that a particular belief is an item of a priori knowledge then he must specify a segment of the causal ancestry of the belief, consisting of states and events internal to the believer, and type-identity conditions which conform to some principle (or set of principles) of classification which are standardly employed in our divisions of belief-forming processes (of which the principles I have indicated above furnish the most obvious examples). If he succeeds in doing this so that the requirements in (2) are met, his claim is sustained; if he cannot, then his claim is defeated.

The final issue which requires discussion in this section is that of explaining the modal and conditional notions I have used. There are all kinds of possibility, and claims about what is possible bear an implicit relativization to a set of facts which are held constant.[16] When we say, in (2), that, given any sufficiently rich life, X could have had a belief which was the product of a particular type of process, should we conceive of this as merely logical possibility or are there some features of the actual world which are tacitly regarded as fixed? I suggest that we are not just envisaging any logically possible world. We imagine a world in which X has similar mental powers to those he has in the actual world. By hypothesis, X's experience is different. Yet the capacities for thinking, reasoning, and acquiring knowledge which X possesses as a member of *homo sapiens* are to remain unaffected: we want to say that X, *with the kinds of cognitive capacities distinctive*

---

[15] Strictly, the sets which do not constitute types are those which violate correct taxonomies. In making present decisions about types, we assume that our current principles of classification are correct. If it should turn out that those principles require revision then our judgments about types will have to be revised accordingly.

[16] For a lucid and entertaining presentation of the point, see David Lewis, "The Paradoxes of Time Travel," (*American Philosophical Quarterly*, 13, 1976, pp. 145–152), pp. 149–151.

of humans, could have undergone processes of the appropriate type, even if his experiences had been different.[17]

Humans might have had more faculties for acquiring knowledge than they actually have. For example, we might have had some strange ability to "see" what happens on the other side of the Earth. When we consider the status of a particular type of process as an a priori warrant, the existence of worlds in which such extra faculties come into play is entirely irrelevant. Our investigation focusses on the question of whether a particular type of process would be available to a person with the kinds of faculties people actually have, not on whether such processes would be available to creatures whose capacities for acquiring knowledge are augmented or diminished. Conditions (2(b)) and (2(c)) are to be read in similar fashion. Rewriting (2(b)) to make the form of the conditional explicit, we obtain: for any life e sufficient for X for p and for any world in which X has e, in which he believes that p, in which his belief is the product of a process of the appropriate kind, and *in which X has the cognitive capacities distinctive of humans*, X is warranted in believing that p. Similarly, (2(c)) becomes: for any life e sufficient for X for p and for any world in which X has e, in which he believes that p, in which his belief is the product of a process of the appropriate kind, *and in which X has the cognitive capacities distinctive of humans*, p. Finally, the notion of a life's being sufficient for X for p also bears an implicit reference to X's native powers. To say that a particular life enables X to form certain concepts is to maintain that, given the genetic programming with which X is endowed, that life allows for the formation of the concepts.

The account I have offered can be presented more graphically in the following way. Consider a human as a cognitive device, endowed initially with a particular kind of structure. Sensory experience is fed into the device and, as a result, the device forms certain concepts. For any proposition p, the class of experiences which are sufficiently rich for p consists of those experiences which would enable the device, with the kind of structure it actually has, to acquire the concepts to believe that p. To decide

---

[17] Of course, X might have been more intelligent, that is, he might have had better versions of the faculties he has. We allow for this type of change. But we are not interested in worlds where X has extra faculties.

whether or not a particular item of knowledge that p is an item of a priori knowledge we consider whether the type of process which produced the belief that p is a process which would have been available to the device, with the kind of structure it actually has, if different sufficiently rich experiences had been fed into it, whether, under such circumstances, processes of the type would warrant belief that p, and would produce true belief that p.

Seen in this way, claims about apriority are implicitly indexical, in that they inherit the indexical features of "actual."[18] If this is not recognized, use of "a priori" in modal contexts can engender confusion. The truth value of "Possibly, X knows a priori that p" can be determined in one of two ways: we may consider the proposition expressed by the sentence at our world, and inquire whether there is a world at which that proposition is true; or we may ask whether there is a world at which the sentence expresses a true proposition. Because of the covert indexicality of "a priori," these lines of investigation may yield different answers. I suspect that failure to appreciate this point has caused trouble in assessing theses about the limits of the a priori. However, I shall not pursue the point here.[19]

V

At this point, I want to address worries that my analysis is too liberal, because it allows some of our knowledge of ourselves and our states to count as a priori. Given its Kantian psychologistic underpinnings, the theory appears to favor claims that some of our self-knowledge is a priori. However, two points should be

---

[18] The idea that "actual" is indexical is defended by David Lewis in "Anselm and Actuality," (*Noûs*, IV, 1970, pp. 175–188). In "The Only Necessity is Verbal Necessity," (*Journal of Philosophy*, LXXIV, 1977, pp. 71–85), Bas van Fraassen puts Lewis' ideas about "actual" in a general context. The machinery which van Fraassen presents in that paper can be used to elaborate the ideas of the present paragraph.

[19] Jaegwon Kim has pointed out to me that, besides the "species-relative" notion of apriority presented in the text, there might be an absolute notion. Perhaps there is a class of propositions which would be knowable a priori by any being whom we would count as a rational being. Absolute a priori knowledge would thus be that a priori knowledge which is available to all possible knowers.

kept in mind. Firstly, the analysis I have proposed can only be applied to cases in which we know enough about the ways in which our beliefs are warranted to decide whether or not the conditions of (2) are met. In some cases, our lack of a detailed account of how our beliefs are generated may mean that no firm decision about the apriority of an item of knowledge can be reached. Secondly, there may be cases, including cases of self-knowledge, in which we have no clear pre-analytic intuitions about whether a piece of knowledge is a priori.

Nevertheless, there are some clear cases. Obviously, any theory which implied that I can know a priori that I am seeing red (when, in fact, I am) would be suspect. But, when we apply my analysis, the unwanted conclusion does not follow. For, if the process which leads me to believe that I am seeing red (when I am) can be triggered in the absence of red, then (2(c)) would be violated. If the process cannot be triggered in the absence of red, then, given some sufficiently rich experiences, the process will not be available, so that (2(a)) will be violated. In general, knowledge of any involuntary mental state—such as pains, itches or hallucinations—will work in the same way. Either the process which leads from the occurrence of pain to the belief that I am in pain can be triggered in the absence of pain, or not: if it can, (2(c)) would be violated, if it cannot, then (2(a)) would be violated.

This line of argument can be sidestepped when we turn to cases in which we have the power, independently of experience, to put ourselves into the appropriate states. For, in such cases, one can propose that the processes which give us knowledge of the states cannot be triggered in the absence of the states themselves *and* that the processes are always available because we can always put ourselves into the states.[20] On this basis, we might try to conclude that we have a priori knowledge that we are imagining red (when we are) or thinking of Ann Arbor (when we are). However, the fact that such cases do not fall victim to the argument of the last paragraph does not mean that we are compelled

---

[20] In characterizing pain as an involuntary state one paragraph back I may seem to have underestimated our powers of self-torture. But even a masochist could be defeated by unkind experience: as he goes to pinch himself his skin is anesthetized.

to view them as cases of a priori knowledge. In the first place, the thesis that the processes through which we come to know our imaginative feats and our voluntary thoughts cannot be triggered in the absence of the states themselves requires evaluation—and, lacking detailed knowledge of those processes, we cannot arrive at a firm judgment here. Secondly, the processes in question will be required to meet (2(b)) if they are to be certified as a priori warrants. This means that, whatever experience hurls at us, beliefs produced by such processes will be warranted. We can cast doubt on this idea by imagining that our experience consists of a lengthy, and apparently reliable, training in neurophysiology, concluding with a presentation to ourselves of our own neurophysiological organization which appears to show that our detection of our imaginative states (say) is slightly defective, that we always make mistakes about the contents of our imaginings. If this type of story can be developed, then (2(b)) will be violated, and the knowledge in question will not count as a priori. But, even if it cannot be coherently extended, and even if my analysis does judge our knowledge of states of imagination (and other "voluntary" states) to be a priori, it is not clear to me that this consequence is counterintuitive.

In fact, I think that one can make a powerful case for supposing that *some* self-knowledge is a priori. At most, if not all, of our waking moments, each of us knows of herself that she exists.[21] Although traditional ideas to the effect that self-knowledge is produced by some "non-optical inner look" are clearly inadequate, I think it is plausible to maintain that there are processes which do warrant us in believing that we exist—processes of reflective thought, for example—and which belong to a general

---

[21] I shall ignore the tricky issue of trying to say exactly what is known when we know this and kindred things. For interesting explorations of this area, see Hector-Neri Castañeda, "Indicators and Quasi-indicators" (*American Philosophical Quarterly*, 4, 1967, pp. 85–100), "On the Logic of Attributions of Self-Knowledge to Others," (*Journal of Philosophy*, LXV, 1968, pp. 439–56); John Perry, "Frege on Demonstratives," (*Philosophical Review*, 86, 1977, pp. 474–97), "The Problem of the Essential Indexical," (*Noûs*, 13, 1979, pp. 3–21). The issue of how to represent the content of items of self-knowledge may force revision of the position taken in footnote 3 above: it may not be possible to identify objects of belief with meanings of sentences. Although such revision would complicate my analysis, I don't think it would necessitate any fundamental modifications.

type whose members would be available to us independently of experience.[22] Trivially, when any such process produces in a person a belief that she exists that belief is true. All that remains, therefore, is to ask if the processes of the type in question inevitably warrant belief in our own existence, or whether they would fail to do so, given a suitably exotic background experience. It is difficult to settle this issue conclusively without a thorough survey of the ways in which reflective belief in one's existence can be challenged by experience, but perhaps there are Cartesian grounds for holding that, so long as the belief is the product of reflective thought, the believer is warranted, no matter how wild his experience may have been. If this is correct, then at least some of our self-knowledge will be a priori. However, in cases like this, attributions of apriority seem even less vulnerable to the criticism that they are obviously incorrect.

At this point we must consider a doctrinaire objection. If the conclusion of the last paragraph is upheld then we can know some contingent propositions a priori.[23] Frequently, however, it is maintained that only necessary truths can be known a priori. Behind this contention stands a popular argument.[24] Assume that a person knows a priori that p. His knowledge is independent of his experience. Hence he can know that p without any information about the kind of world he inhabits. So, necessarily p.

This hazy line of reasoning rests on an intuition which is captured in the analysis given above. The intuition is that a priori warrants must be ultra-reliable: if a person is entitled to ignore empirical information about the type of world she inhabits then that must be because she has at her disposal a method of arriving

---

[22] This presupposes that our knowledge of our existence does not result from some special kind of "inner sensation." For, if it did, different lives would deprive us of the warrant.

[23] Kripke (loc. cit.) has attempted to construct examples of contingent propositions which can be known a priori. I have not tried to decide here whether his examples are successful, since full treatment of this question would lead into issues about the analysis of the propositions in question which are well beyond the scope of the present paper. For a discussion of some of the difficulties involved in Kripke's examples, see Keith Donnellan "The Contingent A Priori and Rigid Designators" (*Mid-West Studies in Philosophy*, Volume 2, 1977, pp. 12–27).

[24] Kripke seems to take this to be the main argument against the contingent a priori. See "Naming and Necessity," p. 263.

at belief which guarantees *true* belief. (This intuition can be defended by pointing out that if a method which could produce false belief were allowed to override experience, then we might be blocked from obtaining knowledge which we might otherwise have gained.) In my analysis, the intuition appears as (2(c)).[25]

However, when we try to clarify the popular argument we see that it contains an invalid step. Presenting it as a *reductio*, we obtain the following line of reasoning. Assume that a person knows a priori that p but that it is not necessary that p. Because p is contingent there are worlds at which p is false. Suppose that the person had inhabited such a world and behaved as she does at the actual world. Then she would have had an a priori warrant for a false belief. This is debarred by (2(c)). So we must conclude that the initial supposition is erroneous: if someone really does know a priori that p then p is necessary.

Spelled out in this way, the argument fails. We are not entitled to conclude from the premise that there are worlds at which p is false the thesis that there are worlds at which p is false *and* at which the person behaves as she does at the actual world. There are a number of propositions which, although they could be false, could not both be false and also believed by us. More generally, there are propositions which could not both be false and also believed by us in particular, definite ways. Obvious examples are propositions about ourselves and their logical consequences: such propositions as those expressed by tokens of the sentences "I exist," "I have some beliefs," "There are thoughts," and so forth. Hence the attempted *reductio* breaks down and allows for the possibility of a priori knowledge of some contingent propositions.

I conclude that my analysis is innocent of the charge of being too liberal in ascribing to us a priori knowledge of propositions

---

[25] As the discussion of this paragraph suggests, there is an intimate relation between my requirements (2(b)) and (2(c)). Indeed, one might argue that (2(b)) would not be met unless (2(c)) were also satisfied—on the grounds that one cannot allow a process to override experience unless it guarantees truth. The subsequent discussion will show that this type of reasoning is more complicated than appears. Hence, although I believe that the idea that a priori warrants function independently of experience does have implications for the reliability of these processes, I have chosen to add (2(c)) as a separate condition.

about ourselves. Although it is plausible to hold that my account construes some of our self-knowledge as a priori, none of the self-knowledge it takes to be a priori is clearly empirical. Moreover, it shows how a popular argument against the contingent a priori is flawed, and how certain types of contingent propositions—most notably propositions about ourselves—escape that argument. Thus I suggest that the analysis illuminates an area of traditional dispute.

VI

I now want to consider two different objections to my analysis. My replies to these objections will show how the approach I have developed can be further refined and extended.

The first objection, like those considered above, charges that the analysis is too liberal. My account apparently allows for the possibility that a priori knowledge could be gained through perception. We can imagine that some propositions are true at any world of which we can have experience, and that, given sufficient experience to entertain those propositions, we could always come to know them on the basis of perception. Promising examples are the proposition that there are objects, the proposition that some objects have shapes, and other, similar propositions. In these cases, one can argue that we cannot experience worlds at which they are false and that any (sufficiently rich) experience would provide perceptual warrant for belief in the propositions, regardless of the specific content of our perceptions. If these points are correct (and I shall concede them both, for the sake of argument), then perceptual processes would qualify as a priori warrants. Given any sufficiently rich experience, some perceptual process would be available to us, would produce warranted belief and, *ex hypothesi*, would produce warranted *true* belief.

Let us call cases of the type envisaged cases of *universally empirical* knowledge. The objection to my account is that it incorrectly classifies universally empirical knowledge as a priori knowledge. My response is that the classical notion of apriority is too vague to decide such cases: rather, this type of knowledge only becomes apparent when the classical notion is articulated. One could defend the classification of universally empirical knowledge as a priori by pointing out that such knowledge requires no particular type of experience (beyond that needed to obtain the concepts, of course). One could oppose that classification by pointing out that, even though the content of the experience is immaterial, the knowledge is still gained by perceiving, so that it should count as a posteriori.

If the second response should seem attractive, it can easily be accommodated by recognizing a stronger and a weaker notion of apriority. The weaker notion is captured in (1) and (2). The stronger adds an extra requirement: no process which involves the operation of a perceptual mechanism is to count as an a priori· warrant.

At this point, it is natural to protest that the new condition makes the prior analysis irrelevant. Why not define a priori knowledge outright as knowledge which is produced by processes which do not involve perceptual mechanisms? The answer is that the prior conditions are not redundant: knowledge which is produced by a process which does not involve perceptual mechanisms need not be independent of experience. For the process may fail to generate warranted belief against a backdrop of misleading experience. (Nor may it generate true belief in all relevant counterfactual situations.) So, for example, certain kinds of thought-experiments may generate items of knowledge given a particular type of experience, but may not be able to sustain that knowledge against misleading experiences. Hence, if we choose to exclude universally empirical knowledge from the realm of the a priori in the way suggested, we are building on the analysis given in (1) and (2), rather than replacing it.

A different kind of criticism of my analysis is to accuse it of revealing the emptiness of the classical notion of apriority. Someone may suggest that, in exposing the constraints on a priori knowledge, I have shown that there could be very little a priori knowledge. Although I believe that this suggestion is incorrect, it is worth pointing out that, even if it is granted, my approach allows for the development of weaker notions which may prove epistemologically useful.

Let me first note that we can introduce approximations to a priori knowledge. Suppose that A is any type of process all of whose instances culminate in belief that p. Define the *supporting class* of A to be that class of lives, e, such that, (a) given e, some process in A could occur (and so produce belief that p), (b) given e, any process in A which occurred would produce warranted true belief that p. (Intuitively, the supporting class consists of those lives which enable processes of the type in question to produce knowledge.) The *defeating class* of A is the complement of the supporting class of A within the class of lives which are sufficient for p. A priori warrants are those processes which belong to a type whose defeating class is null. But we can be more liberal, and allow approximations to a priori knowledge by considering the size and/or nature of the defeating class. We might, for example, permit the defeating class to contain those radically disruptive experiences beloved of sceptics. Or we can define a notion of *contextual* apriority by allowing the defeating class to include experiences which undermine "framework principles."[26] Or we may employ a concept of *comparative* apriority by ordering defeating classes according to inclusion relations. Each of these notions can serve a useful function in delineating the structure of our knowledge.

VII

Finally, I want to address a systematic objection to my analysis. The approach I have taken is blatantly psychologistic. Some philosophers may regard these psychological complications as objectionable intrusions into epistemology. So I shall consider the possibility of rival apsychologistic approaches.

Is there an acceptable view of a priori knowledge which rivals the Kantian conception? The logical positivists hoped to understand a priori knowledge without dabbling in psychology. The simplest of their proposals was the suggestion that X knows a priori that p if and only if X believes that p and p is analytically true.[27]

---

[26] This notion of contextual apriority has been used by Hilary Putnam. See, for example, his paper "It Ain't Necessarily So," (Chapter 15 of H. Putnam, *Mathematics, Matter and Method*, Philosophical Papers, Volume I, Cambridge, 1975) and "There is At Least One A Priori Truth" (*Erkenntnis*, 13, 1978, pp. 153–70), especially p. 154.

[27] See A. J. Ayer, *Language, Truth and Logic*, (London 1936), Chapter IV, and

Gilbert Harman has argued cogently that, in cases of factual belief, the nature of the reasons for which a person believes is relevant to the question of whether he has knowledge. [28] Similar considerations arise with respect to propositions which the positivists took to be a priori. Analytic propositions like synthetic propositions, can be believed for bad reasons, or for no reasons at all, and, when this occurs, we should deny that the believer knows the propositions in question. Assume, as the positivists did, that mathematics is analytic, and imagine a mathematician who comes to believe that some unobvious theorem is true. This belief is exhibited in her continued efforts to prove the theorem. Finally, she succeeds. We naturally describe her progress by saying that she has come to know something she only believed before. The positivistic proposal forces us to attribute knowledge from the beginning. Worse still, we can imagine that the mathematician has many colleagues who believe the theorem because of dreams, trances, fits of Pythagorean ecstasy, and so forth. Not only does the positivistic approach fail to separate the mathematician after she has found the proof from her younger self, but it also gives her the same status as her colleagues.

A natural modification suggests itself: distinguish among the class of analytic truths those which are elementary (basic laws of logic, immediate consequences of definitions, and, perhaps, a few others), and propose that elementary analytic truths can be known merely by being believed, while the rest are known, when they are known a priori, by inference from such truths. Even this restricted version of the original claim is vulnerable. If you believe the basic laws of logic because you have learned them from an eminent mathematician who has deluded himself into believing that the system of *Grundgesetze* is consistent and true, then you do not have a priori knowledge of those laws. Your belief in the laws of logic is undermined by evidence which you do not currently possess, namely the evidence which would expose your teacher as a misguided fanatic. The moral is obvious:

M. Schlick, "The Foundation of Knowledge" (in A. J. Ayer (ed.) *Logical Positivism* (New York, 1959) pp. 209–227) especially p. 224.

[28] *Thought* Chapter 2; see also Goldman "What is Justified Belief?" Section 1.

apsychologistic approaches to a priori knowledge fail because, for a priori knowledge as for factual knowledge, the reasons for which a person believes are relevant to the question of whether he knows.

Although horror of psychologizing prevented the positivists from offering a defensible account of a priori knowledge, I think that my analysis can be used to articulate most of the doctrines that they wished to defend. Indeed, I believe that many classical theses, arguments and debates can be illuminated by applying the analysis presented here. My aim has been to prepare the way for investigations of traditional claims and disputes by developing in some detail Kant's conception of a priori knowledge. "A priori" has too often been a label which philosophers could attach to propositions they favored, without any clear criterion for doing so. I hope to have shown how a more systematic practice is possible.

University of Vermont

RUTH BARCAN MARCUS

MORAL DILEMMAS AND CONSISTENCY *

I WANT to argue that the existence of moral dilemmas, even where the dilemmas arise from a categorical principle or principles, need not and usually does not signify that there is some inconsistency (in a sense to be explained) in the set of principles, duties, and other moral directives under which we define our obligations either individually or socially. I want also to argue that, on the given interpretation, consistency of moral principles or rules does not entail that moral dilemmas are resolvable in the sense that acting with good reasons in accordance with one horn of the dilemma erases the original obligation with respect to the other. The force of this latter claim is not simply to indicate an intractable fact about the human condition and the inevitability of guilt. The point to be made is that, although dilemmas are not settled without residue, the recognition of their reality has a dynamic force. It motivates us to arrange our lives and institutions with a view to avoiding such conflicts. It is the underpinning for a second-order regulative principle: that as rational agents with some control of our lives and institutions, we ought to conduct our lives and arrange our institutions so as to minimize predicaments of moral conflict.

I

Moral dilemmas have usually been presented as predicaments for individuals. Plato, for example, describes a case in which the return of a cache of arms has been promised to a man who, intent on mayhem, comes to claim them. Principles of promise keeping and

* This paper was written during my tenure as a Fellow at the Center for the Advanced Study of the Behavioral Sciences. I am grateful to Robert Stalnaker for his illuminating comments. A version of the paper was delivered on January 17, 1980, at Wayne State University as the Gail Stine Memorial Lecture.

133

benevolence generate conflict. One does not lack for examples. It is safe to say that most individuals for whom moral principles figure in practical reasoning have confronted dilemmas, even though these more commonplace dilemmas may lack the poignancy and tragic proportions of those featured in biblical, mythological, and dramatic literature. In the one-person case there are principles in accordance with which one ought to do x and one ought to do y, where doing y requires that one refrain from doing x; i.e., one ought to do not-x. For the present rough-grained discussion, the one-person case may be seen as an instance of the n-person case under the assumption of shared principles. Antigone's sororal (and religious) obligations conflict with Creon's obligations to keep his word and preserve the peace. Antigone is obliged to arrange for the burial of Polyneices; Creon is obliged to prevent it. Under generality of principles they are each obliged to respect the obligations of the other.

It has been suggested that moral dilemmas, on their face, seem to reflect some kind of inconsistency in the principles from which they derive. It has also been supposed that such conflicts are products of a plurality of principles and that a single-principled moral system does not generate dilemmas.

In the introduction to the *Metaphysics of Morals* Kant[1] says, "Because however duty and obligation are in general concepts that express the objective practical necessity of certain actions . . . it follows . . . that a conflict of duties and obligations is inconceivable (*obligationes non colliduntor*)." More recently John Lemmon,[2] citing a familiar instance of dilemma, says, "It may be argued that our being faced with this moral situation merely reflects an implicit inconsistency in our existing moral code; we are forced, if we are to remain both moral and logical, by the situation to restore consistency to our code by adding exception clauses to our present principles or by giving priority to one principle over another, or by some such device. The situation is as it is in mathematics: there, if an inconsistency is revealed by derivation, we are compelled to modify our axioms; here, if an inconsistency is revealed in appli-

---

[1] Immanuel Kant, *The Metaphysical Elements of Justice:* Part I of the *Metaphysics of Morals*, translated by John Ladd (Indianapolis: Bobbs-Merrill, 1965), p. 24.

[2] "Deontic Logic and the Logic of Imperatives," *Logique et Analyse*, VIII, 29 (April 1965): 39–61. Lemmon originally presented his paper at a symposium of the Western Division meeting of the American Philosophical Association in May 1964. My unpublished comments on that occasion contain some of the ideas here presented.

cation, we are forced to revise our principles." Donald Davidson,[3] also citing examples of conflict, says, "But then unless we take the line that moral principles *cannot* conflict in application to a case, we must give up the concept of the nature of practical reason we have so far been assuming. For how can premises, all of which are true (or acceptable) entail a contradiction? It is astonishing that in contemporary moral philosophy this problem has received little attention and no satisfactory treatment."

The notion of inconsistency which views dilemmas as evidence for inconsistency seems to be something like the following. We have to begin with a set of one or more moral principles which we will call a *moral code*. To count as a principle in such a code, a precept must be of a certain generality; that is, it cannot be tied to specific individuals at particular times or places, except that on any occasion of use it takes the time of that occasion as a zero coordinate. The present rough-grained discussion does not require that a point be made of the distinction between categorical moral principles and conditional moral principles, which impose obligations upon persons in virtue of some condition, such as that of being a parent, or a promise-maker or contractee. For our purposes we may think of categorical principles as imposing obligations in virtue of one's being a person and a member of a moral community.

In the conduct of our lives, actual circumstances may arise in which a code mandates a course of action. Sometimes, as in dilemmas, incompatible actions x and y are mandated; that is, the doing of x precludes the doing of y; y may in fact be the action of refraining from doing x. The underlying view that takes dilemmas as evidence of inconsistency is that a code is consistent if it applies without conflict to all actual—or, more strongly—to all possible cases. Those who see a code as the foundation of moral reasoning and adopt such a view of consistency argue that the puzzle of dilemmas can be resolved by elaboration of the code: by hedging principles with exception clauses, or establishing a rank ordering of principles, or both, or a procedure of assigning weights, or some combination of these. We need not go into the question of whether exception clauses can be assimilated to priority rankings, or priority rankings to weight assignments. In any case, there is some credibility in such solutions, since they fit some of the moral facts. In the question of whether to return the cache of arms, it is clear

<hr/>

[3] "How Is Weakness of the Will Possible?", in Joel Feinberg. ed., *Moral Concepts* (New York: Oxford. 1970), p. 105.

(except perhaps to an unregenerate Kantian) that the principle requiring that the promise be kept is overridden by the principle requiring that we protect human lives. Dilemmas, it is concluded, are merely apparent and not real. For, with a complete set of rules and priorities or a complete set of riders laying out circumstances in which a principle does not apply, in each case one of the obligations will be vitiated. What is incredible in such solutions is the supposition that we could arrive at a complete set of rules, priorities, or qualifications which would, in every possible case, unequivocally mandate a single course of action; that where, on any occasion, doing x conflicts with doing y, the rules with qualifications or priorities will yield better clear reasons for doing one than for doing the other.

The foregoing approach to the problem of moral conflict—ethical formalism—attempts to dispel the reality of dilemmas by expanding or elaborating on the code. An alternative solution, that of moral intuitionism, denies that it is possible to arrive at an elaboration of a set of principles which will apply to all particular circumstances. W. D. Ross,[4] for example, recognizes that estimates of the stringency of different prima facie principles can sometimes be made, but argues that no general universally applicable rules for such rankings can be laid down. However, the moral intuitionists *also* dispute the reality of moral dilemmas. Their claim is that moral codes are only guides; they are not the only and ultimate ground of decision making. Prima facie principles play an important heuristic role in our deliberations, but not as a set of principles that can tell us how we ought to act in all particular circumstances. That ultimate determination is a matter of intuition, albeit rational intuition. Moral dilemmas are prima facie, not real conflicts. In apparent dilemmas there *is* always a correct choice among the conflicting options; it is only that, and here Ross quotes Aristotle, "the decision rests with perception." For Ross, those who are puzzled by moral dilemmas have failed to see that the problem is epistemological and not ontological, or real. Faced with a dilemma generated by prima facie principles, *uncertainty* is increased as to whether, in choosing x over y, we have in fact done the right thing. As Ross puts it, "Our judgments about our actual duty in concrete situations, have none of the certainty that attaches to our recognition of general principles of duty. . . . Where a possible act is seen to have two characteristics in virtue of one of which it is prima facie right and in virtue of the other prima facie wrong we are well aware that we are not certain whether we ought or ought not to do it. Whether we do it or not we are taking a moral risk" (30). For Ross, as well as the formalist, it is only that we may be uncertain of the right way. To say that dilemma is evidence of inconsistency is to confuse inconsistency with uncertainty. There *is* only one right way to go, and hence no problem of inconsistency.

There are, as we see, points of agreement between the formalist and the intuitionist as here described. Both claim that the appearance of dilemma and inconsistency flows from prima facie principles and that dilemmas can be resolved by supplementation. They differ in the nature of the supplementation.[5] They further agree that it is the multiplicity of principles which generates the prima facie conflicts; that if there were one rule or principle or maxim, there would be no conflicts. Quite apart from the unreasonableness of the belief that we can arrive ultimately at a single moral principle, such proposed single principles have played a major role in moral philosophy, Kant's categorical imperative and various versions of the principle of utility being primary examples. Setting aside the casuistic logical claim that a single principle can always be derived by conjunction from a multiplicity, it can be seen that the single-principle solution is mistaken. There is always the analogue of Buridan's ass. Under the single principle of promise keeping, I might make two promises in all good faith and reason that they will not conflict, but then they do, as a result of circumstances that were unpredictable and beyond my control. All other considerations may balance out. The lives of identical twins are in jeopardy, and, through force of circumstances, I am in a position to save only one. Make the situation as symmetrical as you please. A single-principled framework is not necessarily unlike the code with qualifications or priority rule, in that it would appear that, however strong our wills and complete our knowledge, we might be faced with a moral choice in which there are no moral grounds for favoring doing x over y.

Kant imagined that he had provided a single-principled framework from which all maxims flowed. But Kantian ethics is notably deficient in coping with dilemmas. Kant seems to claim that they

---

[5] For the formalist, priority rankings (like Rawls's lexical ordering), or weights permitting some computation, or qualifications of principles to take care of all problematic cases, are supposed possible. For the intuitionist it is intuitive "seeing" in each case which supplements prima facie principles.

don't really arise, and we are provided with no moral grounds for their resolution.

It is true that unregenerate act utilitarianism is a plausible candidate for dilemma-free principle or conjunction of principles, but not because it can be framed as a single principle. It is rather that attribution of rightness or wrongness to certain kinds of acts *per se* is ruled out whether they be acts of promise keeping or promise breaking, acts of trust or betrayal, of respect or contempt. One might, following Moore, call such attributes "non-natural kinds," and they enter into all examples of moral dilemmas. The attribute of having maximal utility as usually understood is not such an attribute. For to the unregenerate utilitarian it is not features of an act *per se* which make it right. The only thing to be counted is certain consequences, and, for any given action, one can imagine possible circumstances, possible worlds if you like, in each of which the action will be assigned different values—depending on different outcomes in those worlds. In the unlikely cases where in fact two conflicting courses of action have the same utility, it is open to the act utilitarian to adopt a procedure for deciding, such as tossing a coin.

In suggesting that, in all examples of dilemma, we are dealing with attributions of rightness *per se* independent of consequences is not to say that principles of utility do not enter into moral dilemmas. It is only that such conflicts will emerge in conjunction with non-utilitarian principles. Indeed, such conflicts are perhaps the most frequently debated examples, but not, as we have seen, the only ones. I would like to claim that it is a better fit with the moral facts that all dilemmas are real, even where the reasons for doing *x* outweigh, and in whatever degree, the reasons for doing *y*. That is, wherever circumstances are such that an obligation to do *x* and an obligation to do *y* cannot as a matter of circumstance be fulfilled, the obligations to do each are not erased, even though they are unfulfillable. Mitigating circumstances may provide an explanation, an excuse, or a defense, but I want to claim that this is not the same as denying one of the obligations altogether.

We have seen that one of the motives for denying the reality of moral dilemmas is to preserve, on some notion of consistency, the consistency of our moral reasoning. But other not unrelated reasons have been advanced for denying their reality which have to do with the notion of guilt. If an agent ought to do *x*, then he is guilty if he fails to do it. But if, however strong his character and however good his will and intentions, meeting other equally weighted or overriding obligations precludes his doing x, then we cannot assign guilt, and, if we cannot, then it is incoherent to suppose that there is an obligation. Attendant feelings of the agent are seen as mistaken or misplaced.

That argument has been rejected by Bas van Fraassen [6] on the ground that normative claims about when we ought to assign guilt are not part of the analysis of the concept of guilt, for if it were, such doctrines as that of "original sin" would be rendered incoherent. The Old Testament assigns guilt to three or four generations of descendants of those who worship false gods. Or consider the burden of guilt borne by all the descendants of the house of Atreus, or, more recently, the readiness of many Germans to assume a burden of guilt for the past actions of others. There are analogous converse cases, as in the assumption of guilt by parents for actions of adult children. Having presented the argument. I am not wholly persuaded that a strong case can be made for the coherence of such doctrines. However, the situation faced by agents in moral dilemmas is not parallel. Where moral conflict occurs, there is a genuine sense in which both what is done and what fails to be done are, before the actual choice among irreconcilable alternatives, within the agent's range of options. But, as the saying goes—and it is not incoherent—you are damned if you do and you are damned if you don't.

I will return to the question of the reality of moral dilemmas, but first let me propose a definition of consistency for a moral code which is compatible with that claim.

---

[6] "Values and the Heart's Command," this JOURNAL, LXX, 1 (Jan. 11, 1973): 5–19. Van Fraassen makes the point that such a claim would make *the* doctrine of "original sin" incoherent. As I see it, there are at least three interesting doctrines, two of them very likely true, which could qualify as doctrines of original sin. One of them, which I call "inherited guilt," is the doctrine that some of the wrongful actions of some persons are such that other persons, usually those with some special connection to the original sinners, are also judged to be sinners; their feelings of guilt are appropriate, their punishment "deserved," and so on. Such is the case described in Exodus and Deuteronomy here mentioned. A second notion of original sin is to be found in the account of the Fall. Here it is suggested that, however happy our living arrangements, however maximal the welfare state, we will each of us succumb to some temptation. There is universality of sin because of universality of weakness of will, but specific sins are neither inherited by nor bequeathed to others.

A third candidate supposes the reality and inevitability, for each of us, of moral dilemma. Here we do not inherit the sins of others, nor need we be weak of will. The circumstances of the world conspire against us. However perfect our will, the contingencies are such that situations arise where, if we are to follow one right course of action, we will be unable to follow another.

II

Consistency, as defined for a set of meaningful sentences or propositions, is a property that such a set has if it is possible for all of
the members of the set to be true, in the sense that contradiction
would not be a logical consequence of supposing that each member
of the set is true. On that definition 'grass is white' and 'snow is
green' compose a consistent set although false to the facts. There is
a possible set of circumstances in which those sentences are true,
i.e., where snow is green and grass is white. Analogously we can
define a set of rules as consistent if there is some possible world in
which they are all obeyable in all circumstances in *that* world.
(Note that I have said "obeyable" rather than "obeyed" for I want
to allow for the partition of cases where a rule-governed action fails
to be done between those cases where the failure is a personal
failure of the agent—an imperfect will in Kant's terms—and those
cases where "external" circumstances prevent the agent from meeting conflicting obligations. To define consistency relative to a king-
dom of ends, a deontically perfect world in which all actions that
ought to be done are done, would be too strong; for that would
require both perfection of will *and* the absence of circumstances
that generate moral conflict.) In such a world, where all rules are
obeyable, persons intent on mayhem have not been promised or do
not simultaneously seek the return of a cache of arms. Sororal obligations such as those of Antigone do not conflict with obligations to preserve peace, and so on. Agents may still fail to fulfill obligations.

Consider, for example, a silly two-person card game. (This is the
partial analogue of a two-person dilemma. One can contrive silly
games of solitaire for the one-person dilemma.) In the two-person
game the deck is shuffled and divided equally, face down between
two players. Players turn up top cards on each play until the cards
are played out. Two rules are in force: black cards trump red cards,
and high cards (ace high) trump lower-valued cards without attention to color. Where no rule applies, e.g., two red deuces, there is
indifference and the players proceed. We could define the winner
as the player with the largest number of tricks when the cards are
played out. There is an inclination to call such a set of rules inconsistent. For suppose the pair turned up is a red ace and a black
deuce; who trumps? This is not a case of rule indifference as in a
pair of red deuces. Rather, two rules apply, and both cannot be
satisfied. But, on the definition here proposed, the rules are consistent in that there are possible circumstances where, in the course

of playing the game, the dilemma would not arise and the game would proceed to a conclusion. It is possible that the cards be so distributed that, when a black card is paired with a red card, the black card happens to be of equal or higher value. Of course, with shuffling, the likelihood of dilemma-free circumstances is small. But we could have invented a similar game where the likelihood of proceeding to a conclusion without dilemma is greater. Indeed a game might be so complex that its being dilemmatic under any circumstances is very small and may not even be known to the players.[7] On the proposed definition, rules are consistent if there are possible circumstances in which no conflict will emerge. By extension, a set of rules is inconsistent if there are *no* circumstances, no possible world, in which all the rules are satisfiable.[8]

A pair of offending rules which generates inconsistency as *here* defined provides *no* guide to action under any circumstance. Choices are thwarted whatever the contingencies. Well, a critic might say, you have made a trivial logical point. What pragmatic difference is there between the inconsistent set of rules and a set, like those of the game described above, where there is a likelihood of irresolvable dilemma? A code is, after all, supposed to guide action. If it allows for conflicts without resolution, if it tells us in some circumstances that we ought to do x and we ought to do y even though x and y are incompatible in those circumstances, that is tantamount to telling us that we ought to do x and we ought to refrain from doing x and similarly for y. The code has failed us as a guide. If it is not inconsistent, then it is surely deficient, and, like the dilemma-provoking game, in need of repair.

But the logical point is not trivial, for there are crucial disanalogies between games and the conduct of our lives. It is part of the canon of the family of games of chance like the game described,

---

[7] There is a question whether, given such rules, the "game" is properly described as a game. Wittgenstein says "Let us suppose that the game [which I have invented] is such that whoever begins can always win by a particular simple trick. But this has not been realized;—so it is a game. Now someone draws our attention to it—and it stops being a game." *Remarks on the Foundations of Mathematics*, ed., G. H. von Wright *et al.*, translated by G. E. M. Anscombe (Oxford: Blackwell, 1956), II 78. p. 100e. Wittgenstein is pointing to that canon of a game which requires that both players have some opportunity to win. The canon that rules out dilemmatic rules is that the game must be playable to a conclusion. (I am beholden to Robert Fogelin for reminding me of this quotation.)

[8] Bernard Williams, in *Problems of the Self* (New York: Cambridge, 1977), chs. 11 and 12, also recognizes that the source of some apparent inconsistencies in imperatives and rules is to be located in the contingency of their simultaneous inapplicability on a given occasion.

that the cards must be shuffled. The distribution of the cards must be "left to chance." To stack the deck, like loading the dice, is to cheat. But, presumably, the moral principles we subscribe to are, whatever their justification, not justified merely in terms of some canon for games. Granted, they must be guides to action and hence not totally defeasible. But consistency in our sense is surely only a necessary but not a sufficient condition for a set of moral rules. Presumably, moral principles have some ground; we adopt principles when we have reasons to believe that they serve to guide us in right action. Our interest is not merely in having a playable game whatever the accidental circumstances, but in doing the right thing to the extent that it is possible. We want to maximize the likelihood that in all circumstances we can act in accordance with each of our rules. To that end, our alternative as moral agents, individually and collectively, as contrasted with the card-game players, is to try to stack the deck so that dilemmas do not arise.

Given the complexity of our lives and the imperfection of our knowledge, the occasions of dilemma cannot always be foreseen or predicted. In playing games, when we are faced with a conflict of rules we abandon the game or invent new playable rules; dissimilarly, in the conduct of our lives we do not abandon action, and there may be no justification for making new rules to fit. We proceed with choices as best we can. Priority rules and the like assist us in those choices and in making the best of predicaments. But, if we do make the best of a predicament, and make a choice, to claim that one of the conflicting obligations has thereby been erased is to claim that it would be mistaken to feel guilt or remorse about having failed to act according to that obligation. So the agent would be said to believe falsely that he is guilty, since his obligation was vitiated and his feelings are inappropriate. But that is false to the facts. Even where priorities are clear and overriding and even though the burden of guilt may be appropriately small, explanations and excuses are in order. But in such tragic cases as that described by Jean-Paul Sartre [9] where the choice to be made

---

[9] Sartre in "Existentialism Is a Humanism" describes a case where a student is faced with a decision between joining the Free French forces and remaining with his mother. He is her only surviving son and her only consolation. Sartre's advice was that "No rule of general morality can show you what you ought to do." His claim is that in such circumstances "nothing remains but to trust our instincts." But what is "trust" here? Does our action reveal to us that we subscribe to a priority principle or that in the absence of some resolving principles we may just as well follow our inclination? In any case to describe our feelings about the rejected alternative as "regret" seems inadequate. See Walter Kaufmann, ed., *Existentialism from Dostoevsky to Sartre* (New York: Meridian, 1956), pp. 295–298.

by the agent is between abandoning a wholly dependent mother and not becoming a freedom fighter, it is inadequate to insist that feelings of guilt about the rejected alternative are mistaken and that assumption of guilt is inappropriate. Nor is it puritanical zeal which insists on the reality of dilemmas and the appropriateness of the attendant feelings. For dilemmas, when they occur, are data of a kind. They are to be taken into account in the future conduct of our lives. If we are to avoid dilemmas we must be motivated to do so. In the absence of associated feelings, motivation to stack the deck, to arrange our lives and institutions so as to minimize or avoid dilemma is tempered or blunted.

Consider, for example, the controversies surrounding nonspontaneous abortion. Philosophers are often criticized for inventing bizarre examples and counterexamples to make a philosophical point. But no contrived example can equal the complexity and the puzzles generated by the actual circumstances of foetal conception, parturation, and ultimate birth of a human being. We have an organism, internal to and parasitic upon a human being, hidden from view but relentlessly developing into a human being, which at some stage of development can live, with nurture, outside of its host. There are arguments that recognize competing claims: the right to life of the foetus (at some stage) versus the right of someone to determine what happens to his body. Arguments that justify choosing the mother over the foetus (or vice-versa) where their survival is in competition. Arguments in which foetuses that are defective are balanced against the welfare of others. Arguments in which the claims to survival of others will be said to override survival of the foetus under conditions of great scarcity. There are even arguments that deny prima facie conflicts altogether on some metaphysical grounds, such as that the foetus is not a human being or a person until quickening, or until it has recognizable human features, or until its life can be sustained external to its host, or until birth, or until after birth when it has interacted with other persons. Various combinations of such arguments are proposed in which the resolution of a dilemma is seen as more uncertain, the more proximate the foetus is to whatever is defined as being human or being a person. What all the arguments seem to share is the assumption that there is, despite uncertainty, a resolution without residue; that there is a correct set of metaphysical claims, principles, and priority rankings of principles which will justify the choice. Then, given the belief that one choice is justified, assignment of guilt relative to the overridden alternative is seen as inappropriate, and feelings of guilt or pangs of conscience are viewed as, at best, sentimental. But as one tries to unravel the tangle of arguments, it is clear that to insist that there is in every case a solution without residue is false to the moral facts.

John Rawls,[10] in his analysis of moral sentiments, says that it is an essential characteristic of a moral feeling that an agent, in explaining the feeling, "invokes a moral concept and its associated principle. His (the agent's) account of his feeling makes reference to an acknowledged right or wrong." Where those ingredients are absent, as, for example, in the case of someone of stern religious background who claims to feel guilty when attending the theater although he no longer believes it is wrong, Rawls wants to say that such a person has certain sensations of uneasiness and the like which resemble those he has when he feels guilty, but, since he is not apologetic for his behavior, does not resolve to absent himself from the theater, does not agree that negative sanctions are deserved, he experiences not a feeling of guilt, but only something like it. Indeed, it is the feeling which needs to be explained; it is not the action which needs to be excused. For, says Rawls, in his discussion of moral feelings and sentiments, "When plagued by feelings of guilt . . . a person wishes to act properly in the future and strives to modify his conduct accordingly. He is inclined to admit what he has done, to acknowledge and accept reproofs and penalties." Guilt qua feeling is here defined not only in terms of sensations but also in terms of the agent's disposition to acknowledge, to have wishes and make resolutions about future actions, to accept certain outcomes, and the like. Where an agent acknowledges conflicting obligations, unlike the theater-goer who acknowledges no obligation, there is sufficient overlap with dilemma-free cases of moral failure to warrant describing the associated feelings where present as guilt, and where absent as appropriate to an agent with moral sensibility. Granted that, unlike agents who fail to meet their obligations simpliciter, the agent who was confronted with a

[10] *A Theory of Justice* (Cambridge, Mass.: Harvard, 1971), pp. 481–483. Rawls's claim is that such sensations, to be properly describable as "guilt feelings" and not something resembling such feelings, must occur in the broader context of beliefs, strivings, acknowledgements, and readiness to accept outcomes, and cannot be detached from that context. He rejects the possibility that there are such "pure" sensations that can occur independent of the broader context. This is partially, perhaps, an empirical claim about identifying sameness of feeling. The theater-goer might claim that he does feel guilty because he has the same feeling he has when he acknowledges that he is guilty, that what remains is to give an account of when such feelings of guilt are justified. Still, Rawls's analysis seems to me to be a better account.

dilemma may finally act on the best available reasons. Still, with respect to the rejected alternative he acknowledges a wrong in that he recognizes that it was within his power to do otherwise. He may be apologetic and inclined to explain and make excuses. He may sometimes be inclined to accept external reproofs and penalties. Not perhaps those which would be a consequence of a simple failure to meet an obligation but rather like the legal cases in which mitigating circumstances evoke a lesser penalty—or reproof.[11]

Even if, as Rawls supposes, or hopes (but as seems to me most unlikely), a complete set of rules and priorities were possible which on rational grounds would provide a basis for choosing among competing claims in all cases of moral conflict that actually arise, it is incorrect to suppose that the feeling evoked on such occasions, if it is evoked, only resembles guilt, and that it is inappropriate on such occasions to ascribe guilt. *Legal* ascriptions of guilt require sanctions beyond the pangs of conscience and self-imposed reproofs. In the absence of clear external sanctions, legal guilt is normally not ascribable. But that is one of the many distinctions between the legal and the moral.

Most important, an agent in a predicament of conflict will also "wish to act properly in the future and strive to modify his actions accordingly." He will strive to arrange his own life and encourage social arrangements that would prevent, to the extent that it is possible, future conflicts from arising. To deny the appropriateness or correctness of ascriptions of guilt is to weaken the impulse to make such arrangements.[12]

III

I have argued that the consistency of a set of moral rules, even in the absence of a complete set of priority rules, is not incompatible with the reality of moral dilemmas. It would appear, however, that at least some versions of the principle " 'ought' implies 'can' " are being denied; for dilemmas are circumstances where, for a pair of

---

[11] To insist that "regret" is appropriate rather than "guilt" or "remorse" is false to the facts. It seems inappropriate, for example, to describe as "regret" the common feelings of guilt that women have in cases of abortion even where they believe (perhaps mistakenly) that there was moral justification in such an undertaking.

[12] Bernard Williams ["Politics and Moral Character," in Stuart Hampshire, ed., *Public and Private Morality* (New York: Cambridge, 1978), pp. 54–74] discusses the question in the context of politics and the predicament of "dirty hands." He argues that, where moral ends of politics justify someone in public life lying, or misleading, or using others, "the moral disagreeableness of these acts is not merely cancelled." In particular, we would not want, as our politicians, those "practical politicians" for whom the disagreeableness does not arise.

obligations, if one is satisfied then the other cannot be. There is, of course, a range of interpretations of the precept resulting from the various interpretations of 'ought', 'can', and 'implies'. Some philosophers who recognize the reality of dilemmas have rejected the precept that " 'ought' implies 'can' "; some have accepted it.[13] If we interpret the 'can' of the precept as "having the ability in this world to bring about," then, as indicated above, in a moral dilemma, 'ought' *does* imply 'can' for *each* of the conflicting obligations, *before* either one is met. And after an agent has chosen one of the alternatives, there is still something which he ought to have done and could have done and which he did not do. 'Can', like 'possible', designates a modality that cannot always be factored out of a conjunction. Just as 'possible P and possible Q' does not imply 'possible both P and Q', so 'A can do x and A can do y' does not imply 'A can do both x and y'. If the precept " 'ought' implies 'can' " is to be preserved, it must also be maintained that 'ought' designates a modality that cannot be factored out of a conjunction. From 'A ought to do x' and 'A ought to do y' it does not follow that 'A ought to do x and y'. Such a claim is of course a departure from familiar systems of deontic logic.

The analysis of consistency and dilemmas advanced in this paper suggests a second-order principle which relates 'ought' and 'can' and which provides a plausible gloss of the Kantian principle "Act so that thou canst will thy maxim to become a universal law of nature." As Kant understood laws of nature, they are, taken together, universally and jointly applicable in all particular circumstances. It is such a second-order principle that has been violated when we knowingly make conflicting promises. It is such a second-order principle that has, for example, been violated when someone knowingly and avoidably conducts himself in such a way that he is confronted with a choice between the life of a foetus, the right to determine what happens to one's body, and benefits to others. To will maxims to become universal laws we must will the means, and

---

[13] For example, John Lemmon, in "Moral Dilemmas," *Philosophical Review*, LXXI, 2 (April 1962): 139–158, p. 150, rejects the principle that 'ought' implies 'can'. Van Fraassen, *op. cit.*, pp. 12/3, accepts it, as does Bernard Williams seemingly in *Problems of the Self, op. cit.*, pp. 179–184. Van Fraassen and Williams see that such acceptance requires modification of the principle of factoring for the deontic "ought." There are other received principles of deontic logic which will have to be rejected, but they will be discussed in a subsequent paper. It should also be noted that, in "Ethical Consistency" and "Consistency and Realism" in *Problems of the Self*, Williams also articulates the contingent source of dilemmas and argues for their "reality."

among those means are the conditions for their compatibility. One ought to act in such a way that, if one ought to do *x* and one ought to do *y*, then one can do both *x* and *y*. But the second-order principle is regulative. This second-order 'ought' does *not* imply 'can'.[14] There is no reason to suppose, this being the actual world, that we can, individually or collectively, however holy our wills or rational our strategies, succeed in foreseeing and wholly avoiding such conflict. It is not merely failure of will, or failure of reason, which thwarts moral maxims from becoming universal laws. It is the contingencies of this world.

IV

Where does that leave us? I have argued that all dilemmas are real in a sense I hope has been made explicit. Also that there is no reason to suppose on considerations of consistency that there *must* be principles which, on moral grounds, will provide a sufficient ordering for deciding all cases. But, it may be argued, when confronted with what are *apparently* symmetrical choices undecidable on moral grounds, agents do, finally, choose. That is sometimes understood as a way in which, given good will, an agent makes explicit the rules under which he acts. It is the way an agent discovers a priority principle under which he orders his actions. I should like to question that claim.

A frequently quoted remark of E. M. Forster[15] is "if I had to choose between betraying my country and betraying my friend, I hope I should have the courage to betray my country." One could of course read that as if Forster had made manifest some priority rule: that certain obligations to friends override obligations to nation. But consider a remark of A. B. Worster, "if I had to choose between betraying my country and betraying my friend, I hope I should have the courage to betray my friend." Both recognize a dilemma, and one can read Worster as subscribing to a different priority rule and, to that extent, a different set of rules from Forster's. But is that the only alternative? Suppose Forster had said that, morally, Worster's position is as valid as his own. That there was no moral reason for generalizing his own choice to all. That there was disagreement between them not about moral principles but rather about the kind of persons they wished to be and the kind of lives they wished to lead. Forster may not want Worster

---

14 See fn 13. The reader is reminded that, on the present analysis, 'ought' is indexical in the sense that applications of principles on given occasions project into the future. They concern bringing something about.

15 *Two Cheers for Democracy* (London: E. Arnold, 1939).

for a friend; a certain possibility of intimacy may be closed to them which perhaps Forster requires in a friend. Worster may see in Forster a sensibility that he does not admire. But there is no reason to suppose that such appraisals are or must be moral appraisals. Not all questions of value are moral questions, and it may be that not all moral dilemmas are resolvable by principles for which moral justification can be given.

RUTH BARCAN MARCUS

Yale University

THOMAS CARSON MARK

ON WORKS OF VIRTUOSITY

THERE are artworks in which technical skill is an important ingredient, not merely as something required to produce the artwork, but in the deeper sense that it penetrates and partly determines the nature of the artwork itself. The Chopin études, for example, are generally admitted to be masterpieces of music, but it is obvious that the development and display of skill in piano playing enters essentially into their composition. Indeed, as I shall explain more fully later, piano playing is what the études are about. As another example, consider the still life paintings by various Dutch artists of the seventeenth century, in which such objects as crystal goblets, jewelry, glass spheres, dewdrops, and oysters

149

on the half shell are consummately represented. Whatever else is true of them, these pictures show a deliberate collecting of hard-to-paint items whose convincing representation counts as a display of the skill of the painter. Or consider the intricate polyphonic music of the late Middle Ages and early Renaissance; the rondeau of Machaut, for example, in which the top two voices are inverted mirror images of each other and the third voice is a perfect palindrome. Or what must surely be the ultimate in rhyme:

> Gall, amant de la Reine, alla, tour magnanime,
> Gallamant de l'arène, à la Tour Magne, à Nîmes.

The concept of skill is elusive, and I shall not try to define it. Accurate specification of just which concrete objects count as examples of outstanding skill is also a difficult task, which—if it can be done at all—can certainly not be done apart from a historical context; as E. H. Gombrich remarks "many a modest amateur has mastered tricks that would have looked like sheer magic to Giotto. Perhaps even the crude colored renderings we find on a box of breakfast cereal would have made Giotto's contemporaries gasp." [1] Furthermore, the point at which skill ceases to be "merely" technical, or, as some might prefer to put it, the point at which skill becomes artistry, may not admit of precise delineation. Nevertheless, despite these unclarities, I think that we do have some grasp of what is meant by skill and of what is meant when a work is said to show technical mastery or a person is described as technically skilled. In what follows I shall rely on this preanalytic notion of what skill is, which will be sufficient for my purpose in this paper. I am setting out not to define the notion of skill but to analyze a certain class of artworks, and even though the works that interest me are works in which technical skill is an important ingredient, what I want to say about them does not depend on being able to state precisely and universally what skill consists in.

Sometimes skill is incidental, a means to an end. Where skill is thus incidental, present merely in that the artwork is a product of skill, I shall say that the artwork *shows* skill. But sometimes skill is not incidental. There are artworks in which the exhibition of skill becomes an end in itself, and in such cases I shall say that the artwork *displays* skill. Artworks in which the display of skill is made a central feature I shall call *works of virtuosity*.

The word 'virtuosity' is most often applied in the performing arts, but, as the above examples suggest, works aimed at the dis-

[1] *Art and Illusion*, 2nd ed. (Princeton, N.J.: University Press, 1972), p. 8.

play of skill can be found in all the arts. Not all works of virtuosity are great art; some are, others—perhaps more numerous—are not; the examples given above range from the sublime to the trivial. But, as a class, works of virtuosity raise interesting questions, for it is not obvious why the display of skill should be part of an artwork. Many aestheticians would say that the display of skill is of no artistic or aesthetic interest at all. Although I believe they are mistaken, I shall not argue the point here, except briefly in section VI.[2] I wish to discuss not the aesthetic but the philosophic characteristics of works of virtuosity, and what makes an artwork important for philosophy is not the same as what determines its stature as a work of art. The central aim of this paper is to offer a philosophic analysis of the concept of a work of virtuosity. In approaching this topic I shall begin with what will seem to be a digression, by considering some distinctions worked out by Richard Wollheim.

I

In a justly celebrated paper,[3] Wollheim has considered the question why certain works of "minimal art" (e.g., monochrome canvasses, unassisted ready-mades) ought to be taken seriously as works of art. He suggests that the claim that they should not be taken seriously might be supported by observing that they do not seem to show "what we have over the centuries come to regard as an essential ingredient in art: work, or manifest effort" (106). The connection between work and art, he thinks, "rightly . . . enjoys such prestige in our aesthetic thinking that it is hard to see how objects of minimal art can justify their claims to the status of art unless it can be shown that the reason for holding that they inadequately exhibit work is based on too narrow or limited a view of what work is" (107). He then offers what he takes to be a more satisfactory conception of work by distinguishing two phases: (1) work *"tout court:* . . . the putting of paint on canvas, the hacking of stone, the welding of metal elements," and (2) "the decision that the work has gone far enough" (107/8). Finally, he claims that some works of art, such as Duchamp's urinal, may single out and "celebrate in isolation" the second of these phases; others, as in the case of "highly undifferentiated objects," may give to the first phase a new direction or significance. Thus, to the suggestion that

---

2 For a defense of the view that skill, as an artistic value, is important in aesthetic experience, see Jerome Stolnitz, "The Artistic Values in Aesthetic Experience," *Journal of Aesthetics and Art Criticism*, XXXII, 1 (Fall 1973): 5–15.

3 "Minimal Art," *Arts Magazine* (January 1965): 26–32. Reprinted in Wollheim, *On Art and the Mind* (Cambridge, Mass.: Harvard, 1974), pp. 101–111. All page references in the text are to this reprint.

certain purported artworks are not rightly regarded as artworks since they do not satisfy a necessary condition, namely the exhibiting of "work or manifest effort," Wollheim replies that, once the necessary condition is properly analyzed and the objects properly understood, these objects can be seen to satisfy the condition after all.

Wollheim's paper is insightful in a number of ways, but it contains some obscurities. Although Wollheim thinks that evidence of work or manifest effort is necessary for an object to be an artwork, he does not give a reason for this contention. He points to the connection between art and work simply as a fact. And yet, without denying that it is a fact, it would seem to be a fact for which an explanation could reasonably be demanded: *why* should an artwork exhibit work or manifest effort? One may easily suspect that the alleged connection between art and work amounts to no more than the familiar (though important) observation that artworks must be made or done; that is, they must be artifacts and not just naturally occurring things in the world. There is perhaps a hint of this foundation for the connection between art and work in Wollheim's essay, at the point where he says that objections to minimal art may rest on the feeling that 'the artist hasn't *done* anything, or not enough (107). Now, it does seem to me that completion of both phases of work is sufficient to make something an artifact. Furthermore, all artworks are artifacts (as Wollheim agrees elsewhere [4]). But not all artifacts are artworks. That means, however, that completion of the two phases of work is not sufficient, though it may be necessary, to make something an artwork. And *that* means that completion of the two phases is not really enough for Wollheim's purpose of showing why objects of minimal art should be taken seriously as artworks. That such objects are artifacts was never in doubt; what was wanted was some reason to think them also art.

A different approach to the connection between art and work might seem to be found in Wollheim's phrase "work or manifest effort," 'manifest effort' presumably being used equivalently with 'work'. Perhaps the sense in which artworks must show work is that they must show effort: they must cost their creators something. But the sheer expending of physical labor cannot be what makes something an artwork, and scarcely less absurd is the claim that the amount of effort—the difficulty experienced by the artist—must be manifest in whatever is to count as an artwork. I once heard a

[4] "The Work of Art as Object," in *On Art and the Mind, op. cit.*, p. 112.

soprano (some years past her prime) take a deep gasp of air as if to "wind up" for a climactic passage, which she then belted out by main force. The result was unfortunate and the applause feeble, although her effort was manifest. For sopranos, apparently, not only is manifest effort not required, it is undesirable.

Take another example. It would be ludicrous to imagine Horo-witz saying to himself, "I'd better drop a few notes lest people think that no effort is needed to play the Rachmaninoff sonata." This is ludicrous because part of the reason Horowitz's performance is out-standing is that effort is *not* manifest. But it would be wrong merely to say that effort should not be manifest—that is, to endorse the view classically expressed by Horace that art (here in the sense of technical skill) should be concealed, artistry consisting, indeed, in this concealment. And it would be equally wrong to fall back on the shallow opinion—often found in journalistic criticism— that a virtue of Horowitz's performance lies in his making the work "sound easy." The difficulty of the Rachmaninoff sonata is not an irrelevant or extrinsic fact about it; it is not easy, nor is it intended to sound easy, nor does Horowitz make it sound easy. He does make it sound as if *he* had no trouble playing it; that is, he shows that he can do something which is extremely hard to do and which is, at the same time, *evidently* hard to do. This is not manifest effort, it is a manifestation of extraordinary skill.

I do not have a satisfactory explanation of the connection Woll-heim finds between work and art, an explanation that would show its foundation without amounting merely to the observation that artworks must be artifacts. But the example offered in the last paragraph brings us to a different though related view, important for the principal topic of this paper, and not discussed by Woll-heim: the notion that an artwork must exhibit some sort of skill or mastery.

II

Taken as a completely general claim, the view that artworks must exhibit skill is false (so merely construing "work" as "skill" would not explain the problematic connection between work and art). It may be that the only thing that is always required of artworks is that they be designated "artwork" by those qualified to make the judgment or bestow the title; something like the institutional the-ory may be the only theory that holds with perfect generality. But within a particular style or period the requirements may be stricter, there may be other or additional demands, which take precedence over an individual's power to bestow a title. Now there are kinds of artworks—historically the majority—such that a person must possess special skill, sometimes highly developed, in order to produce an object that counts as an artwork of one of those kinds. In the seventeenth century, the degree of skill required for one's oil-daubed canvas to count as a painting was quite considerable; similarly for one's hacked marble to count as a statue or one's scribblings as a sonnet. Such cases are governed by a concept of "artwork" which makes skill a necessary condition for the production of an artwork. Thus, although the view that artworks must show skill is not true of all artworks, it is true of some.

That some types of artwork require skill is not exactly a novel observation, or one that is likely to be contested. But it can give rise to two mistaken views, one naive and one more sophisticated. (1) Having observed that some types of artwork require skill and that many acknowledged masterpieces are of these types, someone may make the unjustified generalization that skill is necessary for all artworks. I suspect that this kind of mistake underlies the objections to minimal art that Wollheim wishes to counter; people may think not so much that an artist has done nothing as that his work does not show the skill that they take to be required of artworks. (2) Having observed that skill is not a prerequisite for all artworks, the philosopher or critic may infer that it is prerequisite for none or (and this is the more common error) that, although required in some cases, it is always irrelevant to the artistic or philosophic evaluation of the artworks in which it figures. But neither of these inferences is justified, and neither of the conclusions is true. That the first conclusion is false has been shown already by giving counterinstances; that the second is false will become evident as we proceed.

One last preliminary observation before addressing our main topic. It is an extremely important feature of artworks that they admit of having a subject, of being *about* something. Not that every artwork *must* be about something; some are not about anything. But it is never out of place to ask the question, "What is it about?" of an artwork, even when the answer turns out to be "Nothing." Indeed, it can be plausibly argued that this admitting of having a subject (even when they do not actually have a subject) is part of what distinguishes artworks from ordinary things in the world.[5]

---

[5] See, for instance, Arthur C. Danto, "The Transfiguration of the Commonplace," *Journal of Aesthetics and Art Criticism*, XXXIII, 2 (Winter 1974): 140–148.

This feature of artworks can be used to distinguish works of virtuosity from other displays of skill. For someone might wonder why not just any display of skill—baton twirling, say, or juggling—counts as a work of virtuosity. As actions, baton twirling, juggling, and coloratura singing seem to be equally contrived or artificial; none of them is easy, or likely to occur naturally in the course of daily life. But instances of singing can be works of virtuosity, whereas instances of the others cannot. The difference does not hinge on whether a skill is displayed for its own sake (all three can be so displayed); it comes about because singing, unlike the others, can have a subject. A display of skill in baton twirling, however great the skill, cannot be *about* anything; it is not a work of virtuosity because it is not an artwork, and its not being an artwork results not merely from its having no subject but from its not admitting of having a subject. (Obviously, the facts appealed to in this paragraph reflect simply a present state of affairs; they carry no necessity; which objects can be artworks may change in the course of artistic and cultural evolution.)

III

We are now ready, after a brief and final look at Wollheim, to discuss works of virtuosity. Wollheim distinguishes two phases of artistic work: (1) work *tout court*, and (2) the decision that the work has gone far enough, and he distinguishes two sorts of minimal art. But in his relating of these two sorts of minimal art to the concept of work, there is a certain asymmetry. He says that one type of minimal art amounts to a focus on the second phase of work, which it "celebrates in isolation." Symmetry would demand that the other type of minimal art be a celebration in isolation of the first phase of work. But this is not what we get. Instead, Wollheim speaks of a redirecting or reinterpretation of the first phase of work, a challenge to ordinary notions of what this phase consists in. His account fits—indeed it illuminates—the cases he is concerned to describe, and I do not suggest that for his purpose the asymmetry is a defect. Nevertheless, one may speculate whether there are artworks that *do* complete the symmetry, artworks that "celebrate in isolation" the first phase of work. I claim that there are such artworks, and that among them are the artworks in which the skill of the artist is deliberately displayed as an end in itself.

What would an artwork be like which concentrated on the first phase of work, celebrating it in isolation? I take it that for an artwork to do this would involve taking the first phase of work or some part of the first phase as artistic subject; the first phase is what the artwork would be about. (Just as, if Wollheim's claim is correct that Duchamp's urinal concentrates on the second phase, we can say that the subject of that artwork—what it is about—is artistic judgment, an artist's power of making decisions about his own work, with the artwork seen as constituted by those decisions.) Now, it seems to be a necessary condition of artworks that they include *something* corresponding to the first phase of work, since they must be artifacts and the first phase of work is required for something to be an artifact. Thus, if an artwork concentrates on the first phase of artistic work, we can say that it takes (some of) its own necessary conditions as its subject—or, less prosaically, that art here turns inward on itself, contemplating and exalting the necessary conditions of its own existence.

Concentration on the first phase of work is not sufficient to produce a work of virtuosity. This can be seen, for example, in the works of Jackson Pollock and other abstract expressionists, some of which are plausibly seen as having the physical act of painting as their subject, the "work" of putting paint on canvas, where this is taken as necessary for the production of an artwork. Such artworks can be said to focus on the first phase of work and to take as their artistic subject the necessary conditions of their own existence as artworks. But they are not displays of skill, and therefore not works of virtuosity.

The explanation for this seems obvious: although works of abstract expressionism may be about their own necessary conditions, skill (in the sense that concerns us, namely, technical mastery or craftsmanship) is not one of their necessary conditions. So of course they are not displays of skill. But this suggests a necessary condition for an artwork's being a work of virtuosity: (1) The artwork must be one for which skill is a necessary condition; it must fall in one of the categories of artworks which require that an artwork show skill. This is clearly not sufficient, for a work might be one for which skill is required, and it might take its own necessary conditions as its subject, and yet not focus on skill—skill is, after all, only one of a variety of necessary conditions for the artworks that show it. So let us stipulate a second condition: (2) The artwork must take the skills that are its own necessary conditions as its subject. This requirement, obviously, is a more specific form of the claim that works of virtuosity are artworks that concentrate on the first phase of work. Notice that this second condition is compatible with an artwork's having more than one subject. If a seventeenth-century still life by Kalf is, as I have suggested, a work of virtuosity, thus having skill in representation as (one of) its subject(s), it can perfectly well also reflect the tastes and values of wealthy Dutch merchants and have those as its subject too.

Most artworks that satisfy these two conditions are works of virtuosity. This accords with our intuitive expectations, since it seems plausible that artistic concentration on the skills that are a work's necessary conditions may be brought about by exhibiting those skills developed to an unusual degree. Nevertheless, there are cases in which an artwork that satisfies both conditions is not a work of virtuosity. Consider Mozart's *Musikalischer Spass*. The classical period in music was one in which certain compositional skills were necessary for producing works of music (condition 1), and the *Musikalischer Spass* can reasonably be said to be about those skills (condition 2). Furthermore, it *shows* them, in the sense laid down earlier, since no one lacking them could have written the piece (not, at any rate, as a *joke*). But it does not *display* those skills— that is just its point—and hence it is not a work of virtuosity. Cases like this are no doubt rare, but they are important since they lead us to recognize a third requirement of works of virtuosity: (3) They must display the skills that they are artistically about. The three conditions we have now given—(1) the artwork must require skill; (2) it must be about the skills that it requires; (3) it must display the skills it is about—are sufficient as well as necessary for an artwork's being a work of virtuosity.

IV

The third condition for works of virtuosity has deep consequences: it ensures that any artwork that qualifies as a work of virtuosity will stand as an *instance* of what it is about. This puts works of virtuosity in a philosophically interesting class of artworks that explore the relation between art and reality. For the distinction between an artwork and what it is about normally coincides with the distinction between art and reality; thus, a work that *is* what it is about collapses, as it were, onto reality. This kind of blurring of the separation between art and reality can occur in other ways also, some of which have been deliberately exploited in twentieth-century art. But in works of virtuosity, which have been produced throughout the history of art (since at least Hellenistic times), we can see that artworks in which art and reality merge are not confined to the twentieth century and that the preoccupation of art with its own necessary conditions is not new, although it has perhaps only recently become self-conscious.

It is worth contrasting works of virtuosity with other artworks in which the relation between what the work is and what it is about takes on artistic importance. Frequently, such works rely on a coincidence of the artwork with what it represents. We must therefore insist on the distinction between what a work is *of*—what it represents—and what it is *about,* and describe the ways in which artworks may instantiate their objects of representation and being about. Since I shall take examples from visual art, "representation" will be taken as visual representation or depiction, and I shall speak for simplicity as if each picture had just one object of representation and just one object of being about.

The relations of being about and representing are distinct, and neither one is a subset of the other, since a work can be about something it does not represent, or represent something it is not about. But the two relations do intersect, since what a work represents and what it is about can be the same. Furthermore, a work can be an instance of what it represents, or an instance of what it is about, or of both, or neither. It is not hard to think of examples. Suppose that the objects of representation and of being about are different. Then there are four possibilities:

1. The picture may instantiate neither one: a picture by David is of the Horatii and about Roman virtue, but the picture *is* neither one of the Horatii nor one of the virtues.
2. The picture may instantiate what it is of, but not what it is about: a picture of a flag which is a flag and is about patriotism.
3. The picture may instantiate what it is about, but not what it is of: an impressionist picture that is of a bridge and about the resolution of light into primary colors.
4. The picture may instantiate what it is of and what it is about: a picture of a numeral 5 which is a numeral 5 and is about the traversing of the space between representation and represented.

Where the objects of representation and of being about are the same there are two possibilities:

5. The picture may instantiate neither what it is about nor what it is of: a picture of an oyster which is about oysters.
6. The picture may instantiate both what it is about and what it is of: a picture of a numeral 5 which is about the numeral 5.

Works of virtuosity are instances of what they are about, but, even where representational, they need not be instances of what

THOMAS CARSON MARK   159

they represent. From this it would appear that a work of virtuosity might occur in any of the categories above in which an artwork instantiates what it is about, and that representation could be disregarded. This would mean that works of virtuosity might be of types 3, 4, or 6. But in fact representation is not entirely irrelevant; if the objects of representation and being about are the same, there cannot be a work of virtuosity. This is because a work of virtuosity must be about the skills that are its own necessary conditions, and these, though they can be instantiated, cannot be *represented*. Therefore, representational works of virtuosity cannot be of type 6; they occur only in categories 3 and 4. However, the vast majority of representational works of virtuosity fall in category 3, not category 4, and are instances of what they are about but not of what they are of. Works of virtuosity that fall in category 4 are conceivable, though unusual; an example might be Raphael's famous freehand drawing of a circle, which is a circle, is about the skills necessary for its own existence, and instantiates those skills.

The relation of an artwork to what it is about is the source of the philosophic character of works of virtuosity and some of the other works mentioned in this section. Coincidence of representation and represented is by itself not decisive. There have been representations of circles and spheres in art for centuries, and some of them have been instances of what they represented. But they were not philosophical works. Art becomes philosophical when it explores the relation between art and reality. The coincidence of representation and represented becomes philosophical only when it is made the subject of the work, so that the artwork becomes an instance not just of what it represents but of what it is about; for only then does the coincidence of representation and represented, taken as a coincidence of art and reality, cease to be merely an external accident and become part of the artwork. Representational artworks may become philosophical by taking as object of representation something whose depiction counts not just as depiction but as the thing itself: the artwork becomes a bit of reality. Other philosophical works—ready-mades, some minimal art—proceed in the opposite direction; starting with real things they lift them into the realm of art: a bit of reality becomes an artwork. Works of virtuosity, by contrast, take art itself, through its necessary conditions, as subject, thus placing art from the outset in the position normally occupied by reality. The artwork then constitutes itself an instance of art-seen-as-reality, and we can understand the transformation in both directions at once: the artwork becomes reality and reality becomes an artwork. The line between art and reality has been absorbed into the artwork, with art on both sides of the line.

v

The preceding discussion has taken examples from visual art, but works of virtuosity occur in other arts as well, and there is no need for them to be representational. So we may consider what happens in other arts, and simplify matters by setting representation aside. As noted earlier, the word 'virtuosity' is most often applied in the performing arts. Let us turn now to examining the case of the performer, for it presents a new set of complications which may seem to go counter to the view we have developed. Consider the Chopin études, works of virtuosity, apparently, as well as masterpieces of music. They aim, obviously, at displaying skill in piano playing, and there are a number of senses in which it is true to say that the études are about skill in piano playing. But in fact the études are not works of virtuosity according to the analysis offered here, since of the three conditions for a work of virtuosity they satisfy only one.

The études *are* artworks whose production requires skill, and so they do satisfy the first requirement. The second requirement is that an artwork be about the skills it requires. But the skill required to produce an étude is skill in musical composition, whereas the skill it is about is skill in piano playing. Skill in piano playing is not a necessary condition for producing works of music, even piano pieces. To be sure, many composers of piano music, especially of works like études which are about piano playing as well as for the piano, have been pianists themselves. But there is no necessity here. Schubert, apparently, was not an outstanding pianist (he is said not to have been able to play his own "Wanderer" Fantasy), although he composed many works for piano, some of them very demanding. Therefore, the études do not satisfy the second requirement for works of virtuosity.

The third requirement is that a work of virtuosity be an instance of what it is about, and an étude is not an instance of skill in piano playing. It is an instance of various other things—"work of music," "romantic piano piece," etc.—but whatever its exact ontological status, it is not an instance of piano playing and so not an instance of what it is about. Therefore, the études do not satisfy the third requirement for works of virtuosity.

It may appear from all this that the études, and other examples from performing art, cast doubt on the analysis we have offered of works of virtuosity, especially when we consider that, since virtuosity is thought to be a feature of performing arts in particular, an account that does not fit *them* cannot be worth much. But the appearance is misleading; the analysis does apply to performing art, although we need to look more closely to see that it does. In discussing performance, I shall rely on a concept of performance that I have developed at greater length elsewhere.[6] The relevant features of this account of performance are, first, that performance consists in part in producing an instance of the work one is performing, and, second, that the performer *asserts* the work he performs; that is, his relation to the sounds he produces is very like a person's relation to the words he utters when he not only utters words but asserts the sentences constituted by the words. Finally, the performance should itself be regarded as an artwork, so that in the performance by Horowitz of a piece by Chopin we confront two artworks, not one; we confront an instance of the artwork by Chopin and we confront the performance, which is an artwork by Horowitz.

Consider, now, the performance of a Chopin étude. The performance, I have claimed, is an artwork, and obviously it is one for which skill is required; some technical mastery of the piano is a necessary condition of any performance on the piano. The performance thus satisfies the first condition for a work of virtuosity. Now, a Chopin étude is an artwork which is about skill in piano playing. But the performance, I say, is an *assertion* of the work, and as an assertion of the work it will normally be about whatever the work is about; if the work is about skill in piano playing, so is the performance. If this is correct, then the performance of a Chopin étude satisfies the second condition for a work of virtuosity, since it is about the skills that are its own necessary condition. Finally, the performance of an étude involves the production of an instance of the étude, and this production is an instance of piano playing. Now, it happens that the études are very difficult to play, which has the consequence that whatever counts as a performance of one of them must be an instance not just of piano playing but piano playing of a rather high order; it must be an instance of pianistic skill if it succeeds in giving an instance of the étude at all. But this means that the performance, besides being about skill in piano playing, is an instance of what it is about; therefore it satisfies the third condition for a work of virtuosity.

[6] See my paper "Philosophy of Piano Playing: Reflections on the Concept of Performance," *Philosophy and Phenomenological Research,* forthcoming.

A Chopin étude falls in a special class of artwork. It is not itself a work of virtuosity, but its artistic subject and its construction are such as to ensure that its performance *will be* a work of virtuosity. Although the études do contemplate the necessary conditions of art, the art whose necessary conditions they contemplate is that of the performer. Works of this kind are not uncommon in the performing arts. There could be—indeed there are—musical compositions that *are* works of virtuosity. But such works must have their *own* necessary conditions, not those of their performance, as subject matter, and be about, say, skill in composition. Furthermore, they must be instances of the skills they are about. A plausible example of such a work is the *Art of Fugue*; one might also suggest Brahms's canons, perhaps his Handel Variations, or the rondeau of Machaut described at the beginning of this paper.

VI

The analysis given here of works of virtuosity makes it easy to explain some phenomena that may seem to be paradoxical. For example, in discussing virtuosity it is sometimes asserted that a Beethoven slow movement may be at least as difficult to perform adequately as many a display piece. Schnabel is supposed to have said of a brilliant passage from Liszt that it was easy and of a lyrical passage from Beethoven that it was hard. But there is no paradox here. The truth of Schnabel's contention is compatible with saying that a performance of the Liszt is a work of virtuosity and a performance of the Beethoven is not. The question whether an artwork is a work of virtuosity, or aims at performances that are works of virtuosity, is not simply a question of the intrinsic difficulty of the work. An artwork's being a work of virtuosity depends more on what it is about than on how hard it is. Not all works that are hard make it their purpose to show this about themselves (i.e., not all have their own necessary conditions as subject), whereas some that do aim at display are not especially hard. The slow movement of a Beethoven sonata is not about piano playing, although it is very difficult to play well. Liszt, according to Schnabel, is easy, though Liszt's music often *is* about piano playing. Notice that a performance can be about piano playing even if the work performed is not, since someone can use for display a work that was not intended as a display piece, although this is generally thought to be aesthetically undesirable. Without entering into questions of evaluative aesthetics, we note that support for this general opinion might be derived from the intuitive persuasiveness of the suggestion that a pianist who is more interested in piano playing than in music should confine his performance to works that are about piano playing. This happens, in fact, to a considerable extent, in opera singing; the proportion of the standard opera repertory that is about skill in singing is much larger than the proportion of the standard piano repertory that is about skill in piano playing.

Although an artwork's being a work of virtuosity is not simply a function of its intrinsic difficulty, what it displays must count as skill if it is to be effective. Three observations are worth making in this connection. First, an artwork's effectiveness as a work of virtuosity will be partly dependent on technical developments in art. If an artwork displays skills that are later thought irrelevant or uninteresting, or if technical advance brings it about that what formerly counted as outstanding skill seems commonplace, then continued interest in the work will depend on features other than its status as a work of virtuosity. Second, the effectiveness of a work of virtuosity is less a matter of what is intrinsically difficult than a matter of the work's making the difficulty, hence the skill required for success, evident. I suspect that it is no less difficult to produce a realistic painting of a Dutch interior or street scene than it is to paint convincingly an array of exotic canapés. The latter is a work of virtuosity, however, and I think that the difference comes about because the oysters and such interest us, in the context, principally as objects to be depicted; we are not interested so much in *them* as in the depiction of them, and the skill required for this depiction is made evident by the choice of objects. Third, that an artwork requires or displays skill is not obvious to untutored contemplation; being a product of skill is not a directly perceivable property of the artworks that have it. This means that appreciation of works of virtuosity, in which display of skill is central, presupposes some knowledge. A person must have some notion of the technical demands imposed in a work if he is even to notice the skill required to meet them. Most works of virtuosity are accessible to people whose technical knowledge is slight, but there are some whose effect depends on more than perfunctory knowledge—virtuosity, we might say, for the connoisseur. A plausible example is a performance of the E-flat minor étude of Chopin. An *andante* melody over an insistent *ostinato* in the middle voice, this étude has none of the brilliance of most of the other études. Immense skill is required to sustain and shape the melody without losing the subtle changes in the *ostinato* underneath, but the degree of skill is evident only if one knows something about piano playing.

Nevertheless, this skill is what the work is about—that is to say, we are dealing with a work of virtuosity, not just a work that happens to be very difficult.

The third observation above has some theoretical importance; for it provides a way of seeing the falsity of two opinions that are still sometimes taken to have some cogency, although they have recently been attacked on various grounds. The first is the view that factors having to do with the production of an artwork are always irrelevant to the aesthetic evaluation of the artwork. The second, which can be seen as a more general thesis having the first as a special case, is that all the aesthetically relevant properties of an artwork must be directly perceivable. Since skill has to do with production of an artwork and since it is not directly perceived, a proponent of the views under consideration would insist that people who respond to skill are responding to aesthetically irrelevant properties of artworks. This claim is indeed true of some artworks—that is, there are artworks in which the skill required to produce them *is* irrelevant to aesthetic evaluation of the finished work. Examples might be the interiors of de Hooch, many of Rembrandt's portraits, or the Brahms intermezzi. But in works of virtuosity skill is not irrelevant to aesthetic evaluation. In saying this I am not merely saying that since works of virtuosity are intended as displays of skill, to overlook skill is to miss the artist's intention (although it would be true to say that). Instead, my point is that in a work of virtuosity the display of skill enters essentially into the nature of the work, shaping it and providing its artistic subject. Consider the Mozart piano concertos, which are so constructed as to ensure that a performance of one of them is a work of virtuosity. Charles Rosen has shown how the display of instrumental virtuosity is related to the musical form of these works.[7] As we might expect, the musical material is arranged so as to draw attention to the virtuoso passages, but, besides being a focus of attention, the virtuoso passages serve to complete the tonal balance. Virtuosic display is offered for its own sake, yet it simultaneously provides a way of satisfying the dramatic impulse and the demand for proportions which are at the heart of the classical style. Rosen points out that the concerto is like the operatic aria in some aspects of formal construction, and in opera my point is if anything more striking. The person who does not recognize or thinks it irrel-

---

[7] *The Classical Style* (New York: Norton, 1972), section V, chapter 1, "The Concerto." Scattered through Rosen's book are numerous insightful remarks about virtuosity; see, among others, p. 281, 306, 335, 340, 352.

evant that a performance of the Queen of the Night's *Der Hölle Rache* is a *tour de force* is not overlooking something secondary; on the contrary, he has failed to understand the first thing about the aria. These remarks and examples are intended to support my claim that recognizing their status as displays of skill is essential to the understanding of works of virtuosity as artworks. But this amounts to saying that properties which are not directly perceivable and which have to do with production are relevant to the aesthetic evaluation of some artworks. (I take it as obvious that understanding is an aid to aesthetic evaluation; aesthetic judgment is impaired if one does not recognize or purposely disregards what a work is about.)

We should observe that to determine whether a work is about its own necessary conditions is not always easy, and in some cases there may be no conclusive evidence. Conclusive evidence, when available, is likely to be external. For example, one might try to establish on internal grounds that the études are about piano playing, by looking at the types of figuration, seeking characteristically pianistic writing, and so on, but such evidence would not be decisive. Some of the Bach preludes contain keyboard figuration surprisingly like what is found in the études (and resemble them, stylistically, in other ways as well), yet they are not about harpsichord playing. In the case of the études, we do have conclusive evidence in the fact that they are called "études." In other cases, conclusive evidence may come from other sources; thus, *Ach ich liebte* (from *Die Entführung aus dem Serail*) is partly about singing, in exactly the sense in which the Chopin études are about piano playing, but we know this neither from the title nor from internal evidence; we know it because of a remark in one of Mozart's letters: "I have sacrificed Constanze's aria a bit to the flexible throat (der geläufigen Gurgel) of Mlle Cavallieri" (letter of September 26, 1781). That the subject matter of some artworks must be established externally ought to occasion no misgivings; it is a very common state of affairs. We might easily never discover from internal evidence that a picture by Pollock was about painting, especially if we came to it believing that all pictures are representations. That the *Oath of the Horatii* is about Roman virtue could not be established *just* by looking; we need, at least, the title and some historical knowledge.

The discussion of the last few paragraphs makes clear that the application to concrete cases of the concept of a work of virtuosity is sometimes tentative and uncertain; few artworks are as unequivocal in this respect as the Chopin études. Many artworks combine the characteristics of a work of virtuosity with others. Is a performance of the Waldstein Sonata a work of virtuosity? Think of the *prestissimo* octaves toward the end. Then think of the *Introduzione* and the opening of the last movement. Obviously, any one-word answer is wrong. But my purpose has not been classification; the concept of a work of virtuosity is not derived by induction from some antecedently distinguishable class of artworks. Nevertheless, it illuminates an important dimension of artistic activity which has received comparatively little theoretical attention.

THOMAS CARSON MARK

St. John's College, Annapolis

ILKKA NIINILUOTO

SCIENTIFIC PROGRESS*

1. INTRODUCTION

Science is often distinguished from other human enterprises by its progressive nature. Science, it is said, has "a progressive and public character"[1], and an essential feature of scientific knowledge is its "continued growth"[2]. Just like Kant who complained that metaphysics has not yet found "the sure path of science"[3], so many philosophers have thought that science can be effectively demarcated from religion, art, philosophy and politics by reference to its method; this method is thought to be sufficient to guarantee continuous progress for science or at least to give clear criteria for recognizing 'progressive' developments within science.[4]

This view has recently been challenged by philosophers who argue that there is no deep difference between science and many fields of non-science.[5] But along with other philosophers, most of them would agree that there is some sense in which science can be said to make 'progress'. Even Feyerabend, perhaps the most radical critic of the distinction between science and non-science, goes so far as to claim that his "anarchism helps to achieve progress in any one of the senses one cares to choose".[6]

In many discussions of the development of science, the notion of 'progress' is either left unanalysed or characterized only in vague terms. Semantical, epistemological, and factual questions concerning progress are also often confused with each other. The definitions of progress which in fact have been proposed so far, while disagreeing greatly with each other, have widely different implications for our understanding of the nature of science. The study of this concept seems therefore to be a very important task for philosophers of science – and it is no wonder that increasing attention has been paid to it in recent years.

'Progress' is a normative or goal-relative – rather than purely descriptive – term: saying that the step from one theory A to another theory B constitutes progress means that B is an improvement of A

167

in some respect. In this sense, 'progress' can be contrasted with such neutral terms as 'development', and a philosophical analysis of scientific progress is tantamount to a specification of the aims of science.

One can raise three different questions concerning scientific progress. First, what is meant by the notion of 'progress'? In what different senses can one say that the development of science is 'progressive'? Secondly, how can we identify 'progressive' developments within science? What are the most reliable indicators of scientific progress? Thirdly, has science made and will it make progress? The third question is a factual one, given some answer to the first conceptual question and to the second methodological question.

In this paper, I shall discuss and evaluate the most important types of answers which have been given to these questions. In particular, my aim is to show that it is possible to give a systematic defense of the 'realist' theory progress which claims that science makes progress so far as it succeeds in gaining true or highly truthlike information about reality. This view of progress has been the target of forceful attacks by Kuhn, Feyerabend, Stegmüller, Laudan, and many others. A recent commentator has even argued that "the rate of improvement" of "the various formal analyses of science in terms of truth, approximation to the truth, et cetera" is "diminishing rapidly".[7] This paper is an attempt to support the opposite conclusion.

2. PROGRESS AS CUMULATION

The idea of progress is of a relatively recent origin. In his classical study of this idea, J. Bury argued that the conception of progress in the historical development of mankind was, in spite of its anticipation by some medieval and renaissance thinkers, established only in the 17th and 18th century.[8] An essential ingredient of this conception was the view that scientific knowledge grows by cumulation. Associated with the methodological optimism of classical empiricists (Francis Bacon) and rationalists (Descartes) there was the view that the Scientific Method, if properly used, guarantees that science grows by accumulating reliably established truths.[9] Scientific progress, in this view, means that new truths are added to the body of accepted results of scientific inquiry.

The *accumulation-of-truths view* of progress was effectively criticized by many philosophers and scientists from the 18th century onwards,[10] and it is nowadays widely regarded as giving a naive and oversimplified picture of the development of science.[11] First, it makes unreasonable assumptions of the epistemological status of scientific knowledge: the results of factual sciences are not absolutely certain or conclusively established, but rather they are always to some degree conjectural and corrigible in principle. Secondly, it also makes unreasonable assumptions of the linear or continuous character of scientific growth: the earlier results of science are not only preserved and reorganized in the future development of science, but they may also be reinterpreted, re-evaluated and rejected by new theories and conceptual frameworks. Thirdly, it makes unreasonable assumptions concerning the truth-value of scientific statements: even the best theories in science are in some respects idealized and their claims about the reality may strictly speaking be false.

The traditional view of progress is 'realist' in the sense that it takes truth (or informative truth) to be the aim of science and claims that science makes progress in so far as it succeeds in realizing this aim. Against this sort of a *realist view*, some critics have claimed that the notion of truth need not or should not be used in the characterization of progress. In the sequel, our main interest will be in the contrast between the various non-cumulative versions of the realist view and the non-realist accounts of scientific progress.[12]

3. PROGRESS AS APPROACH TO THE TRUTH

If scientific knowledge is always corrigible, subject to further revision, and possibly false, does it still make sense to speak of scientific progress in the realist sense? An answer to this question can be based on the suggestion of the 17th century physicists Robert Boyle and Robert Hooke who compared the method of science to the rule called *regula falsi* in arithmetic.[13] This rule is a method of solving a linear equation by starting from a conjectural false guess of the solution. Boyle referred to Bacon's remark that "truth does more easily emerge out of error than confusion", and accordingly suggested that false assumptions may be useful in the search for truth in science. In the 18th century, this analogy between the methods of arithmetic and science was extended to cover the so-called iterative methods of approaching the solutions of equations by means of

successive approximation. David Hartley, Joseph Priestley, and
Georges LeSage argued, on the basis of this analogy, that the method
of science is essentially self-corrective and brings scientific theories
gradually to closer approximations to the truth.[14]

The *approach-to-the-truth view* of progress received support also
from a quite different source, viz. from rationalist and idealist
metaphysics. Already in the 15th century, Nicholas of Cusa argued in
his doctrine of "learned ignorance" that the absolute truth about the
infinite universe (or God) is beyond the reach of our finite intellect:
God is "infinitely greater than anything that words can express", but

"it is by the process of elimination and the use of negative propositions that we come
nearer the truth about Him".

For example,

"it is truer to assert that God is intelligence and life than to assert that He is earth, stone or
anything material".[15]

The ideas of the infinity of the world (Spinoza[16]), of the objective
reality of truth as divine thought (Leibniz[17]), and of the self-deter-
mined 'dialectical' development of Objective Spirit towards its perfection (Hegel), had an important influence on many 19th century
philosophers. The British Hegelian Bradley developed, on the basis of
a coherence theory, a doctrine of absolute and relative truths and of
"degrees of truth"[18], while Engels and, following him, Lenin attempted to combine in their "dialectical materialism" the views that the
nature is infinite and "inexhaustible", and that

"the *limits* of approximation of our knowledge to the objective, absolute truth are
historically conditional, but the existence of such truth is *unconditional*, and the fact
that we are approaching nearer to it is also unconditional".[19]

Similar ideas were expressed by many French philosophers in the
19th century. Laplace contrasts the human mind (which is capable of
making progress in its search for truth) with a vast intelligence "from
which it will always remain infinitely removed".[20] Cournot says that,
even though "we do not have the ability to attain absolute reality",
we may be able to gradually move from one stage to another "in the
series whose last term would be absolute reality".[21] Claude Bernard
argues that scientific theories are "only partial and provisional truths"
and "literally speaking" false, but nevertheless we are "constantly

nearing" the "absolute truth" about "complex and infinitely varied phenomena".[22] Duhem suggests that

"to the extent that physical theory makes progress, it becomes more and more similar to a natural classification which is its ideal end".[23]

Perhaps the most important defender of the self-corrective nature of science in the 19th century was Charles Peirce who thought that truth can be defined as the *limit of inquiry*. From a historical perspective, Peirce seems to be a point where the methodological and the metaphysical traditions in the approach-to-the-truth view meet each other. This is illustrated by the fact that in his article 'Methods for Attaining Truth' (1898) on self-corrective methods Peirce refers both to iterative methods in mathematics and to Hegel (CP 5.574-604). (This is also an instance of the two different tendencies in Peirce's thinking that Goudge has called Peirce's 'naturalism' and 'transcendentalism'.) The Peircean account of scientific progress will be discussed in detail in the next section.[24]

4. TRUTH AS THE LIMIT OF INQUIRY

As we mentioned in Section 4, the first defenders of the self-corrective nature of science compared the method of hypothesis in science to the mathematical methods for solving equations.[25] The latter methods typically satisfy the following principles:

(1)   *Monotone convergence*: Each step in the iteration brings us closer to the true solution.

(2)   *Fixed point*: True solution is a fixed point of the iteration, i.e., if the true solution is once found, it will not be lost later.

(Here (2) follows from (1).) Moreover, they usually satisfy one of the following conditions:

(3)   *Finite success*: The true solution is found in a finite number of steps.

(4)   *Success in limit*: The true solution, even though it may in some cases be found in a finite number of steps, is the limit of the successive approximations obtained in the different steps in the iteration.

Assume now that analogous principles could be formulated for the scientific method – let us call them (S1)–(S4). Is there any evidence for the validity of these principles? Peirce once claimed the following[26]:

"But we hope that in the progress of science its error will indefinitely diminish, just as the error of 3.14159, the value given for π, will indefinitely diminish as the calculation is carried to more and more places of decimals." (5.565)

If this analogy were successful, scientific method would satisfy principles (S1) and (S4). However, several philosophers already in the 18th and 19th century pointed out that in fact there is no guarantee for monotone convergence (S1) in science.[27] Peirce, too, argued on many occasions against principles (S1), (S2), and (S3). He realized that convergence to the truth is "irregular" even in the case of enumerative induction (2.775). Even though the opinion of a scientist is "constantly gravitating" to a final conclusion, "the individual may not live to reach the truth" (8.12, cf. 2.654). According to Peirce, induction leads to approximate truth only "in the long run" (1.67, cf. 2.781 and 5.380), so that success is guaranteed only as an "ideal limit" of "endless investigation" (5.565). Moreover, Peirce rejects the idea that the truth, once found, could be effectively recognized as the truth (cf. (S2)).[28]

It is important to observe that the validity of (S1) is not necessary for the validity of (S4). In mathematics, converging sequences need not be monotone – it is sufficient that the upper bound of the absolute error decreases at each step and eventually tends to zero. For this reason, arguments against (S1) and (S2) do not refute (S4). In spite of his rejection of (S1)–(S3), Peirce could thus consistently remain a defender of the limit principle (S4) for scientific knowledge.

In fact, Peirce took the limit principle so seriously that he defined truth as the limit of inquiry. On Peirce's pragmatist theory of meaning, the "absolutely incognizable" reality is "absolutely inconceivable" or merely "a meaningless word" (5.310). Therefore, the reality must have the capacity of influencing our opinion. According to Peirce, "real things" cause our beliefs in such a way that, in scientific research,

"different minds may set out with most antagonist views, but the process of investigation carries them by force outside of themselves to one and the same conclusion ... The opinion which is fated to be ultimately agreed to by all who investigate, is what we mean by the truth, and the object represented in this opinion is the real." (5.407)[29]

Even if Peirce himself was convinced that "that the rule of induction will hold good in the long run may be deduced from the principle that reality is only the object of the final opinion to which sufficient investigation would lead" (2.693), he tried to substantiate his general argument for scientific progress by giving a direct proof for the self-corrective nature of induction.

Enumerative induction, as an inference from sample to a statistical generalization about a population, involves as an essential element the problem of the estimation of physical probabilities. Already James Bernoulli suggested that the convergence of observed relative frequencies to the true values of probabilities is analogous to the approximation of the true value of π (cf. above), but Leibniz was quick to observe the fallacy of this analogy: the convergence of relative frequencies does not satisfy the monotonicity principle (1).[30] But does this convergence satisfy the limit principle (4), as Peirce repeatedly claims? The answer to this question depends on the underlying theory of probability.

In the frequency theory of Venn, Peirce, von Mises, and Reichenbach, probabilities are defined as limits of relative frequencies, so that the limit principle (4) becomes valid *per definitionem* for those cases where limits in fact exist. Reichenbach, who thought that all scientific methods are ultimately reducible to enumerative induction, used this fact as the basis of his pragmatic justification of induction:

"The rule of induction is justified as an instrument of positing because it is a method of which we know that if it is possible to make statements about the future we shall find them by means of this method."

The critics of Reichenbach have acutely observed, however, that "his justification of the principle of induction reduces to the bare tautology that if there is a limit, there is a limit".[31]

According to the propensity theory, which Peirce himself developed in the first decade of this century, probabilities are numerical tendencies which exist objectively as dispositional physical properties of chance set-ups (2.664). In this theory, the limit principle (4) is not valid any more. The strongest result which can be proved is Borel's Theorem (1909):

(5)   The relative frequency of event A in a sequence of independent trials of an experiment *converges almost surely* (i.e., with probability one) to the probability of A.[32]

Another way of writing (5) is the following:

(5') *Probable success in limit*: With probability one, the true solution is the limit of successive approximations obtained in the different steps in the iteration.

Even if this result makes success in the limit extremely probable, it is logically weaker than the limit principle (4). Thus, Peirce's paradigm example for principle (4), viz. enumerative induction, after all fails to satisfy it.[33]

It is remarkable that Peirce seems to have been aware of this difficulty:

"I take it that anything may fairly be said to be *destined* which is sure to come about although there is no necessitating reason for it. Thus, a pair of dice, thrown often enough, will be sure to turn up sixes some time, although there is no necessity that they should. The probability that they will is 1; that is all." (4.547n)

If we assume that, instead of the problematic (S4), Peirce was attempting to defend a principle (S5) which claims that science is "destined" to converge to the truth, i.e., that *very probably* science is successful in the limit, his programme is justifiable at least in some important cases.[34] Moreover, this programme cannot be said to "trivialize" the thesis of the self-corrective nature of science – instead this charge (due to Laudan) should be directed against attempts, such as the recent *consensus theory of truth*[35], which *define* truth in terms of a limiting consensus of an ideal scientific community. The analysis of scientific progress by means of such a consensus theory would be as circular as Reichenbach's pragmatic justification of induction.

5. CAN SCIENCE GROW FOREVER?

One important aspect of the approach-to-the-truth view is the assumption that, in some sense, the world is infinite but human knowledge is finite. Therefore, it is argued, there will be no end for science: as creations of scientists, theories can never exhaust the whole universe in its all variety. A clear expression of this view was given by John Herschel in 1831.[36] Herschel reminds the reader of Newton's famous remark of himself as a boy in the shore of a wide and unexplored ocean. According to Herschel, the world is an "inexhaustible store which only awaits our continued endeavors".

Science is

"essentially incomplete, and incapable of being fully embodied in any system, or embraced by any single mind."

Therefore,

"in whatever state of knowledge we may conceive man to be placed, his progress towards a yet higher state need never fear a check, but most continue till the last existence of society."

More recently, similar arguments against the possibility of a "final state of knowledge" on the basis of the "infinite complexity of the world" have been presented by Popper, Bohm, and Vigier.[37]

On the other hand, there are philosophers and scientists – among them George Gore in 1878 – who have claimed that scientific inquiry will ultimately come to a terminal point, either because all scientific problems become solved or because the resources for investigation will be exhausted.[38]

William Kneale has argued that the principle of perpetual revolution in science cannot be justified by appeal to the infinite complexity of nature.[39] In other words, the infinity of nature does not preclude the possibility that science comes to an end through the acceptance of a wholly true single theory. Kneale distinguishes between three different versions of the infinity doctrine:

(i) the world contains an infinite multiplicity of particulars

(ii) the natural phenomena have an infinite variety

(iii) there is in the world an infinite number of distinguishable layers of fine structure.

Of these possibilities, (i) is irrelevant since "theories are not concerned with particulars as such", and (ii) does not rule out a final theory since e.g. Newton's law of gravitation covers "infinitely many different mechanical phenomena". Further, (iii) would in fact mean that there is no single or unitary theory about the whole world but at best an infinite conjunction of explanatory theories. In this case, Kneale argues, there would be no point in speaking about "approximations to truth" (as Bohm and Vigier want to do).[40]

Kneale's argument do not seem quite conclusive. In the first place, it is not clear that those who think that science will continue and grow forever have to assume a strong principle of the unity of science. It is an important feature of scientific progress that advances towards generality have at the same time been "steps towards simplification", as Herschel said.[41] But this tendency towards unification – "consilience of inductions", as Whewell called it[42] – may have limits which are due to the existence of different irreducible levels or 'layers' of the world. Then, instead of being interested in one single overall theory which is an "organic unity",[43] we would consider separately theories for the different 'layers' of reality – and there might be at least one 'layer' where scientific inquiry may continue forever without reaching a final state.

In the second place, it is not quite clear what logical requirements should be imposed on a theory. In the sixties and the seventies, logicians have developed different sorts of infinitary languages, such as (a) languages with arbitrary large infinite vocabularies, (b) languages which infinite conjunctions and disjunctions and with quantification over infinite sequences of variables, and (c) languages with formulas which have infinitely long nested subformulas.[44] How complex the world ever is, it seems that there is a suitable infinitary language in which we can express 'theories' about the whole world – and if no restrictions are given to the notion of a theory, these 'theories' may also be infinitely complex. But, on the other hand, as soon as restrictions are given, the possibility arises that there is no single theory of the admissible kind which would completely describe the reality.

For example, as Gödel showed in 1931, there cannot be any *recursive* axiomatization of the class of all truths about natural numbers. Nevertheless, we may say that our knowledge in arithmetic (if it has to be expressed as a recursive theory) can grow indefinitely and make progress towards the so-called complete arithmetic without ever reaching it.[45]

Kneale's other argument for the possibility of the terminal state of science is the following: Bohm and others can show at most that no theory is *known* to be final. In other words, we may find the final theory without knowing that it is final. Let us distinguish two kinds of successions of theories:

(6) $\qquad T_1, T_2, \ldots, T_{n-1}, T_n, T_n, T_n, \ldots$

where T_n is true, and

(7) $T_1, T_2, \ldots, T_{n-1}, T_n, T_{n+1}, \ldots$

where T_n is false and $T_n \neq T_{n+1}$ for all n. Then Kneale seems to be right: the 'fallibilist' view of the corrigibility of scientific knowledge is not incompatible with the possibility of theory successions of type (6). But, on the other hand, there are philosophers – I have called them "strong fallibilists" elsewhere[46] – who would claim that, as all theories are strictly speaking false, only sequences of type (7) are possible.

Sequences (6) and (7) may represent successive solutions to a single scientific problem. In the case of (6), the correct solution is found in a finite time, while in (7) the solution is at best the limit of endless investigation. For example, (7) might represent a sequence of successive and increasingly accurate point estimates of some unknown physical constant, or it might correspond to successive steps in a problem involving enumerative induction (cf. Section 4). Now, in order that science would come to an end in a finite time, it should be the case that all sequences of problem solutions are of type (6). If there is even *one* sequence of type (7), then science will continue for ever – and there is no way of ruling out this possibility. Thus one need not accept 'strong fallibilism' to defend the view that science will not reach a terminal state: it is enough that there exist problems which may require an indefinite time for their solution.

One further problem with Kneale's view is the fact that, *if* we find the 'final' true theory without knowing it, it seems that we may also lose it later. To find this theory is not the same thing as to accept it permanently.[47]

Robert Almeder has argued that

"if the process of scientific inquiry were to continue forever, then science would ultimately terminate in the acceptance of a single theoretical framework better than all conceivable other, and ... there is some evidence in favor of the view that science will continue unto eternity but no evidence in favor of the contrary view."[48]

Almeder thinks that it is implausible to suppose that we can approach the final theory as a limit without actually accepting it already after some finite time. He says that there is "no real difference between endorsing a final theory and approaching it by a margin of error infinitely small". Almeder seems thus to think that principle (S4) or (S5), i.e., success in limit, entails (S3), i.e., finite success. Indeed, he explicitly supports this view by claiming that (5) entails (3). This argument is mistaken, since there *is* a difference – as the mathematical notion of limit shows us – between reaching a limit in a finite time and approaching a limit indefinitely, i.e., between sequences of types (6) and (7).[49]

Even if Almeder were right in thinking that a final theory will ultimately be found, his argument does not show that this theory could not be an incomplete true theory. Indeed, to claim that science, pursued indefinitely, *will* terminate in a final and irreversible answer to any question that may be asked and admits of an answer sounds like an instance of the notorious Principle of Plenitude (i.e., the thesis that all genuine possibilities will eventually be realized).

We may thus conclude that there are no strong arguments for denying the possibility that science will grow forever – or at least "till the end of society", as Herschel put it.

6. ARE THERE IDEAL CONCEPTUAL STRUCTURES AND THEORIES?

What does it mean to say that truth is the ideal *limit* of endless investigation? In the preceding section, we have spoken of theses (S1)–(S5) as if their content would be more or less unproblematic. It is by no means clear, however, what 'nearness to the truth' means in connection with scientific theories. Indeed, Quine has argued that this idea involves a false numerical analogy.[50] Moreover, Quine adds, even if we could speak of 'limits' of theories, what would guarantee the existence and the uniqueness of such limits?

If the accumulation-of-truths view were acceptable, Quine's problems could be easily solved. In speaking of 'the truth' as the aim of inquiry we would mean 'the truth, the whole truth, and nothing but the truth', i.e., the class T of all true (general) statements about the world. A true theory h (as a deductively closed set of statements) would then simply be a subset of the class T; a true theory h' would be closer to T than another true theory h if and only if h is contained in h', i.e., h' is logically stronger that h. (See Fig. 1.) Moreover, to say that T is the limit of the true theories $h_1, h_2, \ldots$ would mean that T is the set-theoretical union of $h_1, h_2, \ldots$.

For false theories the situation is much more problematic, however, since they always have a non-empty intersection with both T and $-T$ (the complement of T). In 1865, Bernard defined progress as follows:

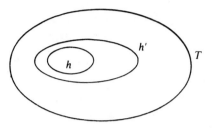

Fig. 1.

"the sum of truths grows larger in proportion as the sum of error grows less".[51] A more explicit version of essentially the same idea was given by Karl Popper in 1960: h' is *more truthlike* than h if and only if

  (a) $h \cap T \subseteq h' \cap T$
  (b) $h' \cap -T \subseteq h \cap -T$

where one of the inclusions (a) and (b) is strict.[52] (See Fig. 2.) However, it turned out that this definition does not work in the intended way: h' is more truthlike than h, in this sense, *only if h' is true*.[53]

Another approach to defining the notion of 'more true' is due to Wilfrid Sellars – who views this enterprise as an attempt to "revitalize central themes in nineteenth-century Idealism".[54] Sellars says that a proposition is true if it is correctly S-assertible, i.e., assertible in accordance with the semantical rules describing a conceptual structure. More precisely, a proposition p in a conceptual structure CS_i is *true in* CS_i if p is S-assertible in CS_i. Further, p in CS_i is *true quoad*

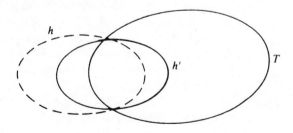

Fig. 2.

CS_j if the 'counterpart' proposition of p in CS_i is true in CS_j. For Sellars, truth as such does not admit of degrees, but still

"one conceptual framework can be more 'adequate' than another, and this fact can be used to define a sense in which one proposition can be said to be 'more true' than another."

The adequacy of a conceptual system CS_i depends on the adequacy of the 'pictures' of genuinely extra-linguistic objects that the atomic statements of CS_i can give.

A language CSP which enables its users to form "*ideally* adequate pictures of objects" is called "Peirceish" by Sellars. Then a proposition p in CS_i (e.g., in *our* conceptual system CSO) is true *quoad* CSP if its counterpart in CSP is S-assertible by the users of CSP. This notion of ultimate truth is, for Sellars, a "regulative ideal": the ideal "Peirceish community" need not exist.

Assuming that the notion of a 'linguistic picture' is viable,[56] one may ask: When is one picture 'more adequate' than another? What is an 'ideally adequate' picture of objects? Is it possible, and on what conditions, to say that of two propositions in CSO which are false *quoad* CSP one is 'more true' than another? If Sellars does not have answers to these questions – as it seems to me – then the whole talk about the Peirceish conceptual structure does not give us much help in analysing the idea of scientific progress.

Rosenberg has tried to supplement Sellars' view by pointing out that there may be successions of theories which generate converging (in Cauchy's sense) sequences of numbers.[57] The ideal Peirceish theory could then be identified with the limit of such succession. However, it is not clear that all interesting theories are of the required kind: qualitative theories seem to be excluded in any case. Moreover, assume that a succession of theories satisfies up to the present time Cauchy's criterion for all the sequences of numbers that it generates. What guarantees that it will satisfy this condition in the future? What excludes the possibility that this sequence has two or more alternative converging continuations? And even if the existence and the uniqueness of the limit theory were guaranteed, this theory might concern only some restricted aspects of the world – unless some strong principle for the unity of science is presupposed.

Michael Hooker has also suggested that the notion of an ideal Peirceish theory is contradictory in the sense that this theory should

both *be* a member of the series of theories which converges towards
it (otherwise it would not be a candidate for replacing these theories)
and *not be* a member of this series (otherwise it could be replaced by
a better theory).[58]

To avoid the difficulties with the notion of "Peirceish", we might
suggest the following two theses:

(6)   There is no unique, ideally adequate conceptual framework
        for describing the world.

(7)   The comparative notion of 'more true' can be defined
        relative to each choice of a conceptual framework for
        describing the world.

To deny thesis (6) would amount to the claim that there is an ideal
language which has a privileged status in the description of the
reality. This seems to be at least part of the view that Putnam calls
"metaphysical realism" as opposed to "internal realism".[59] However,
one can argue against such metaphysical realism that the world is not
carved up into 'pieces' and 'facts' without human conceptualizing
activity. THE WORLD *exists* independently of any conceptualization
(to claim otherwise would lead us to linguistic idealism), but it can be
approached and described only *via* different conceptual frameworks.

THE WORLD conceptualized by language L will be called the
L-world. More precisely, let L be a language with vocabulary λ, and
let $\mathcal{M}_L$ be the class of L-structures (in the ordinary model-theoretical
sense). Thus, $\mathcal{M}_L$ is the class of those set-theoretical structures which
contain interpretations for the terms in λ. (Hence, one may speak of
the truth of sentences of L in members of $\mathcal{M}_L$ in Tarski's sense.) If L
is a semantically determinate language which does not contain vague
or 'fuzzy' terms, then there is a *unique* member W_L of $\mathcal{M}_L$ which
represents THE WORLD as far it can be represented in L.

Each L-world W_L is, in an obvious sense, a fragment of the reality
and can be the object of scientific investigation. Moreover, the
L-worlds and THE WORLD constitute a partially ordered structure
where L_j-world is higher than L_i-world if language L_j is an extension
of language L_i (see Fig. 3.).

The theses (6) and (7) together suggest that one can make pictures
only of the L-worlds but not of THE WORLD. To think that THE
WORLD looks like something, and that one can make pictures of it,
already involves a presupposed way of composing this world into
facts. On the other hand, more or less adequate pictures can be made

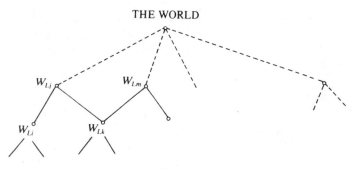

Fig. 3.

of the L-worlds. But as the L-worlds are fragments of THE WORLD, pictures of the former can, in a derivative sense, be said to be pictures of the latter.

It is worth pointing out that, independently of the validity of (6), our position seems to be better off than the Sellarsian view. Namely, if (6) is valid, then Sellars' treatment is inadequate; and if (6) is not valid, i.e., if the Peircean framework CSP exists, then we may utilize our solution of (7) and define the notion of truthlikeness *relative to CSP*.

It is important to add that thesis (6) is compatible with the view that, for inquiries which have more restricted or 'local' aims than the description of the whole truth,[60] there may exist languages which include all (or almost all) relevant factors:

(8)   For each scientific problem or problem area, there exists an ideal or practically ideal language.

The aim of a whole field of science (e.g., genetics) may be to investigate certain objects (e.g., animals) from a certain viewpoint. In this case, the ideal conceptual structure L for this field should include all those features of the objects under study which are relevant for this general aim.[61] The task of this field would not, then, be the description of THE WORLD but rather of the L-world W_L. In practice, we do not have absolute criteria for choosing L, so that the study of the L-world W_L starts with some language L' in which we attempt to include at least what we expect to be the most relevant features of the objects. This method of *idealization* is then complemented by a process of 'concretization' which means that new factors are added to the language L' – with the aim of reaching eventually the most adequate language L and the most truthlike theory in L.[62]

In the next section, we shall outline an approach to 'truthlikeness' which takes the theses (6), (7), and (8) as its starting point.

The following mathematical analogy may clarify the underlying idea (cf. the different branches of Fig. 3). Let us consider the sequence of natural numbers

$$1, 2, 3, \ldots, n, \ldots$$

which has the infinite number ω as its 'ideal limit'. Here ω is not a natural number any more. If we ask how close to ω two numbers m and n are, we cannot answer this by measuring the distance of m and n from ω – for the simple reason that $\omega - m = \omega - n = \omega$. But, in another sense, we can say that m is closer to ω than n if and only if $k - m \geqslant k - n$ for some (and hence all) natural number $k \geqslant m, k \geqslant n$.

7. DEGREES OF TRUTHLIKENESS

Let L be a first-order language with a finite vocabulary λ. Here λ may consist of several families of predicates (in Carnap's sense) where some of these families may be based upon quantitative concepts. Then each generalization h in L has a distributive normal form, i.e., h is logically equivalent to a finite disjunction of mutually exclusive constituents.[63] Assuming that one can define a distance $d(C_i, C_j)$ between two constituents, the distance $d(h, C_j)$ of the generalization h from C_j can be defined as a function of the distances $d(C_i, C_j)$, where C_i is in the normal form of L.[64]

For each language L, there is one and only one constituent which is (actually) true. Let us denote it by C_*. As C_* expresses the whole truth about the L-world W_L (cf. Section 6), it seems natural to say that the *degree of L-truthlikeness* of h is measured by

$$(9) \qquad M(h, C_*) = 1 - d(h, C_*).$$

(Cf. Fig. 4.) Given a suitable choice of d, this measure M has intuitively satisfactory properties. For example, C_* itself has the maximum degree of L-truthlikeness. If h' is logically stronger than h, and both h' and h are true, then $M(h, C_*) \leqslant M(h', C_*)$.

If C_* is unknown (as it in most cases is), we cannot apply formula (9). However, given some evidence e which can be used to evaluate

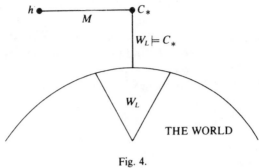

Fig. 4.

the inductive probabilities $P(C_i/e)$ of the constituents C_i, we can propose to estimate the value of $M(h, C_*)$ by the following:

(10) $\text{ver}(h/e) = \sum_i P(C_i/e)M(h, C_i)$

where i ranges over the indices of all constituents in L.[65] Thus, $\text{ver}(h/e)$ is the *estimated degree of L-truthlikeness* of h on the basis of evidence e.

In Hintikka's system of inductive logic, when the size n of evidence e (in L) grows without limit, there is a unique constituent C_c such that $P(C_c/e) \to 1$. This C_c is the constituent which says that the L-world is of the same kind as sample e, i.e., that those and only those Q-predicates are instantiated in the L-world which are exemplified in e. Here c indicates the number of different *kinds* of individuals in sample e. Hence,

(11) $\text{ver}(h/e) \to M(h, C_c)$, when $n \to \infty$.

Here $C_c = C_*$ if e is both true (no empty Q-predicates are claimed to be non-empty be e) and fully informative (all non-empty Q-predicates are exemplified in e). In particular,

(12) $\text{ver}(C_c/e) \to 1$, when $n \to \infty$ and c remains fixed.

On the basis of measures M and ver, we can say that a theory h' in L is *closer to the truth* than another theory h in L if $M(h', C_*) > M(h, C_*)$. Similarly, h' *seems* on e to be *closer to the truth* than h if $\text{ver}(h'/e) > \text{ver}(h/e)$.[66]

A sequence of theories $h_1, h_2, \ldots$ in L can be said to *converge* *towards the truth* if $M(h_i, C_*) \to 1$ when $i = 1, 2, \ldots$. Similarly, this sequence *seems to converge* towards the truth if $\text{ver}(h_i/e) \to 1$ when $i = 1, 2, \ldots$.

The notion of L-truthlikeness is relative to language in the sense that there are cases where h has greater L-truthlikeness than h' but h' has greater L'-truthlikeness than h, when L' is an extension of L.[67] We might say that h' in L has, in an absolute sense, greater truthlikeness than h in L if h' has greater L'-truthlikeness than h in all extensions L' of L.

8. IN DEFENCE OF THE REALIST THEORY OF PROGRESS

The theory of truthlikeness, which was outlined in Section 7, gives us a systematic tool for defending a realist theory of scientific progress. Let h and h' be rival theories which are concerned with the same problem area of science. Let L be the ideal language for this problem area (cf. (9)). Then h' is closer to the truth than h if and only if h' has a greater degree of L-truthlikeness than h; in this case, the step from h to h' is *progressive*.[68] In practice, L may be unknown to us, and the evaluation of h and h' has to be made by appeal to evidence e in our conceptual structure, say L'. Then we can say that, relative to L', the step from h to h' *seems progressive* on evidence e if and only if $\text{ver}(h'/e)$ is greater than $\text{ver}(h/e)$ in L'. The rational appraisal of theories is, in this sense, historical – bound to the best conceptual systems that we so far have been able to find.

One difficulty – which is related to the problem of 'incommensurability' – should be mentioned. If a language consists of a vocabulary and a set of meaning postulates, then two languages L and L' with partly overlapping vocabularies may contain contradictory sets of meaning postulates (MP and MP', say), so that there cannot be any common extension of L and L' which preserves the meaning postulates of both languages. In this case, the following can be suggested: let h be a theory in L and h' in L', and let L'' be a common extension of L and L'. Then L'' is chosen to contain only the meaning postulates, if any, in MP $\cap$ MP', and h' is said to be more truthlike than h relative to L'' if and only if h' *together with* postulates MP' – MP has a greater degree of L''-truthlikeness (relative to MP $\cap$ MP') than h *together with* postulates MP – MP'. In other words, we treat the specific meaning postulates of L (resp. L') as a part of the theory h (resp. h').

This account of progress seems to give an answer to many well-known arguments against the approach-to-the-truth view. For example, we have answered Laudan's challenge that

"no one has been able even to say what it would mean to be 'closer to the truth', let alone to offer criteria for determining how we could assess such proximity."[69]

Laudan adds that

"we apparently do not have any way of knowing for sure (or even with some confidence) that science is true, or probable, or that it is getting closer to the truth. Such aims are *utopian*, in the literal sense that we can never know whether they are being achieved."[70]

But these aims do not seem *more* problematic than the task of finding a correct estimate of some unknown quantity. In particular, we can never know for sure whether the task of simple enumerative induction has been achieved. Such 'utopian' tasks belong to the everyday practice of science.

Kuhn argues that we need not assume that the evolution of science is directed toward some goal:

"Does it really help to imagine that there is some one full, objective, true account of nature and that the proper measure of scientific achievement is the extent to which it brings us closer to that ultimate goal? If we can learn to substitute evolution-from-what-we-do-know for evolution-toward-what-we-wish-to-know, a number of vexing problems may vanish in the process. Somewhere in this maze, for example, must lie the problem of induction."[71]

In our account, there is no *unique* goal for science, since, for *any* L-world, knowing the whole truth about it is a legitimate goal for science. However, science is a goal-directed process: there indeed are things which we wish to know but do not yet know. But, of course, the estimates of truthlikeness, i.e., values of ver, are based on evidence which we already know. Kuhn argues further that

"there is, I think, no theory-independent way to reconstruct phrases like 'really there'; the notion of a match between the ontology of a theory and its 'real' counterpart in nature now seems to me illusive in principle."[72]

If the word 'theory-independent' is replaced by 'language-independent', this quotation seems to agree with our treatment of the difference between the L-worlds and THE WORLD (cf. (7)). But, as

we have seen, the truth of (7) does not preclude the possibility, denied
by Kuhn, of seeing (from our conceptual system) a "coherent direction of ontological development" in actual historical cases of theory
succession. We need not assume, though, that such successions are
uniformly or monotonely convergent.

Are later results of science worthier of acceptance than earlier ones
because they are 'truer'? Or are later results 'truer' because they are
better grounded and thus worthier of acceptance? According to
Rescher's "methodological pragmatism", the latter alternative is the
correct one – but 'truer' is a methodological notion equivalent to
'presumably truer'.[73] This argument leads Rescher to conclude that
the progress of science should be analyzed only on the "pragmatic"
level, where progress means "the increasing success of applications in
problem solving and control".[74]

In view of our results – in particular, our distinction between 'true'
and 'estimated' verisimilitude, i.e., between functions M and ver –
Rescher's considerations do not constitute an argument against the
realist view of progress. The pragmatic success of theories increases
their degree of corroboration which can be shown to covary with
their estimated verisimilitude or their degree of 'presumed truth'.[75]
There are evidential situations e and hypotheses h such that ver(h/e)
is high. In such cases, it is rational for us to claim that the unknown
degree of truthlikeness $M(h, C_*)$ is also high, but this estimate may of
course be wrong (and corrigible by further evidence). Thus, in addition to the methodological level of estimated progress, it is
meaningful to speak of 'real' progress on the semantical level of the
content of theories.

Most philosophers would agree that science makes progress in the
scope of its practical applications. But why is science pragmatically
successful? This problem has puzzled both Kuhn:

"how a value-based enterprise of the sort I have described can develop as a science
does, repeatedly producing powerful new techniques for prediction and control. To that
question, unfortunately, I have no answer at all, but that is only another way of saying
that I make no claim to have solved the problem of induction."[76]

and Laudan:

"Until and unless we can show why science can be an effective instrument for the
solution of problems, then its past success at problem solving can always be viewed as
an accidental piece of good fortune which may, at any time, simply dry up."[77]

The realist theory of progress is able to provide an answer to this query: pragmatically successful theories have a high degree of estimated truthlikeness, and their continued success can be *explained* by the *hypothesis* that they in fact are close to the truth at least in the relevant respects.[78]

Isaac Levi has recently argued, in his 'Truth, Fallibility and the Growth of Knowledge', that

"it is fallibilism together with the doctrine that getting closer to the truth is the ultimate aim of inquiry which renders knowledge irrelevant to practice and truth irrelevant to the revision of knowledge".

Against Peirce and Popper (and his own earlier views), Levi endorses the doctrine of *infallibilism* which says that what we know or believe is, from our point of view, infallibly and certainly true. He argues further that infallibilism is consistent with *corrigibilism* (i.e., the view that our knowledge is always open to revision) if we abandon the idea that all specific inquiries should promote the ultimate aim of getting closer to the truth. Thus, replacement of a theory by another which contradicts it may be rational for an infallibilist – to whom this move seems to be a deliberate replacement of a certain truth by a falsity – if he extols "the virtues of myopia" and holds that avoidance of error is an invariant feature of the *proximate* (rather than ultimate) goals of specific inquiries.

Levi's argument shows, I think, successfully that the combination
          infallibilism & corrigibilism & myopic realism
is a coherent alternative to
          fallibilism & corrigibilism & long-sighted realism.
But, on the other hand, I do not find his reasons for rejecting the latter alternative compelling – at least when this alternative is presented in the form that has been defended in this paper.

First, the notion of estimated verisimilitude gives us a unified way of appraising theoretical revisions of knowledge. It gives emphasis to both information *and* truth, so that "avoidance of error" is not the only relevant consideration. Indeed, according to the measures mentioned in Section 7, there are false theories which have a greater degree of truthlikeness than some true theories. Moreover, it is even possible that a step from one theory h to another h', where h and h' are incompatible, may seem progressive relative to an evidential situation which contains h. Second, Levi himself admits that the problems concerning the rationality of the contraction of knowledge systems do not arise for a fallibilist. Thirdly, I take it that decision theory – or the theory of rational decision making under *uncertainty* – is sufficient to show how fallible knowledge is relevant to the guidance of practical action. In contrast with Levi's present position, I thus admit that there is "a gulf between theory and practice", but this gulf is not wider – and not narrower – than the difference between epistemic and practical utilities.

9. SCIENTIFIC PROGRESS AND PROBLEM-SOLVING

In arguing against the approach-to-the-truth view, Kuhn characterizes his own position as follows:

"Later scientific theories are better than earlier ones for solving puzzles in the often quite different environments to which they are applied. This is not a relativist's position, and it displays the sense in which I am a convinced believer in scientific progress."[79]

The idea that scientific progress can be defined by means of the *problem-solving ability* of theories has been further developed by Laudan in his *Progress and its Problems*. For Laudan, science is "a problem-solving rather than a truth-seeking progress"[80], and he assumes that scientific progress can be analyzed without the notions of 'truth' and 'confirmation'.[81] Laudan summarizes his definition of progress as follows:

"progress can occur if and only if the succession of scientific theories in any domain shows an increasing degree of problem solving effectiveness",

where

"the overall problem-solving effectiveness of a theory is determined by assessing the number and importance of the empirical problems which the theory solves and deducting therefrom the number and importance of the anomalies and conceptual problems which the theory generates."[82]

In the preceding section, we have found reasons to think that the problem-solving ability of theories is not unconnected with the truthlikeness of these theories: a problem about a domain gets a good solution (which guarantees continued problem-solving ability) only if the theory gives a sufficiently truthlike description of this domain. For this reason, we might suggest that the *value* of the solution that a theory h gives relative to a domain z is measured either by $M(h, C_z)$, where C_z is the true constituent about domain z in an appropriate language L, or by ver(h/e), evaluated in L relative to our evidence e. Let t be the degree of truthlikeness of a tautology,[83] and let J be the set of all problems (domains) which h is supposed to solve. Then the problem-solving effectiveness of h relative J could be defined either by

$$(10) \quad \sum_{z \in J} a_z(M(h, C_z) - t)$$

or by

$$(11) \quad \sum_{z \in J} a_z(\text{ver}(h/e) - t),$$

where $a_z \geq 0$ is the *weight* given to problem z. (The penalties for the conceptual anomalies of h are ignored in these formulas.)[84]

This notion of problem-solving capacity can be applied also to Sneed's and Stegmüller's set-theoretical reconstruction of "Kuhn-theories" as nets of systematically related 'solutions' to theoretical problems.[85] A "theory-element" is a pair $\langle K, J \rangle$ consisting of a class of domains J and a mathematical core K; the claim associated with $\langle K, J \rangle$ is that the members of J satisfy the fundamental law of K and the "constraints" of K binding them together.[86] In this sense, the core K is supposed to solve several problems at the same and its effectiveness can be measured by (10) or (11). As a special case where J contains only one element z, the evaluation of (10) and (11) reduces to the problem of truthlikeness with respect to one domain.

University of Helsinki

NOTES

* The first version of this paper was read at the symposium on 'Aspects of Scientific Realism', organized by the Philosophical Society of Finland in Helsinki, May 17, 1979. In writing this paper I have benefited from the critical remarks of many colleagues who do not share my views. Among them I should like to mention especially Larry Laudan and Isaac Levi.

[1] See Randall and Buchler (1942), p. 57.

[2] See Popper (1963), p. 125.

[3] See the Introduction to the 2nd edition of *Kritik der reinen Vernunft* (1787).

[4] An authoritative representative of this view is George Sarton who wrote in 1936 in *The Study of the History of Science* as follows:

> "*Definition*. Science is systematized positive knowledge, or what has been taken as such at different ages and in different places.

Theorem. The acquisition and systematization of positive knowledge are the only human activities which are truly cumulative and progressive.
Corollary. The history of science is the only history which can illustrate the progress of mankind. In fact, progress has no definite and unquestionable meaning in other fields than the field of science." (Sarton, 1957, p. 5.)

In his Herbert Spencer Lecture of 1973, Karl Popper argued that "progress in science can be assessed rationally" and that "science seems to be the only field of human endeavour of which this can be said" (Popper, 1975, p. 83). For an attempt to defend progress as a demarcation criterion for science, see also Quay (1974). (The term 'science' is used in a wide meaning in this paper, so that it covers not only natural science but also systematic social and human sciences.)

[5] Cf. Kuhn (1970), Ch. XIII, Feyerabend (1975), p. 306, and Rorty (1978).

[6] Feyerabend (1975), p. 27.

[7] Hull (1979), p. 465. I have earlier discussed the problems of scientific progress in Niiniluoto (1978a), (1978c). Section 4 of this paper is based upon Niiniluoto (1978b).

[8] See Bury (1932). Cp. Zilsel (1945), who claims that the idea of scientific progress was created by the "artisans" of the 16th century. See also Crombie (1975). One of the early expressions of the idea that science is a cumulative enterprise was the image, originally due to Bernard of Chartes in the 12th century, of the modern scholars as dwarfs on the shoulders of giants (see Molland, 1978).

[9] Bacon compares his method to a "machine" which produces results when the "stuff" for it is "gathered from the facts of nature" (Bacon, 1960, p. 6). In the same spirit, Comte describes the cumulative ideal of science (or "philosophy" in its "positive stage") as follows: "Its character will be henceforth unchangeable, and it will then have only to develop itself indefinitely, by incorporating the constantly increasing knowledge that inevitably results from new observations or more profound meditations" (Comte, 1970, p. 13).

[10] See, for example, Laudan (1973).

[11] See, for example, Kuhn (1970) and Feyerabend (1975). In spite of these criticisms, the cumulative view may be valid in some fields (such as some branches of mathematics) or in some periods of science (such as Kuhnian normal science). Perhaps it should be noted that, in speaking about cumulation in science, we mean the *content* of the results of science (i.e., science as a cognitive enterprise), rather than simply the amount of scientific output (books, articles, journals, etc.). The latter amount has increased exponentially since the latter part of the 18th century. In his interesting discussion of the quantitative growth of science, Rescher (1978a) suggests that the number of "first-rate" results has increased linearly rather than exponentially. However, no cognitive criteria are given by him for defining what results are "first-rate". (Cf. Section 8.)

[12] It should be noted that this use of the term 'realism' in connection with scientific progress is not intended to be the same as in the realism-instrumentalism issue concerning scientific theories. (This is not sufficiently emphasized in Niiniluoto, 1978b.) A person may support a realist interpretation of theories without accepting a realist theory of progress (cf. Kuhn, Feyerabend, and also Laudan, 1980); and a person may support an instrumentalist interpretation of theories even if he supports some sort of a realist view of scientific progress (cf. Duhem). What I want to suggest with my choice

of the terminology, however, is that a consistent philosopher who defends the realist view of theories should also subscribe to a realist view of progress in science, and *vice versa.*

[13] Boyle's discussion is in *Certain Physiological Essays* of 1661 (see Boas Hall, 1966, pp. 123–124). See also Laudan (1966). Cf. Bernard (1957), p. 40.

[14] A useful account of this tradition has been given by Laudan (1973). However, there is not much evidence to show that Peirce knew Hartley's and LeSage's work on progress. It is perhaps interesting to add that Mach, in his *Erkenntnis und Irrtum* of 1905, refers to Priestley and LeSage, and further explains the idea of coming nearer to the truth by means of an example of a procedure for approximating to the roots of an equation (see Mach, 1976, pp. 176, 183–184).

[15] See the chapter on Cusanus in de Santillana (1956), pp. 47–63. For Cusanus, the truth itself is something indivisible, not capable of more or less, whereas our understanding of the truth can always be further developed. See Duhem (1969), pp. 57–58.

[16] Spinoza's doctrine on the infinite structure of God turns out to involve non-trivial set-theoretical assumptions (see Friedman, 1976).

[17] See, for example, Martin (1967), Ch. VII.

[18] See Bradley (1893). For a revival of the coherence theory of truth as a criterion of truth, see Rescher (1973).

[19] See Lenin (1927), Ch. 2.5 and 5.2.

[20] See Laplace (1951), p. 4.

[21] See Cournot (1956), pp. 15–16.

[22] See Bernard (1957), pp. 12, 31, 35–36, 40–42, 54.

[23] See Duhem (1954), p. 298. Cf. also pp. 26–28, 177, 297, 334–335.

[24] Cf. Laudan (1973), Niiniluoto (1978a), (1978b), Rescher (1977), (1978b), Skagestad (1979), and Levi (1980).

[25] For iterative methods, see Henrici (1964).

[26] 5.565 refers to paragraph 565 in the fifth volume of Peirce's *Collected Papers* (1931–35).

[27] See Laudan (1973).

[28] "There is nothing, then, to prevent our knowing outward things as they really are, and it is most likely that we do thus know them in numberless cases, although we can never be absolutely certain of doing so in any special case." (5.311)

[29] For an earlier but similar argument, to the effect that external influence on our opinions forces us to a consensus, see Cournot (1956), p. 103.

[30] See von Wright (1957), p. 225.

[31] See Reichenbach (1949), p. 475, and Lenz (1966), p. 435–440.

[32] This result says that the set of infinite sequences with inappropriate limiting behaviour has the measure zero. Borel's theorem is a special case of the Strong Law of Large Numbers. Its weaker counterpart is Bernoulli's Theorem: for any $\epsilon > 0$, $P(|rf_n(A) - P(A)| > \epsilon) \to 0$, when $n \to \infty$, where $rf_n(A)$ is the relative frequency of A in n independent trials.

[33] Isaac Levi (1980) has argued convincingly that, at least in the articles 'The Probability of Induction' and 'The Theory of Probable Inference', Peirce regarded induction as interval estimation essentially in the style of Neyman and Pearson. According to Levi, induction is self-corrective for Peirce in the following sense: either the conclusion reached via an inductive rule is correct or, if wrong, the revised estimate

emerging from a new attempt at estimation based on a different sample will with a preassigned probability k be correct. This guarantees that, if the scientist would repeat drawing samples from the same population *ad infinitum*, the relative frequency of correct inferences would converge on k in the long run; but it does not show that "an inductive rule will, in the messianic long run, reveal the true value".

If Levi is right, then Peirce did not support the limit thesis (4). But this, it seems to me, is contradicted by the evidence that Peirce repeatedly spoke about convergence *towards the truth* rather than towards some limiting *truth-frequency* among inferences – and this happens both in his general theory of reality and truth and in his theory of induction. For example, in 1902, he says:

> "The validity of induction of an inductive argument consists, then, in the fact that it pursues a method which, if duly persisted in, must, in the very nature of things, lead to a result indefinitely approximating to the truth in the long run." (2.781)

Moreover, convergence towards the truth was, for Peirce, related to the solution of specific problems or to the evaluation of single hypotheses (cf. 8.12, 5.565), and not only to the 'messianic' idea of approaching to the final and complete true theory of the world. For these reasons, Levi's observations seem to indicate that Peirce had difficulties in trying to reconcile his new theory of inductive inference with his commitment to the thesis that truth is the limit of endless scientific investigation – but they do not show that Peirce would have abandoned the thesis (4) (or its weaker variant (5)).

Michael Friedman (1979) has recently argued that, instead of long-run justifications, one should try to show that scientific method tends to produce true hypotheses "in the class of actual and physically possible inferences". This seems to be (even though Friedman does not notice it) very close to Peirce's idea that the 'probability of induction' should be defined as the proportion in which a particular method of inference produces true conclusions from true premises. According to Peirce,

> "all human certainty consists merely in our knowing that the processes by which our knowledge has been derived are such as must generally have led to true conclusions." (2.692)

Essentially the same idea is incorporated in the Neyman–Pearson theory of statistical testing: the probability of rejecting the true hypothesis is chosen to be low, and the probability of rejecting the false hypothesis should be made as high as possible.

Friedman's more specific suggestion is the following: it should be possible to derive from confirmation theory law-like "reliability statements" of the form

(A)   The probability that S is true, given that S is accepted (rejected) by method M, is r,

where r is an objective physical probability (distinct from mere actual relative frequency). In order that this is possible, he further claims, the theory of truth should be supplemented with something like Putnam's causal theory of reference. This argument is not convincing, however. There is no analysis available which would allow us to assign physical probabilities to scientific hypotheses – and if r in (A) were interpreted as an epistemic probability, then all inductive rules of acceptance M which take high probability as a necessary condition for acceptance would automatically satisfy the condition: if S is accepted by M, then the probability that S is true is high.

Friedman seems to confuse (A) with a perfectly legitimate physical probability statement

(B)   The probability that method M accepts (rejects) S, given that S is true, is r.

Such statements constitute the essential ingredients of the 'orthodox' theory of statistical tests and, as Levi argues, of Peirce's mature theory of induction – and these theories have been created and practiced for a long time before 'causal theories of reference' were invented.

[34] Bruno de Finetti proved in the 1930's a theorem which erroneously may seem to establish Peirce's limit thesis in its strong form. de Finetti showed that, assuming fairly general conditions of 'exchangeability', the subjective probabilities of agents starting from different non-dogmatic prior beliefs will, on the basis of common evidence, tend towards observed relative frequencies and thus also towards each other. (See de Finetti, 1964.) de Finetti interprets this result only as showing the intersubjective nature of rational beliefs, but some other theorists have suggested that his results show precisely how subjective probabilities can be used to estimate physical probabilities (see Good, 1965).

An interesting variant of de Finetti's result has been given by Savage (1954), pp. 46–50. Let $e_1, e_2, \ldots$ be the successive independent results of a random experiment, and let h be a hypothesis such that $P(e_n/h) \neq P(e_n/\sim h)$. Then the following holds:

(A)   If $P(h) > 0$, then $P\left[\dfrac{P(h/e_1 \ldots e_n)}{P(\sim h/e_1 \ldots e_n)} \xrightarrow[n \to \infty]{} \infty /h\right] = 1$.

If we define $h^* = h$ if h is true and $h^* = \sim h$ if h is false, then (A) entails

(B)   If $P(h^*) > 0$, then $P(P(h^*/e_1 \ldots e_n) \approx 1) \xrightarrow[n \to \infty]{} 1$.

These results, which concern the approach of beliefs towards certainty, are confused with results concerning approach to the truth by Aulin-Ahmavaara (1977), pp. 210–211. He seems to think that, instead of (B), the following result is provable:

(C)   If $P(h^*) > 0$, then $P(h^*/e_1 \ldots e_n) \xrightarrow[n \to \infty]{} 1$.

There is a crucial difference between (B) and (C), however.

[35] In the consensus theory, truth is defined as the limit of ideal communication (see Habermas, 1973). This definition seems to be problematic at least in the following sense: to say whether the conditions for communication really were 'ideal', we should know whether the limit result is really true (in some realist sense). Cf. also Niiniluoto (1980).

[36] See Herschel (1831), p. 360.

[37] See Popper (1963), p. 125, Bohm (1957) and Vigier (1957).

[38] Ravetz (1975) argues that, for Bacon, the significance of scientific progress lies in the fact that it helps to bring about the Millennium – progress is good evidence that the 'last days' are coming closer. For an interesting discussion of the future of scientific progress, with many bibliographical references, see Rescher (1978a), Chs. I–III. Rescher's own well-argued position is that, even though the advance of science will

decelerate, there are "unlimited horizons" for further progress in science. See also Rescher (1979).

[39] See Kneale (1967).

[40] Kneale also suggests that Bohm and Vigier confuse (i) and (ii) – or move without justification from (i) to (ii).

[41] See Herschel (1831), p. 360.

[42] See Whewell (1840). Cp. Niiniluoto (1978a).

[43] See Kneale (1967), p. 36.

[44] For infinitary languages of type (a) and (b), see Monk (1976), and of type (c), see Hintikka and Rantala (1976).

[45] Complete arithmetic is just the class of true statements about natural numbers. As it is not recursively axiomatizable, one may say – as Sellars (1968), p. 135, does – that "in arithmetic there is no end to the series of 'more adequate' axiomatic systems". But it might be equally natural to say that complete arithmetic is the ideal theory which axiomatic systems of arithmetic approximate from within (cf. Fig. 1 in Section 6).

[46] See Niiniluoto (1978a). Many philosophers (like Peirce and Popper) have combined both 'weak' and 'strong' fallibilistic elements in their epistemology.

[47] Kneale suggests that the final theory would be "irrefutable", but it is not clear why this should be the case.

[48] See Almeder (1973). See also Almeder (1975).

[49] A more charitable interpretation of Almeder's discussion of enumerative induction would be the assumption that he is speaking of more and more precise interval estimates rather than point estimates. In other words, the thesis about finite success would be the following: given $\epsilon > 0$, we shall find in a finite number of steps an interval of length less than 2ϵ which covers the unknown true value. However, while Borel's Theorem entails that this kind of success is overwhelmingly probable, it does not guarantee that it also will be achieved in all cases.

[50] See Quine (1960), p. 23.

[51] See Bernard (1957), p. 42.

[52] See Popper (1962), (1972).

[53] See Miller (1974) and Tichy (1974).

[54] See Sellars (1968), Ch. 3. It is interesting to note that both Popper's theory of verisimilitude and the approach to truthlikeness in Section 7 below are related to the coherence theory of truth (even if they both presuppose the correspondence theory in the Tarskian form): for example, Popper's definition, given Fig. 2, essentially measures the degree of 'compatibility' or 'coherence' between two sets of *sentences* (h and T). Cf. also Fig. 4 below.

[55] Sellars thinks that in the evolution of theories one can find 'counterparts' of propositions in earlier and later theories, but it is not quite clear how this notion is to be defined. Cf. Burian (1979), pp. 203–205.

[56] For a lucid analysis of this question, see Rosenberg (1974).

[57] See Rosenberg (1974), pp. 54–55, and the critical remarks in Hooker (1978).

[58] See Hooker (1978).

[59] See Putnam (1978). Putnam's internal realism combines three theses: (i) there is an epistemically ideal theory, (ii) the epistemically ideal theory coincides with the true theory, and (iii) the truth or approximate truth of theories in mature science explains the success of science.

Michael Bradie (1979), who rejects the task (iii) as unnecessary, has claimed that Putnam's position is indistinguishable from a "sophisticated pragmatism" which replaces 'truth' with 'warranted assertibility (in the long run)'. However, there is a crucial difference between pragmatists who accept (ii) as a *definition* of truth and (internal) realists who accept (ii) as a principle which gives a *de facto* valid *methodological characterization* of truth. Among the latter we may include Peirce whose fundamental point is that the ideal theory is destined to correspond with the reality just because it is in effect produced or caused by the reality. (Thus, to define 'Peircean realism' simply by thesis (i), as Putnam does, is clearly too weak to do justice to Peirce's realism.)

Moreover, Bradie's reasons for rejecting (iii) are not convincing. He claims that only the success of particular theories has to be explained, and that this is to be done by other scientific theories. But, to explain the success of a theory T_1 by another theory T_2, a *potential* explanation is not enough: T_2 has to be true or at least more truthlike than T_1 – so that Bradie's suggestion gives no escape from a realist notion of truth.

According to the view defended in Sections 4 and 5 above, thesis (ii) is justifiable only in some special cases. No non-circular epistemic characterization of the 'ideal theory' is sufficient to guarantee its truth (cf. also Koethe, 1979). For this reason, I think, both pragmatists, consensus theorists, and Putnam are wrong. In defending the view that truth is "radically non-epistemic", I thus support part of the view that Putnam calls 'metaphysical realism'.

To classify Sellarsian realism in these terms is difficult. On the one hand, 'truth' is an 'internal' notion for Sellars, since it is relative to a conceptual framework. On the other hand, Sellars has a notion of an ideal conceptual framework which transcends the internal viewpoint, since its ideality is defined in terms of correct picturing of non-linguistic objects. Thus, truth relative to this ideal framework is not characterized in purely epistemic terms.

[60] For a discussion of 'inquiries', 'problems', and 'questions' in science, see Niiniluoto (1976). I am not suggesting that the problem of finding the true constituent of some language L is the only legitimate way of defining a scientific inquiry. For other ways of setting up 'ultimate partitions' of hypotheses, see Levi (1976).

[61] I am not suggesting that we can *know* for sure that some particular language L is 'ideal' in this restricted sense. In this paper, I cannot say much of the important problem of how a conceptual framework should be chosen. What we would need is a definition for the *theoretical effectiveness* of a language. It would tell, following Whewell's principle, how simply and how effectively one can express true general sentences in the language (cf. Niiniluoto, 1978c). In this sense, the criteria for the choice of a language are partly empirical or *a posteriori*. Moreover, Goodman's problem of the simplicity of conceptual systems seems to be a part of this more general question.

[62] For an interesting analysis of the method of idealization, see Nowak (1976) and Krajewski (1977). This analysis is used for a defense of a realist view scientific progress in Nowak (1975).

[63] The theory of distributive normal forms is due to Hintikka. If L is a polyadic language, then the normal form is relative to a given 'depth' which indicates the number of layers of connected quantifiers in a statement. Cf. Niiniluoto (1978d).

[64] For details, see Niiniluoto (1977), (1978d), (1979). It seems that there are many

alternatives in defining the distance measure d, and it is not certain that the best ones have been found so far. For the argument of this paper, the most important thing is that there are at least *some* reasonable alternatives available. For example, it seems reasonable to define

$$d(h, C_*) = \gamma d_{min}(h, C_*) + (1 - \gamma)d_{max}(h, C_*)$$

where $0 < \gamma < 1$,

$$d_{min}(h, C_*) = \min_{i \in I_h} d(C_i, C_*)$$

$$d_{max}(h, C_*) = \max_{i \in I_h} d(C_i, C_*)$$

and

$$\vdash h \equiv \bigvee_{i \in I_h} C_i.$$

[65] For detailed studies of (10), see Niiniluoto (1977) and (1978c). Lakatos has suggested that some weak, conjectural "metaphysical principle of induction" has to be assumed in order to connect "scientific standards with verisimilitude" (Lakatos, 1974, pp. 260–262). In our approach, such an assumption is provided by the premise that there are rational systems of inductive probabilities $P(C_i/e)$ for constituents. For a review of this problem, see Niiniluoto (1981).

[66] This notion has interesting connections with Lakatos' notion of progress (see Niiniluoto, 1978c). Cf. the papers by John Watkins, John Worrall, and Elie Zahar in Radnitzky and Andersson (1978). It can also be shown that Hintikka's measure of corroboration, viz.

$$\text{corr}(h/e) = \min\{P(C_i/e) \mid i \in I_h\}$$

(cf. note 64), covaries with $\text{ver}(h/e)$, if e and h are compatible. Hence, degrees of corroboration may serve as an indicator of scientific progress.

[67] Cf. Niiniluoto (1977), pp. 127–129; (1978d), pp. 308–313. Note that truth itself is not relative to language in this sense: for example, if C_* is the true constituent of L, and if L' is an extension of L, then C_* is entailed by the true constituent C'_* of L'. For comparative purposes, degrees of truthlikeness may be taken to be relative to agreed meaning postulates (cf. Niiniluoto, 1977, p. 145; Niiniluoto, 1978). However, if we have to compare sentences in different conceptual frameworks, the rival meaning postulates have to be taken into account in the comparison (see the next Section).

[68] If h and h' belong to different languages, the ideal language L is one of the common extensions of these languages (cf. Fig. 3). Therefore, h and h' (or their 'counterparts') are expressible in L, too.

[69] See Laudan (1977), pp. 125–126.

[70] *Ibid.*, p. 127.

[71] See Kuhn (1970), p. 171.

[72] *Ibid.*, pp. 206–207.

[73] See Rescher (1977), p. 179.

[74] *Ibid.*, p. 185.

[75] See Niiniluoto (1977), p. 140. Cf. note 66.

[76] See Kuhn (1978), pp. 332–333.

[77] See Laudan (1977), p. 224.

[78] This argument has been given by Shimony (1976), Niiniluoto (1978a), p. 323, and Putnam (1978), pp. 18–21. As true theories have only true deductive consequences, it is clear that true theories are also pragmatically successful for predictive purposes. It is not equally clear why this should be so for highly truthlike but false theories. To outline an argument to this effect, assume that h is the disjunction of constituents $C_1, \ldots, C_m$. If $M(h, C_*)$ is high, say larger than $1 - \epsilon$, then

$$M(h, C_*) = 1 - d(h, C_*) \geq 1 - \epsilon$$

or

$$d(h, C_*) = \tfrac{1}{2} d_{\min}(h, C_*) + \tfrac{1}{2} d_{\max}(h, C_*) \leq \epsilon$$

(cf. note 64). This entails that

$$d(C_i, C_*) \leq 2\epsilon \text{ for all } i = 1, \ldots, m.$$

In other words, no constituent in the normal form of h can be at a great distance from the true constituent C_* – and the larger this distance is, the greater disappointments we may encounter in dealing with the world.

[79] See Kuhn (1970), p. 206.

[80] See Laudan (1977), pp. 7, 70. For discussions about Laudan's views, see Musgrave (1979) and the Laudan Symposia in PSA 1978, vol. 2, and Philosophy of the Social Sciences 9 (1979). For a definition of 'progress' in mathematics in terms of problem-solving ability, see Hallett (1979).

[81] Laudan also argues that empirical problem-solving differs from explanation in important respects (ibid., pp. 22–26), but here he seems to forget about the notions of 'approximate' and 'potential' explanations.

[82] Ibid., p. 68. Lugg (1979) argues that Laudan's view is ambiguous between 'total problem-solving effectiveness' and 'problem-solving capacity relative to a specified set of problems'. However, Laudan (1980) makes it clear that he wishes to appraise theories relative to the finite number of problems that they have solved up to a certain time. In fact, we have here (as in Section 8) the possibility of distinguishing 'real' and 'apparent' progress, i.e., progress defined by the unknown potential ability and progress defined by the known performance so far. But here it would be problematic whether the latter notion may be regarded as an 'estimate' of the former (cf. below). The same distinction can be made, if the notion of empirical problem-solving is replaced by explanation (cf. note 81). This would bring us close to the notion that the Finnish philosopher Eino Kaila (1939) called 'relative simplicity': a theory has high relative simplicity if it is conceptually simple (cf. Laudan's 'conceptual problems') and has high explanatory power. As (actual) explanatory power and degree of confirmation may also be taken to be proportional to each other, this concept of relative simplicity is also related to Sober's (1975) criterion 'confirmation + simplicity' for theory appraisal.

[83] For some natural choices of measure M, we have $t = \tfrac{1}{2}$.

[84] Essentially this proposal has been given in Niiniluoto (1980).

[85] Stegmüller (1976) thinks that to speak of verisimilitude is questionable "teleological metaphysics", but I try to argue in Niiniluoto (1980) that the problem concerning progress for Sneedian Kuhn-theories contains as a special case the ordinary problem of truthlikeness.

[86] I assume here that J is a class of "potential", rather than "partial potential", models in Sneed's sense. Cf. Niiniluoto (1980) for the reasons of this stipulation.

BIBLIOGRAPHY

Almeder, R., 'Science and Idealism', *Philosophy of Science* **40** (1973), 242–254.
Almeder, R., 'Fallibilism and the Ultimate Irreversible Opinion', in N. Rescher (ed.), *Studies in Epistemology* (APQ Monograph Series No. 9), Blackwell, Oxford, 1975, pp. 33–54.
Aulin-Ahmavaara, Y., 'A General Theory of Acts, with Application to the Distinction between Rational and Irrational "Social Cognition", *Zeitschrift für allgemeine Wissenschaftstheorie* **8** (1977), 195–220.
Bacon, F., *The New Organon*, Bobbs-Merrill, Indianapolis, 1960.
Bernard, C., *An Introduction to the Study of Experimental Medicine*, Dover, New York, 1957.
Bieri, P., Horstmann, R.-P., and Krüger, L. (eds.), *Transcendental Arguments and Science*, D. Reidel, Dordrecht, Boston, and London, 1979.
Boas Hall, M., *Robert Boyle on Natural Philosophy*, Indiana University Press, Bloomington, 1966.
Bohm, D., *Causality and Chance in Modern Physics*, Routledge and Kegan Paul, London, 1957.
Bradie, M., 'Pragmatism and Internal Realism', *Analysis* **39** (1979), 4–10.
Bradley, F. H., *Appearance and Reality*, Clarendon Press, Oxford, 1893.
Burian, R., 'Sellarsian Realism and Conceptual Change in Science', in Bieri *et al.* (1979), pp. 197–225.
Bury, J. B., *The Idea of Progress*, Macmillan, New York, 1932. (Dover, New York, 1955).
Comte, A., *Introduction to Positive Philosophy*, Bobbs–Merrill, Indianapolis, 1970.
Cournot, A. A., *An Essay on the Foundations of our Knowledge*, The Liberal Arts Press, New York, 1956.
Crombie, A. C., 'Some Attitudes to Scientific Progress, Ancient, Medieval and Early Modern', *History of Science* **13** (1975) 213–230.
Duhem, P., *The Aim and Structure of Physical Theory*, Princeton University Press, Princeton, 1954.
Duhem, P., *To Save the Phenomena*, The University of Chicago Press, Chicago, 1969.
Feyerabend, P., *Against Method*, NLB, London, 1975.
de Finetti, B., 'Foresight: Its Logical Laws, Its Subjective Sources', in H. E. Kyburg and H. E. Smokler (eds.), *Studies in Subjective Probability*, Wiley, New York, 1964, pp. 93–158.
Friedman, J., 'The Universal Class has a Spinozistic Partitioning', *Synthese* **32** (1976), 403–418.
Friedman, M., 'Truth and Confirmation', *The Journal of Philosophy* **76** (1979), 361–382.
Good, I. J., *Estimation of Probabilities*, The M.I.T. Press, Cambridge, Mass., 1965.
Habermas, J., 'Wahrheitstheorien', in H. Fahrenbach (ed.), *Wirklichkeit und Reflexion*, Pfullingen, 1973, pp. 211–265.

Hallett, M., 'Towards a Theory of Mathematical Research Programmes', *The British Journal for the Philosophy of Science* **30** (1979), 1–25.

Harré, R. (ed.), *Problems of Scientific Revolution: Progress and Obstacles to Progress in the Sciences*, Clarendon Press, Oxford, 1975.

Henrici, P., *Elements of Numerical Analysis*, Wiley, New York, 1964.

Herschel, J., *A Preliminary Discourse on the Study of Natural Philosophy*, Longman, Rees, Orme, Brown & Green and Taylor, London, 1831.

Hintikka, J. and Rantala, V., 'A New Approach to Infinitary Languages', *Annals of Mathematical Logic* **10** (1976), 95–115.

Hooker, M., 'Peirce's Conception of Truth', in J. C. Pitt (ed.), *The Philosophy of Wilfrid Sellars: Queries and Extensions*, Reidel, Dordrecht, Boston, London, 1978, pp. 129–133.

Hull, D., 'Laudan's Progress and Its Problems', *Philosophy of the Social Sciences* **9** (1979), 457–465.

Kaila, E., *Inhimillinen tieto*, Otava, Helsinki, 1939.

Kneale, W., 'Scientific Revolutions for Ever?', *The British Journal for the Philosophy of Science* **19** (1967), 27–42.

Koethe, J., 'Putnam's Argument Against Realism', *The Philosophical Review* **88** (1979), 92–99.

Krajewski, W., *Correspondence Principle and the Growth of Knowledge*, Reidel, Dordrecht and Boston, 1977.

Kuhn, T. S., *The Structure of Scientific Revolutions*, 2nd ed., The University of Chicago Press, Chicago, 1970.

Kuhn, T. S., *The Essential Tension*, The University of Chicago Press, Chicago, 1978.

Lakatos, I., 'Popper on Demarcation and Induction', in P. A. Schilpp (ed.), *The Philosophy of Karl Popper*, Open Court, LaSalle, 1974, pp. 241–273.

Laplace, P. S., *A Philosophical Essay on Probabilities*, Dover, New York, 1951.

Laudan, L., 'The Clock Metaphor and Probabilism: The Impact of Descartes on English Methodological Thought, 1650–65', *Annals of Science* **22** (1966), 73–104.

Laudan, L., 'Peirce and the Trivialization of the Self-Correcting Thesis', in R. N. Giere and R. S. Westfall (eds.), *Foundations of Scientific Method: The Nineteenth Century*, Indiana University Press, Bloomington, 1973, pp. 275–306.

Laudan, L., *Progress and Its Problems*, Routledge and Kegan Paul, London, 1977.

Laudan, L., 'The Philosophy of Progress . . .', in P. D. Asquith and I. Hacking (eds.), *PSA 1978*, vol. 2. Philosophy of Science Association, East Lansing, forthcoming in 1980.

Lenin, V. I., *Materialism and Empirio-Criticism*, International Publishers, New York, 1927.

Lenz, J., 'Reichenbach's Defense of Induction', in M. H. Foster and M. L. Martin (eds.), *Probability, Confirmation, and Simplicity*, The Odyssey Press, New York, 1966, pp. 435–440.

Levi, I., 'Acceptance Revisited', in R. J. Bogdan (ed.), *Local Induction*, Reidel, Dordrecht and Boston, 1976, pp. 1–71.

Levi, I., 'Truth, Fallibility, and the Growth of Knowledge', forthcoming 1980.

Levi, I., 'Induction as Self Correcting According to Peirce', forthcoming in D. H. Mellor (ed.), *Science, Belief, and Behaviour*, Cambridge, 1980.

Lugg, A., 'Laudan and the Problem-Solving Approach to Scientific Progress and Rationality', *Philosophy of the Social Sciences* **9** (1979), 466–474.

Mach, E., *Knowledge and Error*, Reidel, Dordrecht and Boston, 1976.

Martin, G., *Leibniz: Logic and Metaphysics*, Barnes & Noble, New York, 1967.

Miller, D., 'Popper's Qualitative Theory of Verisimilitude', *The Britith Journal for the Philosophy of Science* **25** (1974), 166–177.

Molland, A. G., 'Medieval Ideas of Scientific Progress', *Journal of the History of Ideas* **39** (1978), 561–578.

Monk, J. D., *Mathematical Logic*, Springer-Verlag, New York, Berlin, Heidelberg, 1976.

Musgrave, A., 'Problems with Progress', *Synthese* **42** (1979), 443–464.

Niiniluoto, I., 'Inquiries, Problems, and Questions: Remarks on Local Induction', in R. J. Bogdan (ed.), *Local Induction*, Reidel, Dordrecht and Boston, 1976, pp. 263–296.

Niiniluoto, I., 'On the Truthlikeness of Generalizations', in R. E. Butts and J. Hintikka (eds.), *Basic Problems in Methodology and Linguistics*, Reidel, Dordrecht and Boston, 1977, pp. 121–147.

Niiniluoto, I., 'Notes on Popper as Follower of Whewell and Peirce', *Ajatus* **37** (1978), 272–327. [1978a.]

Niiniluoto, I., 'On the Realist Theory of Scientific Progress', *Section Papers, 16th World Congress of Philosophy*, Düsseldorf, 1978, pp. 463–466. [1978b.]

Niiniluoto, I., 'Verisimilitude, Theory-Change, and Scientific Progress', in I. Niiniluoto and R. Tuomela (eds.), *The Logic and Epistemology of Scientific Change* (Acta Philosophica Fennica 30, 1978), North-Holland, Amsterdam, 1979, pp. 243–264. [1978c.]

Niiniluoto, I., 'Truthlikeness: Comments on Recent Discussion', *Synthese* **38** (1978), 281–330. [1978d.]

Niiniluoto, I., 'Degrees of Truthlikeness: From Singular Sentences to Generalizations', *The British Journal for the Philosophy of Science* **30** (1979), 371–376.

Niiniluoto, I., 'The Growth of Theories: Comments of the Structuralist Approach', forthcoming in *Proceedings of Second International Congress for History and Philosophy of Science, Pisa, 1978*, D. Reidel, Dordrecht, 1980.

Niiniluoto, I., 'On Truth and Argumentation in Legal Dogmatics', to appear in *Rechtstheorie* 1980.

Niiniluoto, I., 'Inductive Logic as a Methodological Research Programme', forthcoming in *Scientia* 1981.

Nowak, L., 'Relative Truth, the Correspondence Principle, and Absolute Truth', *Philosophy of Science* **42** (1975), 187–202.

Nowak, L., 'Essence-Idealization-Praxis', *Poznan Studies in the Philosophy of the Sciences and the Humanities* **2** (1976), 1–28.

Peirce, C. S., *Collected Papers* (ed. by C. Hartshorne and P. Weiss), Harvard University Press, Cambridge, Mass., 1931–35.

Popper, K. R., 'Some Comments on Truth and the Growth of Knowledge', in E. Nagel, P. Suppes, and A. Tarski (eds.), *Logic, Methodology, and Philosophy of Science*, Stanford University Press, Stanford, 1962, pp. 285–292.

Popper, K. R., *Conjectures and Refutations*, Routledge and Kegan Paul, London, 1963.

Popper, K. R., *Objective Knowledge*, Oxford University Press, Oxford, 1972.

Popper, K. R., 'The Rationality of Scientific Revolutions', in Harré (1975), pp. 72–101.

Putnam, H., *Meaning and the Moral Sciences*, Routledge and Kegan Paul, London, 1978.

Quay, P. M., 'Progress as a Demarcation Criterion for the Sciences', *Philosophy of Science* **41** (1974), 154–170.

Quine, W. V. O., *Word and Object*, The M.I.T. Press, Cambridge, Mass., 1960.

Radnitzky, G. and Andersson, G., *Progress and Rationality in Science*, Reidel, Dordrecht and Boston, 1978.

Radnitzky, G. and Andersson, G. (eds.), *The Structure and Development of Science*, D. Reidel, Dordrecht, 1979.

Randall, J. H. and Buchler, J., *Philosophy: An Introduction*, Barnes & Noble, New York, 1942.

Ravetz, J., '... *et augebitur scientia*', in Harré (1975), pp. 42–57.

Reichenbach, H., *Theory of Probability*, University of California Press, Berkeley, 1949.

Rescher, N., *The Coherence Theory of Truth*, Oxford University Press, Oxford, 1973.

Rescher, N., *Methodological Pragmatism*, Blackwell, Oxford, 1977.

Rescher, N., *Scientific Progress*, Biackwell, Oxford, 1978. [1978a.]

Rescher, N., *Peirce's Philosophy of Science*, University of Notre Dame Press, Notre Dame, 1978. [1978b.]

Rescher, N., 'Some Issues Regarding the Completeness of Science and the Limits of Scientific Knowledge', in Radnitzky and Andersson (1979), pp. 19–40.

Rorty, R., 'From Epistemology to Hermeneutics', in I. Niiniluoto and R. Tuomela (eds.), *The Logic and Epistemology of Scientific Change* (Acta Philosophica Fennica **30**, 1978), North-Holland, Amsterdam, 1979.

Rosenberg, J., *Linguistic Representation*, Reidel, Dordrecht and Boston, 1974.

de Santillana, G., *The Age of Adventure: The Renaissance Philosophers*, Mentor Books, The New American Library, New York, 1956.

Sarton, G., *The Study of the History of Science*, Harvard University Press, Harvard, 1936. (Dover, New York, 1957.)

Savage, L. J., *The Foundations of Statistics*, Wiley, New York, 1954. (Dover, New York, 1972.)

Sellars, W., *Science and Metaphysics*, Routledge and Kegan Paul, London, 1968.

Shimony, A., 'Comments on Two Epistemological Theses of Thomas Kuhn', in R. S. Cohen *et al.* (eds.), *Essays in Memory of Imre Lakatos*, Reidel, Dordrecht and Boston, 1976, pp. 569–588.

Skagestad, P., 'C. S. Peirce on Biological Evolution and Scientific Progress', *Synthese* **41** (1979), 85–114.

Sober, E., *Simplicity*, Oxford University Press, Oxford, 1975.

Stegmüller, W., *The Structure and Dynamics of Theories*, Springer-Verlag, Berlin, New York and Heidelberg, 1976.

Tichý, P., 'On Popper's Definition of Verisimilitude', *The British Journal for the Philosophy of Science* **25** (1974), 155–160.

Whewell, W., *Philosophy of the Inductive Sciences*, Parker and Sons, London, 1840. (Reprinted 1967.)

Vigier, J.-P., 'The Concept of Probability in the Frame of the Probabilistic and the Causal Interpretation of Quantum Mechanics', in S. Körner (ed.), *Observation and Interpretation*, Butterworth, London, 1957, pp. 71–77.

von Wright, G. H., *The Logical Problem of Induction*, 2nd ed., Blackwell, Oxford, 1957.

Zilsel, E., 'The Genesis of the Concept of Scientific Progress', *The Journal of the History of Ideas* **6** (1945), 325–349.

MODELS AND REALITY[1]

HILARY PUTNAM

In 1922 Skolem delivered an address before the Fifth Congress of Scandinavian Mathematicians in which he pointed out what he called a "relativity of set-theoretic notions". This "relativity" has frequently been regarded as paradoxical; but today, although one hears the expression "the Löwenheim-Skolem Paradox", it seems to be thought of as only an *apparent* paradox, something the cognoscenti enjoy but are not seriously troubled by. Thus van Heijenoort writes, "The existence of such a 'relativity' is sometimes referred to as the Löwenheim-Skolem Paradox. But, of course, it is not a paradox in the sense of an antinomy; it is a novel and unexpected feature of formal systems." In this address I want to take up Skolem's arguments, not with the aim of refuting them but with the aim of extending them in somewhat the direction he seemed to be indicating. It is not my claim that the "Löwenheim-Skolem Paradox" is an antinomy *in formal logic*; but I shall argue that it *is* an antinomy, or something close to it, in *philosophy of language*. Moreover, I shall argue that the resolution of the antinomy—the only resolution that I myself can see as making sense—has profound implications for the great metaphysical dispute about realism which has always been the central dispute in the philosophy of language.

The structure of my argument will be as follows: I shall point out that in many different areas there are three main positions on reference and truth: there is the extreme Platonist position, which posits nonnatural mental powers of directly "grasping" forms (it is characteristic of this position that "understanding" or "grasping" is itself an irreducible and unexplicated notion); there is the verificationist position which replaces the classical notion of truth with the notion of verification or proof, at least when it comes to describing how the language is understood; and there is the moderate realist position which seeks to preserve the centrality of the classical notions of truth and reference without postulating nonnatural mental powers. I shall argue that it is, unfortunately, the *moderate* realist position which is put into deep trouble by the Löwenheim-Skolem Theorem and related model-theoretic results. Finally I will opt for verificationism as a way of preserving the outlook of scientific or empirical realism, which is totally jettisoned by Platonism, even though this means giving up *metaphysical* realism.

The Löwenheim-Skolem Theorem says that a satisfiable first-order theory (in

Received January 30, 1978

[1]Presidential Address delivered before the Winter Meeting of the Association for Symbolic Logic in Washington, D. C., December 29, 1977. I wish to thank Bas van Fraassen for valuable comments on and criticisms of an earlier version.

a countable language) has a countable model. Consider the sentence:

(i) $-(ER)(R$ is *one-to-one. The domain of* $R \subset N$. *The range of values of* R *is* S)

where 'N' is a formal term for the set of all whole numbers and the three conjuncts in the matrix have the obvious first-order definitions.

Replace 'S' with the formal term for the set of all real numbers in your favorite formalized set theory. Then (i) will be a *theorem* (proved by Cantor's celebrated "diagonal argument"). So your formalized set theory *says* that a certain set (call it "S") is nondenumerable. So S must *be* nondenumerable in all *models* of your set theory. So your set theory—say ZF (Zermelo-Fraenkel set theory) has only nondenumerable models. But this is impossible! For, by the Löwenheim-Skolem Theorem, *no* theory can have *only* nondenumerable models; if a theory has a nondenumerable model, it must have denumerably infinite ones as well. Contradiction.

The resolution of this apparent contradiction is not hard, as Skolem points out (and it is not this apparent contradiction that I referred to as an antinomy, or close to an antinomy). For (i) only "says that S is nondenumerable when the quantifier (ER) is interpreted as ranging over *all* relations on $N \times S$. But when we pick a *denumerable* model for the language of set theory, "(ER)" does not range over *all* relations; it ranges only over relations *in the model*. (i) only "says" that S is nondenumerable in a *relative* sense: the sense that the members of S cannot be put in one-to-one correspondence with a subset of N by any R *in the model*. A set S can be "nondenumerable" in this *relative* sense and yet be denumerable "in reality". This happens when there *are* one-to-one correspondences between S and N but all of them lie outside the given model. What is a "countable" set from the point of view of one model may be an uncountable set from the point of view of another model. As Skolem sums it up, "even the notions 'finite', 'infinite', 'simply infinite sequence' and so forth turn out to be merely relative within axiomatic set theory".

The philosophical problem. Up to a point all commentators agree on the significance of the existence of "unintended" interpretations, e.g., models in which what are "supposed to be" nondenumerable sets are "in reality" denumerable. All commentators agree that the existence of such models shows that the "intended" interpretation, or, as some prefer to speak, the "intuitive notion of a set", is not "captured" by the formal system. But if *axioms* cannot capture the "intuitive notion of a set", what possibly could?

A technical fact is of relevance here. The Löwenheim-Skolem Theorem has a strong form (the so-called "downward Löwenheim-Skolem Theorem"), which requires the axiom of choice to prove, and which tells us that a satisfiable first-order theory (in a countable language) has a countable model which is a submodel of any given model. In other words if we are given a nondenumerable model M for a theory, then we can find a countable model M' of that same theory in which the predicate symbols stand for the same relations (restricted to the smaller universe in the obvious way) as they did in the original model. The only difference between M and M' is that the "universe" of M'—i.e., the totality that the variables of quantification range over— is a proper subset of the "universe" of M.

Now the argument that Skolem gave, and that shows that "the intuitive notion of a set" (if there is such a thing) is not "captured" by any formal system, shows that even a *formalization of total science* (if one could construct such a thing), or even a *formalization of all our beliefs* (whether they count as "science" or not), could not rule out denumerable interpretations, and, *a fortiori*, such a formalization could not rule out *unintended* interpretations of this notion.

This shows that "theoretical constraints", whether they come from set theory itself or from "total science", cannot fix the interpretation of the notion *set* in the "intended" way. What of "operational constraints"?

Even if we allow that there might be a *denumerable infinity* of measurable "magnitudes", and that each of them might be measured to *arbitrary rational accuracy* (which certainly seems a utopian assumption), it would not help. For, by the "downward Löwenheim-Skolem Theorem", we can find a countable submodel of the "standard" model (if there is such a thing) in which countably many predicates (each of which may have countably many things in its extension) have their extensions preserved. In particular, we can fix the values of countable many magnitudes at all rational space-time points, and still find a countable submodel which meets all the constraints. In short, there certainly seems to be a *countable* model of our *entire body of belief* which meets all operational constraints.

The philosophical problem appears at just this point. If we are told, "axiomatic set theory does not capture the intuitive notion of a set", then it is natural to think that *something else*—our "understanding"—does capture it. But what can our "understanding" come to, at least for a naturalistically minded philosopher, which is more than *the way we use our language*? The Skolem argument can be extended, as we have just seen, to show that the *total use of the language* (operational plus theoretical constraints) does not "fix" a unique "intended interpretation" any more than axiomatic set theory by itself does.

This observation can push a philosopher of mathematics in two different ways. If he is inclined to Platonism, he will take this as evidence that the mind has mysterious faculties of "grasping concepts" (or "perceiving mathematical objects") which the naturalistically minded philosopher will never succeed in giving an account of. But if he is inclined to some species of verificationism (i.e., to indentifying truth with verifiability, rather than with some classical "correspondence with reality") he will say, "Nonsense! All the 'paradox' shows is that our understanding of 'The real numbers are nondenumerable' consists in our knowing *what it is for this to be proved*, and not in our 'grasp' of a 'model'." In short, the extreme positions—Platonism and verificationism—seem to receive comfort from the Löwenheim-Skolem Parodox; it is only the "moderate" position (which tries to avoid mysterious "perceptions" of "mathematical objects" while retaining a classical notion of truth) which is in deep trouble.

An epistemological/logical digression. The problem just pointed out is a serious problem for any philosopher or philosophically minded logician who wishes to view set theory as the description of a determinate independently existing reality. But from a mathematical point of view, it may appear immaterial: what does it matter if there are many different models of set theory, and not a unique "intended model" *if they all satisfy the same sentences?* What we want to know as mathematicians is what sentences of set theory are true; we do not want to have the sets themselves in our hands.

Unfortunately, the argument can be extended. First of all, the theoretical constraints we have been speaking of must, on a naturalistic view, come from only two sources: they must come from something like human decision or convention, whatever the source of the "naturalness" of the decisions or conventions may be, or from human experience, both experience with nature (which is undoubtedly the source of our most basic "mathematical intuitions", even if it be unfashionable to say so), and experience with "doing mathematics". It is hard to believe that either or both of these sources together can ever give us a *complete* set of axioms for set theory (since, for one thing, a complete set of axioms would have to be nonrecursive, and it is hard to envisage coming to have a nonrecursive set of axioms in the literature or in our heads even in the unlikely event that the human race went on forever doing set theory); and if a complete set of axioms is impossible, and the intended model*s* (in the plural) are singled out only by theoretical plus operational constraints then sentences which are independent of the axioms which we will arrive at in the limit of set-theoretic inquiry really have *no* determinate truth value; they are just true in some intended models and false in others.

To show what bearing this fact may have on actual set-theoretic inquiry, I will have to digress for a moment into technical logic. In 1938 Gödel put forward a new axiom for set theory: the axiom "$V = L$". Here L is the class of all constructible sets, that is, the class of all sets which can be defined by a certain constructive procedure if we pretend to have names available for all the ordinals, however large. (Of course, this sense of "constructible" would be anathema to constructive mathematicians.) V is the universe of all sets. So "$V = L$" just says *all sets are constructible.* By considering the inner model for set theory in which "$V = L$" is true, Gödel was able to prove the relative consistency of ZF and ZF *plus* the axiom of choice and the generalized continuum hypothesis.

"$V = L$" is certainly an important sentence, mathematically speaking. Is it *true?*

Gödel briefly considered proposing that we *add* "$V = L$" to the accepted axioms for set theory, as a sort of meaning stipulation, but he soon changed his mind. His later view was that "$V = L$" is *really* false, even though it is consistent with set theory, if set theory is itself consistent.

Gödel's intuition is widely shared among working set theorists. But does this "intuition" make sense?

Let *MAG* be a countable set of physical magnitudes which includes all magnitudes that sentient beings in this physical universe can actually measure (it certainly seems plausible that we cannot hope to measure more than a countable number of physical magnitudes). Let *OP* be the "correct" assignment of values; that is, the assignment which assigns to each member of *MAG* the value that that magnitude actually has at each rational space-time point. Then all the information "operational constraints" might give us (and, in fact, infinitely more) is coded into *OP*.

One technical term: an *ω-model* for a set theory is a model in which the *natural numbers* are ordered as they are "supposed to be"; that is, the sequence of "natural numbers" of the model is an *ω*-sequence.

Now for a small theorem.[2]

THEOREM. *ZF plus V = L has an ω-model which contains any given countable set of real numbers.*

PROOF. Since a countable set of reals can be coded as a single real by well-known techniques, it suffices to prove that *for every real s, there is an M such that M is an ω-model for ZF plus V = L and s is represented in M.*

By the "downward Löwenheim-Skolem Theorem", this statement is true if and only if the following statement is:

For every real s, there is a countable M such that M is an ω-model for ZF plus V = L and s is represented in M.

Countable structures with the property that the "natural numbers" of the structure form an ω-sequence can be coded as reals by standard techniques. When this is properly done, the predicate "*M is an ω-model for ZF plus V = L and s is represented in M*" becomes a two-place *arithmetical* predicate of reals M, s. The above sentence thus has the logical form (*for every real s*) (*there is a real M*) $(\cdots M, s, \cdots)$. In short, the sentence is a Π_2-sentence.

Now, consider this sentence *in the inner model V = L*. For every *s in the inner model*—that is, for every *s* in *L*—there is a model—namely *L* itself—which satisfies "*V = L*" and contains *s*. By the downward Löwenheim-Skolem Theorem, there is a countable submodel which is elementary equivalent to *L* and contains *s*. (Strictly speaking, we need here not just the downward Löwenheim-Skolem Theorem, but the "Skolem hull" construction which is used to prove that theorem.) By Gödel's work, this countable submodel itself lies in *L*, and as is easily verified, so does the real that codes it. So the above Π_2-sentence is true in the inner model *V = L*.

But Schoenfield has proved that Π_2-sentences are *absolute:* if a Π_2-sentence is true in *L*, then it must be true in *V*. So the above sentence is true in *V*. □

What makes this theorem startling is the following reflection: suppose that Gödel is right, and "*V = L*" is *false* ("in reality"). Suppose that there is, in fact, a *nonconstructible real number* (as Gödel also believes). Since the predicate "is constructible" is absolute in β-*models*—that is, in models in which the "wellorderings" *relative to the model* are wellorderings "in reality" (recall Skolem's "relativity of set-theoretic notions"!), no model containing such a nonconstructible *s* can satisfy "*s* is constructible" and be a β-*model*. But, by the above theorem, a model containing *s can* satisfy "*s* is constructible" (because it satisfies "*V = L*", and "*V = L*" says *everything* is constructible) and be an ω-*model*.

Now, suppose we formalize *the entire language of science* within the set theory ZF *plus V = L*. Any model for ZF which contains an abstract set isomorphic to *OP* can be extended to a model for this formalized language of science which is *standard with respect to OP*—hence, even if *OP* is nonconstructible "in reality", we can find a model *for the entire language of science* which satisfies *everything is constructible* and which assigns the correct values to all the physical magnitudes in *MAG* at all rational space-time points.

---

[2] Barwise has proved the much stronger theorem that every countable model of ZF has a proper end extension which is a model of ZF + *V = L* (in *Infinitary methods in the model theory of set theory*, published in *Logic Colloquium '69*). The theorem in the text was proved by me before 1963.

The claim Gödel makes is that "$V = L$" is false "in reality". But what on earth can this mean? It must mean, at the very least, that in the case just envisaged, the model we have described in which "$V = L$" holds would not be *the intended model*. But why not? It satisfies all theoretical constraints; and we have gone to great length to make sure it satisfies all operational constraints as well.

Perhaps someone will say that "$V \neq L$" (or something which implies that V does not equal L) should be added to the axioms of ZF as an additional "theoretical constraint". (Gödel often speaks of new axioms someday becoming evident.) But, while this may be acceptable from a nonrealist standpoint, it can hardly be acceptable from a realist standpoint. For the realist standpoint is that there is *a fact of the matter*—a fact independent of our legislation—as to whether $V = L$ or not. A realist like Gödel holds that we have access to an "intended interpretation" of ZF, where the access is not simply by linguistic stipulation.

What the above argument shows is that if the "intended interpretation" is fixed only by theoretical plus operational constraints, then if "$V \neq L$" does not follow from those theoretical constraints—if we do not *decide* to make $V = L$ true or to make $V = L$ false—then there will be "intended" models in which $V = L$ is *true*. If I am right, then the "relativity of set-theoretic notions" extends to a *relativity of the truth value of* "$V = L$" (and, by similar arguments, of the axiom of choice and the continuum hypothesis as well).

Operational constraints and counterfactuals. It may seem to some that there is a major equivocation in the notion of what *can* be measured, or observed, which endangers the apparently crucial claim that the evidence we *could* have amounts to at most denumerably many facts. Imagine a measuring apparatus that simply detects the presence of a particle within a finite volume dv around its own geometric center during each full minute on its clock. Certainly it comes up with at most denumerably many reports (each *yes* or *no*) even if it is left to run forever. But how many are the facts it *could* report? Well, if it were jiggled a little, by chance let us say, its geometric center would shift r centimeters in a given direction. It would then report totally different facts. Since for each number r it could be jiggled that way, the number of reports it could produce is nondenumerable—and it does not matter to this that we, and the apparatus itself, are incapable of distinguishing every real number r from every other one. The problem is simply one of scope for the modal word "can". In my argument, I must be identifying what I call operational constraints, not with the totality of facts that could be registered by observation—i.e., ones that either will be registered, or would be registered if certain chance perturbations occurred—but with the totality of facts that will in actuality be registered or observed, whatever those be.

In reply, I would point out that even if the measuring apparatus *were* jiggled r centimeters in a given direction, we could only know the real number r to some rational approximation. Now, if the intervals involved are all rational, there are only *countably* many facts of the form: if *action A* (an action described with respect to place, time, and character up to some finite "tolerance") were performed, then the result $r \pm \varepsilon$ (a result described up to some rational tolerance) *would be obtained with probability in the interval a, b*. To know all facts of this form would be to know the *probability distribution* of all possible observable results of all possible actions. Our argument shows that a model could be constructed which agrees with all of these facts.

There is a deeper point to be made about this objection, however. Suppose we "first orderize" counterfactual talk, say, by including *events* in the ontology of our theory and introducing a predicate ("subjunctively necessitates") for the counterfactual connection between unactualized event types at a given place-time. Then our argument shows that a model exists which fits all the facts that will actually be registered or observed and fits our theoretical constraints, and this model *induces* an interpretation of the counterfactual idiom (a "similarity metric on possible worlds", in David Lewis' theory) which renders true just the counterfactuals that are true according to some completion of our theory. Thus appeal to counterfactual observations cannot rule out any models at all unless the interpretation of the counterfactual idiom itself is *already* fixed by something beyond operational and theoretical constraints.

(A related point is made by Wittgenstein in his *Philosophical Investigations*: talk about what an ideal machine—or God—could compute is talk *within* mathematics—in disguise—and cannot serve to fix the interpretation of mathematics. "God", too, has many interpretations.)

"Decision" and "convention". I have used the word "decision" in connection with open questions in set theory, and obviously this is a poor word. One cannot simply sit down in one's study and "decide" that "$V = L$" is to be true, or that the axiom of choice is to be true. Nor would it be appropriate for the mathematical community to call an international convention and legislate these matters. Yet, it seems to me that if we encountered an extra-terrestrial species of intelligent beings who had developed a high level of mathematics, and it turned out that they *rejected* the axiom of choice (perhaps because of the Tarski-Banach Theorem[3]), it would be wrong to regard them as simply making a *mistake*. To do *that* would, on my view, amount to saying that acceptance of the axiom of choice is built into our notion of rationality itself; that does not seem to me to be the case. To be sure, our acceptance of choice is not arbitrary; all kinds of "intuitions" (based, most likely, on experience with the finite) support it; its mathematical fertility supports it; but none of this is *so* strong that we could say that an equally successful culture which based *its* mathematics on principles *incompatible* with choice (e.g., on the so-called "axiom of determinacy"[4]) was *irrational*.

---

[3] This is a very counterintuitive consequence of the axiom of choice. Call two objects A, B "congruent by finite decomposition" if they can be divided into finitely many disjoint point sets $A_1, ..., A_n, B_1, ...B_n$, such that $A = A_1 \cup A_2 \cup \cdots \cup A_n$, $B = B_1 \cup B_2 \cup \cdots \cup B_n$, and (for $i = 1, 2, ..., n$) A_i is congruent to B_i. Then Tarski and Banach showed that *all spheres are congruent by finite decomposition*.

[4] This axiom, first studied by J. Mycielski (*On the axiom of determinacy*", **Fundamenta Mathematicae**, 1963) asserts that infinite games with perfect information are determined, i.e. there is a winning strategy for either the first or second player. AD (the axiom of determinacy) implies the existence of a nontrivial countably additive two-valued measure on the real numbers, contradicting a well-known consequence of the axiom of choice.

But if both systems of set theory—ours and the extra-terrestrials'—count as *rational*, what sense does it make to call one *true* and the others *false*? From the Platonist's point of view there is no trouble in answering this question. "The axiom of choice is true—true in *the* model", he will say (if he believes the axiom of choice). "We are right and the extra-terrestrials are wrong." But what is *the* model? If the intended model is singled out by theoretical and operational constraints, then, first, "the" intended model is plural not singular (so the "the" is inappropriate— our theoretical and operational constraints fit many models, not just one, and so do those of the extra-terrestrials as we saw before. Secondly, the intended models for us do satisfy the axiom of choice and the extra-terrestrially intended models do not; we are not talking about the same models, so there is no question of a "mistake" on one side or the other.

The Platonist will reply that what this really shows is that we have some mysterious faculty of "grasping concepts" (or "intuiting mathematical objects") and it is *this* that enables us to fix a model as *the* model, and not just operational and theoretical constraints; but this appeal to mysterious faculties seems both unhelpful as epistemology and unpersuasive as science. What neural process, after all, could be described as the perception of a mathematical object? Why of *one* mathematical object rather than another? I do not doubt that *some* mathematical axioms are built in to our notion of rationality ("every number has a successor"); but, if the axiom of choice and the continuum hypothesis are not, then, I am suggesting, Skolem's argument, or the foregoing extension of it, casts doubt on the view that these statements have a truth value independent of the theory in which they are embedded.

Now, suppose this is right and the axiom of choice is true when taken in the sense that it receives from *our* embedding theory and false when taken in the sense that it receives from extra-terrestrial theory. Urging this relativism is not advocating *unbridled* relativism; I do not doubt that there are some objective (if evolving) canons of rationality; I simply doubt that we would regard them as settling this sort of question, let alone as singling out *one* unique "rationally acceptable set theory". If this is right, then one is inclined to say that the extra-terrestrials have decided to let the axiom of choice be false and we have decided to let it be true; or that we have different "conventions"; but, of course, none of these words is literally right. It may well be the case that the idea that statements have their truth values *independent* of embedding theory is so deeply built into our ways of talking that there is simply no "ordinary language" word or short phrase which refers to the theory-dependence of meaning and truth. Perhaps this is why Poincaré was driven to exclaim "Convention, yes! Arbitrary, no!" when he was trying to express a similar idea in another context.

Is the problem a problem with the notion of a "set"? It would be natural to suppose that the problem Skolem points out, the problem of a surprising "relativity" of our notions, has to do with the notion of a "set", given the various problems which are *known* to surround *that* notion, or, at least, has to do with the problem of reference to "mathematical objects". But this is not so.

To see why it is not so, let us consider briefly the vexed problem of reference to theoretical entities in physical science. Although this may seem to be a problem more for philosophers of science or philosophers of language than for logicians, it is a problem whose logical aspects have frequently been of interest to logicians, as is witnessed by the expressions "Ramsey sentence", "Craig translation", etc. Here again, the realist—or, at least, the hard-core metaphysical realist—wishes it to be the case that *truth* and *rational acceptability* should be *independent* notions. He wishes it to be the case that what, e.g., electrons *are* should be distinct (and possibly different from) what we believe them to be or even what we would believe them to be given the best experiments and the epistemically best theory. Once again, the realist—the hard-core metaphysical realist—holds that our intentions single out "the" model, and that our beliefs are then either true or false in "the" model *whether we can find out their truth values or not.*

To see the bearing of the Löwenheim-Skolem Theorem (or of the intimately related Gödel Completeness Theorem and its model-theoretic generalizations) on this problem, let us again do a bit of model construction. This time the operational constraints have to be handled a little more delicately, since we have need to distinguish operational concepts (concepts that describe what we see, feel, hear, etc., as we perform various experiments, and also concepts that describe our acts of picking up, pushing, pulling, twisting, looking at, sniffing, listening to, etc.) from nonoperational concepts.

To describe our operational constraints we shall need three things. First, we shall have to fix a sufficiently large "observational vocabulary". Like the "observational vocabulary" of the logical empiricists, we will want to include in this set—call it the set of "0-terms"—such words as "red", "touches", "hard", "push", "look at", etc. Second, we shall assume that there *exists* (whether we can define it or not) a set of S which can be taken to be the set of macroscopically observable things and events (observable with the human sensorium, that means). The notion of an observable thing or event is surely vague; so we shall want S to be a generous set, that is, God is to err in the direction of counting too many things and events as "observable for humans" when He defines the set S, if it is necessary to err in either direction, rather than to err in the direction of leaving out some things that might be counted as borderline "observables". If one is a realist, then such a set S must exist, of course, even if our knowledge of the world and the human sensorium does not permit *us* to define it at the present time. The reason we allow S to contain events (and not just things) is that, as Richard Boyd has pointed out, some of the entities we can directly observe are *forces*—we can *feel* forces—and forces are not objects. But I assume that forces can be construed as predicates of either objects, e.g., our bodies, or of suitable events.

The third thing we shall assume given is a valuation (call it, once again 'OP') which assigns the correct truth value to each n-place 0-term (for $n = 1, 2, 3, ...$) on each n-tuple of elements of S on which it is defined. 0-terms are in general also defined on things not in S; for example, two molecules too small to see with the naked eye may touch, a dust-mote too small to see may be black, etc. Thus OP is a *partial* valuation in a double sense; it is defined on only a subset of the predicates of the language, namely the 0-terms, and even on these it only fixes a part of the extension, namely the extension of $T \upharpoonright S$ (the restriction of T to S), for each 0-term T.

Once again, it is the valuation OP that captures our "operational constraints". Indeed, it captures these "from above", since it may well contain *more* information than we could actually get by using our bodies and our senses in the world.

What shall we do about "theoretical constraints"? Let us assume that there exists a possible formalization of present-day total science, call it 'T', and also that there exists a possible formalization of *ideal* scientific theory, call it 'T_I'. T_I is to be "ideal" in the sense of being *epistemically* ideal *for humans*. Ideality, in this sense, is a rather vague notion; but we shall assume that, when God makes up T_I, He constructs a theory which it would be rational for scientists to accept, or which is a limit of theories that it would be rational to accept, as more and more evidence accumulates, and also that he makes up a theory which is compatible with the valuation OP.

Now, the theory T is, we may suppose, well confirmed at the present time, and hence rationally acceptable on the evidence we *now* have; but there is a clear sense in which it may be false. Indeed, it may well lead to false predictions, and thus conflict with OP. But T_I, by hypothesis, does not lead to any false predictions. Still, the metaphysical realist claims—and it is just this claim that makes him a *metaphysical* as opposed to an empirical realist—that T_I may be, in reality, false. What is not knowable as true may nonetheless be true; what is epistemically most justifiable to believe may nonetheless be false, on this kind of realist view. The striking connection between issues and debates in the philosophy of science and issues and debates in the philosophy of mathematics is that this sort of realism runs into *precisely* the same difficulties that we saw Platonism run into. Let us pause to verify this.

Since the ideal theory T_I must, whatever other properties it may or may not have, have the property of being *consistent*, it follows from the Gödel Completeness Theorem (whose proof, as all logicians know, is intimately related to one of Skolem's proofs of the Löwenheim-Skolem Theorem), that T_I has models. We shall assume that T_I contains a primitive or defined term denoting each member of S, the set of "observable things and events". The assumption that we made, that T_I agrees with OP, means that all those sentences about members of S which OP requires to be true are theorems of T_I. Thus if M is any model of T_I, M has to have a member corresponding to each member of S. We can even replace each member of M which corresponds to a member of S by that member of S itself, modifying the interpretation of the predicate letters accordingly, and obtain a model M' in which each term denoting a member of S in the "intended" interpretation does denote that member of S. Then the extension of each 0-term in that model will be partially correct to the extent determined by OP: that is, everything that OP "says" is in the extension of P is in the extension of P, and everything that OP "says" is in the extension of the complement of P is in the extension of the complement of P, for each 0-term, in any such model. In short, such a model is standard with respect to $P \restriction S$ (P restricted to S) for each 0-term P.

Now, such a model satisfies all operational constraints, since it agrees with OP. It satisfies those theoretical constraints we would impose in the ideal limit of inquiry. So, once again, it looks as if any such model is "intended"—for what else could single out a model as "intended" than this? But if this is what it *is* to be an "intended model", T_I must be *true*—true in all intended models! The metaphysical realist's claim that even the ideal theory T_I might be false "in reality" seems to collapse into unintelligibility.

Of course, it might be contended that "true" does not follow from "true in all intended models". But "true" is the same as "true in the intended *interpretation*" (or "in *all* intended interpretations", if there may be more than one interpretation intended—or permitted—by the speaker), on any view. So to follow this line— which is, indeed, the right one, in my view—one needs to develop a theory on which interpretations are specified *other* than my specifying models.

Once again, an appeal to mysterious powers of the mind is made by some. Chisholm (following the tradition of Brentano) contends that the mind has a faculty of *referring to external objects* (or perhaps to external properties) which he calls by the good old name "intentionality". Once again most naturalistically minded philosophers (and, of course, psychologists), find the postulation of unexplained mental faculties unhelpful epistemology and almost certainly bad science as well.

There are two main tendencies in the philosophy of science (I hesitate to call them "views", because each tendency is represented by many different detailed views) about the way in which the reference of theoretical terms gets fixed. According to one tendency, which we may call the Ramsey tendency, and whose various versions constituted the received view for many years, theoretical terms come in batches or clumps. Each clump—for example, the clump consisting of the primitives of electromagnetic theory—is defined by a theory, in the sense that all the models of that theory which are standard on the observation terms count as intended models. The theory is "true" just in case it has such a model. (The "Ramsey sentence" of the theory is just the second-order sentence that asserts the existence of such a model.) A sophisticated version of this view, which amounts to relativizing the Ramsey sentence to an open set of "intended applications", has recently been advanced by Joseph Sneed.

The other tendency is the realist tendency. While realists differ among themselves even more than proponents of the (former) received view do, realists unite in agreeing that a theory may have a true Ramsey sentence and not be (in reality) true.

The first of the two tendencies I described, the Ramsey tendency, represented in the United States by the school of Rudolf Carnap, accepted the "relativity of theoretical notions", and abandoned the realist intuitions. The second tendency is more complex. Its, so to speak, conservative wing, represented by Chisholm, joins Plato and the ancients in postulating mysterious powers wherewith the mind "grasps" concepts, as we have already said. If we have more available with which to fix the intended model than merely theoretical and operational constraints, then the problem disappears. The radical pragmatist wing, represented, perhaps, by Quine, is willing to give up the intuition that T_I might be false "in reality". This radical wing is "realist" in the sense of being willing to assert that present-day science, taken more or less at face value (i.e., without philosophical reinterpretation) is at least approximately true; "realist" in the sense of regarding reference as trans-theoretic (a theory with a true Ramsey sentence may be false, because later inquiry may establish an incompatible theory as better); but not *metaphysical* realist. It is the moderate "center" of the realist tendency, the center that would like to hold on to metaphysical realism *without* postulating mysterious powers of the mind that is once again in deep trouble.

Pushing the problem back: the Skolemization of absolutely everything. We have seen that issues in the philosophy of science having to do with reference of theoretical terms and issues in the philosophy of mathematics having to do with the problem of singling out a unique "intended model" for set theory are both connected with the Löwenheim-Skolem Theorem and its near relative, the Gödel Completeness Theorem. Issues having to do with reference also arise in philosophy in connection with sense data and material objects and, once again, these connect with the model-theoretic problems we have been discussing. (In some way, it really seems that the Skolem Paradox underlies the *characteristic* problems of 20th century philosophy.)

Although the philosopher John Austin and the psychologist Fred Skinner both tried to drive sense data out of existence, it seems to me that most philosophers and psychologists think that there are such things as *sensations*, or *qualia*. They may not be objects of perception, as was once thought (it is becoming increasingly fashionable to view them as states or conditions of the sentient subject, as Reichenbach long ago urged we should); we may not have incorrigible knowledge concerning them; they may be somewhat ill-defined entities rather than the perfectly sharp particulars they were once taken to be; but it seems reasonable to hold that they are part of the legitimate subject matter of cognitive psychology and philosophy and not mere pseudo-entities invented by bad psychology and bad philosophy.

Accepting this, and taking the operational constraint this time to be that we wish the ideal theory to correctly predict all sense data, it is easily seen that the previous argument can be repeated here, this time to show that (if the "intended" models are the ones which satisfy the operational and theoretical constraints we now have, or even the operational and theoretical constraints we would impose in some limit) then, either the present theory is "true", in the sense of being "true in all intended models", provided it leads to no false predictions about sense data, or else the ideal theory is "true". The first alternative corresponds to taking the theoretical constraints to be represented by current theory; the second alternative corresponds to taking the theoretical constraints to be represented by the ideal theory. This time, however, it will be the case that even terms referring to ordinary material objects—terms like 'cat' and 'dog'—get differently interpreted in the different "intended" models. It seems, this time, as if we cannot even refer to ordinary middle sized physical objects except as formal constructs variously interpreted in various models.

Moreover, if we agree with Wittgenstein that the *similarity relation* between sense data we have at different times is not itself something present to my mind—that "fixing one's attention" on a sense datum and thinking "by 'red' I mean whatever is like *this*" does not really pick out any relation of similarity at all—and make the natural move of supposing that the intended models of my language when I now and in the future talk of the sense data I had at some past time t_0 are singled out by operational and theoretical constraints, then, again, it will turn out that my *past* sense data are mere formal constructs which get differently interpreted in various models. If we further agree with Wittgenstein that the notion of truth requires a *public* language (or requires at least states of the self at more than one time —that a "private language for one specious present" makes no sense), then even my *present* sense data are in this same boat . . .. In short, one can "Skolemize" absolutely everything. It seems to be absolutely impossible to fix a determinate reference (without appeal to nonnatural mental powers) for *any* term at all. If we apply the argument to the very metalanguage we use to talk about the predicament . . .?

The same problem has even surfaced recently in the field of cognitive psychology. The standard model for the brain/mind in this field is the modern computing machine. This computing machine is thought of as having something analogous to a formalized language in which it computes. (This hypothetical brain language has even received a name—"mentalese".) What makes the model of cognitive psychology a *cognitive* model is that "mentalese" is thought to be a medium whereby the brain constructs an *internal representation* of the external world. This idea runs immediately into the following problem: if "mentalese" is to be a vehicle for describing the external world, then the various predicate letters must have extensions which are sets of external things (or sets of *n*-tuples of external things). But if the way "mentalese" is "understood" by the deep structures in the brain that compute, record, etc. in this "language" is *via* what artificial intelligence people call "procedural semantics"—that is, if the brain's *program for using* "mentalese" comprises its entire "understanding" of "mentalese"—where the program for using "mentalese", like any program, refers only to what is *inside* the computer—then how do *extensions* ever come into the picture at all? In the terminology I have been employing in this address, the problem is this: if the extension of predicates in "mentalese" is fixed by the theoretical and operational constraints "hard wired in" to the brain, or even by theoretical and operational constraints that it evolves in the course of inquiry, then these will not fix a *determinate* extension for any predicate. If thinking is ultimately done in "mentalese", then *no concept we have will have a determinate extension*. Or so it seems.

The bearing of causal theories of reference. The term "causal theory of reference" was originally applied to my theory of the reference of natural kind terms and Kripke's theory of the reference of proper names. These theories did not attempt to *define* reference, but rather attempted to say something about how reference is fixed, if it is not fixed by associating definite descriptions with the terms and names in question. Kripke and I argued that the intention to preserve reference through a historical chain of uses and the intention to cooperate socially in the fixing of reference make it possible to use terms successfully to refer although no one definite description is associated with any term by all speakers who use that term. These theories assume that individuals can be singled out for the purpose of a "naming ceremony" and that inferences to the existence of definite theoretical entities (to which names can then be attached) can be successfully made. Thus these theories did not address the question as to how any term can acquire a determinate reference (or any gesture, e.g., pointing—of course, the "reference" of gestures is just as problematic as the reference of terms, if not more so). Recently, however, it has been suggested by various authors that some account can be given of how at least some basic sorts of terms refer in terms of the notion of a "causal chain". In one version,[5] a version strikingly reminiscent of the theories of Ockham and other 14th century logicians, it is held that a term refers to "the dominant source" of the beliefs that contain the term. Assuming we can circumvent the problem that the dominant cause of our beliefs concerning *electrons* may well be *textbooks*,[6] it is important to notice that even if a *correct* view of this kind can be elaborated, it will do nothing to resolve the problem we have been discussing.

The problem is that adding to our hypothetical formalized language of science a body of theory titled "causal theory of reference" *is* just adding more *theory*. But Skolem's argument, and our extensions of it, are not affected by enlarging the theory. Indeed, you can even take the theory to consist of *all true sentences*, and there will be many models—models differing on the extension of every term not fixed by *OP* (or whatever you take *OP* to be in a given context)—which satisfy the entire theory. If "refers" can be defined in terms of some causal predicate or predicates in the metalanguage of our theory, then, since each model of the object language extends in an obvious way to a corresponding model of the metalanguage, it will turn out that, *in each model M, reference$_M$ is definable in terms of causes$_M$*; but, unless the word 'causes' (or whatever the causal predicate or predicates may be) is already glued to one definite relation with metaphysical glue, this does not fix a determinate extension for 'refers' at all.

This is not to say that the construction of such a theory would be worthless as philosophy or as natural science. The program of cognitive psychology already alluded to—the program of describing our brains as computers which construct an "internal representation of the environment" seems to require that "mentalese" utterances be, in some cases at least, describable as the causal product of devices in the brain and nervous system which "transduce" information from the environment, and such a description might well be what the causal theorists are looking for. The program of realism in the philosophy of science—of *empirical* realism, not metaphysical realism—is to show that scientific theories can be regarded as better and better representations of an objective world with which we are interacting; if such a view is to be part of science itself, as empirical realists contend it should be, then the interactions with the world by means of which this representation is formed and modified must themselves be part of the subject matter of the representation. But the problem as to how the *whole representation*, including the empirical theory of knowledge that is a part of it, can determinately refer is not a problem that can be solved by developing more and better empirical theory.

Ideal theories and truth. One reaction to the problem I have posed would be to say: there are many ideal theories in the sense of theories which satisfy the operational constraints, and in addition have all the virtues (simplicity, coherence, con-

---

[5] Cf. Gareth Evans, *The causal theory of names,* **Aristotelian Society Supplementary Volume** XLVII, pp. 187–208, reprinted in **Naming, necessity and natural kinds,** (Stephen P. Schwartz, Editor), Cornell University Press, 1977.

[6] Evans handles this case by saying that there are appropriateness conditions on the type of causal chain which must exist between the item referred to and the speaker's body of information.

taining the axiom of choice, whatever) that humans like to demand. But there are no "facts of the matter" not reflected in constraints on ideal theories in this sense. Therefore, what is really true is what is common to all such ideal theories; what is really false is what they all deny; all other statements are neither true nor false.

Such a reaction would lead to too few truths, however. It may well be that there are rational beings—even rational human species—which do not employ our color predicates, or who do not employ the predicate "person", or who do not employ the predicate "earthquake".[7] I see no reason to conclude from this that *our* talk of red things, or of persons, or of earthquakes, lacks truth value. If there are many ideal theories (and if "ideal" is itself a somewhat interest-relative notion), if there are many theories which (given appropriate circumstances) it is perfectly rational to accept, then it seems better to say that, insofar as these theories say different (and sometimes, apparently incompatible) things, that some facts are "soft" in the sense of depending for their truth value on the speaker, the circumstances of utterance, etc. This is what we have to say in any case about cases of ordinary vagueness, about ordinary causal talk, etc. It is what we say about apparently incompatible statements of simultaneity in the special theory of relativity. To grant that there is more than one true version of reality is not to deny that some versions are false.

It may be, of course, that there *are* some truths that *any* species of rational inquirers would eventually acknowledge. (On the other hand, the set of these may be empty, or almost empty.) But to say that *by definition* these are all the truths there are is to redefine the notion in a highly restrictive way. (It also assumes that the notion of an "ideal theory" is perfectly clear; an assumption which seems plainly false.)

Intuitionism. It is a striking fact that this entire problem does *not* arise for the standpoint of mathematical intuitionism. This would not be a surprise to Skolem: it was precisely his conclusion that "most mathematicians want mathematics to deal, ultimately, with performable computing operations and not to consist of formal propositions about objects called this or that."

In intuitionism, knowing the meaning of a sentence or predicate consists in associating the sentence or predicate with a procedure which enables one to recognize when one has a proof that the sentence is constructively true (i.e., that it is possible to carry out the constructions that the sentence asserts can be carried out) or that the predicate applies to a certain entity (i.e., that a certain full sentence of the predicate is constructively true). The most striking thing about this standpoint is that the *classical notion of truth is nowhere used*—the semantics is entirely given in terms of the notion of "constructive proof", *including the semantics of "constructive proof" itself.*

Of course, the intuitionists do not think that "constructive proof' can be formalized, or that "mental constructions" can be identified with operations in our *brains*. Generally, they assume a strongly intentionalist and *a prioristic* posture in philosophy—that is, they assume the existence of mental entities called "meanings" and of a special faculty of intuiting constructive relations between these entities.

---

[7] For a discussion of this very point, cf. David Wiggins, *Truth, invention and the meaning of life*, British Academy, 1978.

These are not the aspects of intuitionism I shall be concerned with. Rather I wish to look on intuitionism as an example of what Michael Dummett has called "non-realist semantics"—that is, a semantic theory which holds that *a language is completely understood when a verification procedure is suitably mastered*, and not when truth conditions (in the classical sense) are learned.

The problem with realist semantics—truth-conditional semantics—as Dummett has emphasized, is that if we hold that the understanding of the sentences of, say, set theory consists in our knowledge of their "truth conditions", then how can we possibly say what *that* knowledge in turn consists in? (It cannot, as we have just seen, consist in the use of language or "mentalese" under the control of operational plus theoretical constraints, be they fixed or evolving, since such constraints are too weak to provide a determinate extension for the terms, and it is this that the realist wants.)

If, however, the understanding of the sentences of a mathematical theory consists in the mastery of verification procedures (which need not be fixed once and for all—we can allow a certain amount of "creativity"), then a mathematical theory can be completely understood, and this understanding does not presuppose the notion of a "model" at all, let alone an "intended model".

Nor does the intuitionist (or, more generally, the "nonrealist" semanticist) have to foreswear *forever* the notion of a model. He has to foreswear reference to models in his account of *understanding*; but, once he has succeeded in understanding a rich enough language to serve as a metalanguage for some theory *T* (which may itself be simply a sublanguage of the metalanguage, in the familiar way), he can define 'true in *T*' à la Tarski, he can talk about "models" for *T*, etc. He can even define 'reference' or ('satisfaction') exactly as Tarski did.

Does the whole "Skolem Paradox" arise again to plague him at this stage? The answer is that it does not. To see why it does not, one has to realize what the "existence of a model" means in *constructive* mathematics.

"Objects" in constructive mathematics are *given through descriptions*. Those descriptions do not have to be mysteriously attached to those objects by some nonnatural process (or by metaphysical glue). Rather the possibility of *proving* that a certain construction (the "sense", so to speak, of the description of the model) has certain constructive properties is what is asserted and *all* that is asserted by saying the model "exists". In short, *reference is given through sense, and sense is given through verification-procedures and not through truth-conditions*. The "gap" between our theory and the "objects" simply disappears—or, rather, it never appears in the first place.

Intuitionism liberalized. It is not my aim, however, to try to convert my audience to intuitionism. Set theory may not be the "paradise" Cantor thought it was, but it is not such a bad neighborhood that I want to leave of my own accord, either. Can we separate the philosophical idea behind intuitionism, the idea of "nonrealist" semantics, from the restrictions and prohibitions that the historic intuitionists wished to impose upon mathematics?

The answer is that we can. First, as to set theory: the objection to *impredicativity*, which is the intuitionist ground for rejecting much of classical set theory, has little or no connection with the insistence upon verificationism itself. Indeed, intuitionist mathematics is itself "impredicative", inasmuch as the intuitionist notion of constructive proof presupposes constructive proofs which refer to the totality of *all* constructive proofs.

Second, as to the propositional calculus: it is well known that the classical connectives can be reintroduced into an intuitionist theory by reinterpretation. The important thing is not whether one uses "classical propositional calculus" or not, but how one *understands* the logic if one does use it. Using classical logic as an intuitionist would understand it, means, for example, keeping track of when a disjunction is selective (i.e., one of the disjuncts is constructively provable), and when it is nonselective; but this does not seem like too bad an idea.

In short, while intuitionism may go with a greater interest in constructive mathematics, a liberalized version of the intuitionist standpoint need not rule out "classical" mathematics as either illegitimate or unintelligible. What about the language of empirical science? Here there are greater difficulties. Intuitionist logic is given in terms of a notion of *proof*, and proof is supposed to be a *permanent* feature of statements. Moreover, proof is nonholistic; there is such a thing as the proof (in either the classical or the constructive sense) of an isolated mathematical statement. But verification in empirical science is a matter of degree, not a "yes-or-no" affair; even if we made it a "yes-or-no" affair in some arbitrary way, verification is a property of empirical sentences that can be *lost*; in general the "unit of verification" in empirical science is the theory and not the isolated statement.

These difficulties show that sticking to the intuitionist standpoint, however liberalized, would be a bad idea in the context of formalizing empirical science. But they are not incompatible with "nonrealist" semantics. The crucial question is this: do we think of the *understanding* of the language as consisting in the fact that speakers possess (collectively if not individually) an evolving network of verification procedures, or as consisting in their possession of a set of "truth conditions"? If we choose the first alternative, the alternative of "nonrealist" semantics, then the "gap" between words and world, between our *use* of the language and its "objects", never appears.[8] Moreover, the "nonrealist" semantics is not *inconsistent* with

---

[8] To the suggestion that we identify truth with being verified, or accepted, or accepted in the long run, it may be objected that a person could reasonably, and possibly truly, make the assertion:

> A; but it could have been the case that A and our scientific development differ in such a way to make Ā part of the ideal theory accepted in the long run; in that circumstance, it would have been the case that A but it was not true that A.

This argument is fallacious, however, because the different "scientific development" means here the choice of a different version; we cannot assume the *sentence* ⌜A⌝ has a fixed meaning independent of what version we accept.

More deeply, as Michael Dummett first pointed out, what is involved is not that we *identify* truth with acceptability in the long run (is there a fact of the matter about what would be accepted in the long run?), but that we distinguish two truth-related notions: the *internal* notion of truth ("snow is white" is true if and only if snow is white), which can be introduced into any theory at all, but which does not explain how the theory is understood (because "snow is white" is true is *understood as meaning that snow is white and not vice versa*, and the notion of verification, no longer thought of as a mere *index* of some theory-independent kind of truth, but as the very thing in terms of which we understand the language.

realist semantics; it is simply *prior* to it, in the sense that it is the "nonrealist" semantics that must be internalized if the language is to be understood.

Even if it is not inconsistent with realist semantics, taking the nonrealist semantics as our picture of how the language is understood undoubtedly will affect the way we view questions about reality and truth. For one thing, verification in empirical science (and, to a lesser extent, in mathematics as well, perhaps) sometimes depends on what we before called "decision" or "convention". Thus facts may, on this picture, depend on our interests, saliencies and decisions. There will be many "soft facts". (Perhaps whether $V = L$ or not is a "soft fact".) I cannot, myself, regret this. If appearance and reality end up being endpoints on a continuum rather than being the two halves of a monster Dedekind cut in all we conceive and do not conceive, it seems to me that philosophy will be much better off. The search for the "furniture of the Universe" will have ended with the discovery that the Universe is not a furnished room.

Where did we go wrong?—The problem solved. What Skolem really pointed out is this: no interesting theory (in the sense of first-order theory) can, in and of itself, determine its own objects up to isomorphism. Skolem's argument can be extended as we saw, to show that if theoretical constraints do not determine reference, then the addition of operational constraints will not do it either. It is at this point that reference itself begins to seem "occult"; that it begins to seem that one cannot be any kind of a realist without being a believer in nonnatural mental powers. Many moves have been made in response to this predicament, as we noted above. Some have proposed that *second-order* formalizations are the solution, at least for mathematics; but the "intended" interpretation of the second-order formalism is not fixed by the use of the formalism (the formalism itself admits so-called "Henkin models", i.e., models in which the second-order variables fail to range over the *full* power set of the universe of individuals), and it becomes necessary to attribute to the mind special powers of "grasping second-order notions". Some have proposed to accept the conclusion that mathematical language is only partially interpreted, and likewise for the language we use to speak of "theoretical entities" in empirical science; but then are "ordinary material objects" any better off? Are sense data better off? Both Platonism and phenomenalism have run rampant at different times and in different places in response to this predicament.

The problem, however, lies with the predicament itself. The predicament only *is* a predicament because we did two things: first, we gave an account of understanding the language in terms of programs and procedures for *using* the language (what else?); then, secondly, we asked what the possible "models" for the language were, thinking of the models as existing "out there" *independent of any description*. At this point, something really weird had already happened, had we stopped to notice. On any view, the understanding of the language must determine the reference of the terms, or, rather, must determine the reference given the context of use. If the use, even in a fixed context, does not determine reference, then use is not understanding. The language, on the perspective we talked ourselves into, has a full program of use; but it still lacks an *interpretation*.

This is the fatal step. To adopt a theory of meaning according to which a language whose whole use is specified still lacks something—viz. its "interpretation"— is to accept a problem which *can* only have crazy solutions. To speak as if *this* were my problem, "I know how to use my language, but, now, how shall I single out an interpretation?" is to speak nonsense. Either the use *already* fixes the "interpretation" or *nothing* can.

Nor do "causal theories of reference", etc., help. Basically, trying to get out of this predicament by *these* means is hoping that the *world* will pick one definite extension for each of our terms even if *we* cannot. But the world does not pick models or interpret languages. *We* interpret our languages or nothing does.

We need, therefore, a standpoint which links use and reference in just the way that the metaphysical realist standpoint refuses to do. The standpoint of "nonrealist semantics" is precisely that standpoint. From that standpoint, it is trivial to say that a model in which, as it might be, the set of cats and the set of dogs are permuted (i.e., 'cat' is assigned the set of dogs as its extension, and 'dog' is assigned the set of cats) is "unintended" even if corresponding adjustments in the extensions of all the other predicates make it end up that the operational and theoretical constraints of total science or total belief are all "preserved". Such a model would be unintended *because we do not intend the word 'cat' to refer to dogs*. From the metaphysical realist standpoint, this answer does not work; it just pushes the question back to the metalanguage. The axiom of the metalanguage, " 'cat' refers to cats" cannot rule out such an unintended interpretation of the object language, unless the metalanguage itself already has had *its* intended interpretation singled out; but we are in the same predicament with respect to the metalanguage that we are in with respect to the object language, from that standpoint, so all is in vain. However, from the viewpoint of "nonrealist" semantics, the metalanguage is completely understood, and so is the object language. So we can *say and understand*, " 'cat' refers to cats". Even though the model referred to satisfies the theory, etc., it is "unintended"; we recognize that it is unintended *from the description through which it is given* (as in the intuitionist case). Models are not lost noumenal waifs looking for someone to name them; they are constructions within our theory itself, and they have names from birth.

DEPARTMENT OF PHILOSOPHY
HARVARD UNIVERSITY
CAMBRIDGE, MASSACHUSETTS 02138

SYDNEY SHOEMAKER

CAUSALITY AND PROPERTIES

I

It is events, rather then objects or properties, that are usually taken by philosophers to be the terms of the causal relationship. But an event typically consists of a change in the properties or relationships of one or more objects, the latter being what Jaegwon Kim has called the "constituent objects" of the event.[1] And when one event causes another, this will be in part because of the properties possessed by their constituent objects. Suppose, for example, that a man takes a pill and, as a result, breaks out into a rash. Here the cause and effect are, respectively, the taking of the pill and the breaking out into a rash. Why did the first event cause the second? Well, the pill was penicillin, and the man was allergic to penicillin. No doubt one could want to know more — for example, about the biochemistry of allergies in general and this one in particular. But there is a good sense in which what has been said already explains why the one event caused the other. Here the pill and the man are the constituent objects of the cause event, and the man is the constituent object of the effect event. Following Kim we can also speak of events as having "constituent properties" and "constituent times". In this case the constituent property of the cause event is the relation expressed by the verb 'takes', while the constituent property of the effect event is expressed by the predicate 'breaks out into a rash'. The constituent times of the events are their times of occurrence. Specifying the constituent objects and properties of the cause and effect will tell us what these events consisted in, and together with a specification of their constituent times will serve to identify them; but it will not, typically, explain why the one brought about the other. We explain this by mentioning certain properties of their constituent objects. Given that the pill was penicillin, and that the man was allergic to penicillin, the taking of the pill by the man was certain, or at any rate very likely, to result in an allergic response like a rash. To take another example, suppose a branch is blown against a window and breaks it. Here the constituent objects include the branch and the window, and the causal relationship holds because of, among other things, the massiveness of the one and the fragility of the other.

It would appear from this that any account of causality as a relation

223

between events should involve, in a central way, reference to the properties of the constituent objects of the events. But this should not encourage us to suppose that the notion of causality is to be analyzed away, in Humean fashion, in terms of some relationship between properties – for example, in terms of regularities in their instantiation. For as I shall try to show, the relevant notion of a property is itself to be explained in terms of the notion of causality in a way that has some strikingly non-Humean consequences.

II

Philosophers sometimes use the term 'property' in such a way that for every predicate F true of a thing there is a property of the thing which is designated by the corresponding expression of the form 'being F'. If 'property' is used in this broad way, every object will have innumerable properties that are unlikely to be mentioned in any causal explanation involving an event of which the object is a constituent. For example, my typewriter has the property of being over one hundred miles from the current heavyweight boxing champion of the world. It is not easy to think of a way in which its having this property could help to explain why an event involving it has a certain effect, and it seems artificial, at best, to speak of my typewriter's acquisition of this property as one of the causal effects of the movements of the heavyweight champion.

It is natural, however, to feel that such properties are not 'real' or 'genuine' properties. Our intuitions as to what are, and what are not, genuine properties are closely related to our intuitions as to what are, and what are not, genuine changes. A property is genuine if and only if its acquisition or loss by a thing constitutes a genuine change in that thing. One criterion for a thing's having changed is what Peter Geach calls the "Cambridge criterion". He formulates this as follows: "The thing called 'x' has changed if we have '$F(x)$' at time t' true and '$F(x)$' at time t^1' false, for some interpretations of 'F', 't', and 't^1' ".[2] But as Geach points out, this gives the result that Socrates undergoes a change when he comes to be shorter than Theaetetus in virtue of the latter's growth, and even that he undergoes a change every time a fresh schoolboy comes to admire him. Such 'changes', those that intuitively are not genuine changes, Geach calls "mere 'Cambridge' changes". For Geach, real changes are Cambridge changes, since they satisfy the Cambridge criterion, but some Cambridge changes, namely those that are *mere* Cambridge changes, fail to be real changes. Since it is mere Cambridge changes, rather than Cambridge changes in general, that are to be contrasted with real or genuine changes, I shall introduce the hyphenated expression 'mere-Cambridge' to characterize these. And I shall apply the terms 'Cambridge' and 'mere-Cambridge' to properties as well as to changes. Mere-Cambridge properties will include such properties as being 'grue' (in Nelson Goodman's sense), historical properties like being over twenty years old and having been slept in by George Washington, relational properties like being fifty miles south of burning barn,[3] and such properties as being such that Jimmy Carter is President of the United States.

It is worth mentioning that in addition to distinguishing between real and mere-Cambridge properties and changes, we must also distinguish between real and mere-Cambridge resemblance or similarity, and between real and mere-Cambridge differences. Cambridge similarities hold in virtue of the sharing of Cambridge properties. And mere-Cambridge similarities hold in virtue of the sharing of mere-Cambridge properties: there is such a similarity between all grue things; there is one between all things fifty miles south of a burning barn; there is one between all beds slept in by George Washington; and there is one between all things such that Jimmy Carter is President of the United States. It will be recalled that the notion of similarity, or resemblance, plays a prominent role in Hume's account of causality. His first definition of *cause* in the *Treatise* is "an object precedent and contiguous to another, and where all the objects resembling the former are plac'd in a like relation of priority and contiguity to those objects, that resemble the latter."[4] Hume clearly regarded the notion of resemblance as quite unproblematical and in no need of elucidation.[5] Yet it is plain that he needs a narrower notion of resemblance than that of Cambridge resemblance if his definition of causality is to have the desired content. Cambridge resemblances are too easily come by; any two objects share infinitely many Cambridge properties, and so 'resemble' one another in infinitely many ways. There are also infinitely many Cambridge differences between any two objects. What Hume needs is a notion of resemblance and difference which is such that some things resemble a given thing more than others do, and such that some things may resemble a thing exactly (without being numerically identical to it) while others resemble it hardly at all. Only 'real' or 'genuine' resemblance will serve his purposes. If it turns out, as I think it does, that in order to give a satisfactory account of the distinction between real and mere-Cambridge properties, changes, similarities, and difference we must make use of the notion of causality, the Humean project of defining causality in terms of regularity or 'constant conjunction', notions that plainly involve the notion of resemblance, is seriously undermined.

I have no wish to legislate concerning the correct use of the terms 'property', 'change', 'similar', and so forth. It would be rash to claim that the accepted use of the term 'property' is such that what I have classified as mere-Cambridge properties are not properties. But I do think that we have *a* notion of what it is to be a property which is such that this is so – in other words, which is such that not every phrase of the form 'being so and so' stands for a property which something has just in case the corresponding predicate of the form 'is so and so' is true of it, and is such that sometimes a predicate is true of a thing, not because (or only because) of any properties *it* has, but because something else, perhaps something related to it in certain ways, has certain properties. It is this narrow conception of what it is to be a property, and the correlative notions of change and similarity, that I am concerned to elucidate in this paper. (I should mention that I am concerned here only with the sorts of properties with respect to which change is possible; my account is not intended to apply to such properties of numbers as being even and being prime.)

III

John locke held that "powers make a great part of our complex ideas of substances."[6] And there is one passage in which Locke seems to suggest that all qualities of substances are powers; he says, in explanation of his usage of the term 'quality', that "the power to produce any idea in our mind, I call *quality* of the subject wherein that power is ".[7] This suggests a theory of properties, namely that properties are causal powers, which is akin to the theory I shall be defending. As it happens, this is not Locke's view. If one ascribed it to him on the basis of the passage just quoted, one would have to ascribe to him the view that all qualities are what he called 'secondary qualities' – powers to produce certain mental effects ('ideas') in us. But Locke recognized the existence of powers that are not secondary qualities, namely powers (for example, the power in the sun to melt wax) to produce effects in material objects. These have been called 'tertiary qualities'. And he distinguished both of these sorts of powers from the 'primary qualities' on which they 'depend'. Nevertheless, the view which Locke's words unintentionally suggest is worth considering.

What would seem to be the same view is sometimes put by saying that all properties are dispositional properties. But as thus formulated, this view seems plainly mistaken. Surely we make a distinction between dispositional and nondispositional properties, and can mention paradigms of both sorts. Moreover, it seems plain that what dispositional properties something has, what powers it has, depends on what nondispositional properties it has – just as Locke thought that the powers of things depend on their primary qualities and those of their parts.

In fact, I believe, there are two different distinctions to be made here, and these are often conflated. One is not a distinction between kinds of *properties* at all, but rather a distinction between kinds of *predicates*. Sometimes it belongs to the meaning, or sense, of a predicate that if it is true of a thing then under certain circumstances the thing will undergo certain changes or will produce certain changes in other things. This is true of what are standardly counted as dispositional predicates, for example, 'flexible', 'soluble', 'malleable', 'magnetized', and 'poisonous'. Plainly not all predicates are of this sort. Whether color predicates are is a matter of controversy. But whatever we say about this, it seems plain that predicates like 'square', 'round' and 'made of copper' are not dispositional in this sense. There are causal powers associated with being made of copper — for example, being an electrical conductor. But presumably this association is not incorporated into the meaning of the term 'copper'.

The first distinction, then, is between different sorts of predicates, and I think that the term 'dispositional' is best employed as a predicate of predicates, not of properties. A different distinction is between powers, in a sense I am about to explain, and the properties in virtue of which things have the powers they have.[8] For something to have a power, in this sense, is for it to be such that its presence in circumstances of a particular sort will have certain effects.[9] One can think of such a power as a function from circumstances to effects. Thus if something is poisonous its presence in someone's body will produce death or illness; in virtue of this, being poisonous is a power. Here it is possible for things to have the same power in virtue of having very different properties. Suppose that one poisonous substance kills by affecting the heart, while another kills by directly affecting the nervous system and brain. They produce these different effects in virtue of having very different chemical compositions. They will of course differ in their powers as well as in their properties, for one will have the power to produce certain physiological effects in the nervous system, while the other will have the power to produce quite different physiological effects in the heart. But there is one power they will share, in virtue of having these different powers, namely that of producing death if ingested by a human being. Properties here play the role, vis-à-vis powers, that primary qualities play in Locke; it is in virtue of a thing's properies that the thing has the powers (Locke's secondary and tertiary qualities) that it has.

There is a rough correspondence between this distinction between powers and properties and the earlier distinction between dispositional and nondispositional predicates. By and large, dispositional predicates ascribe powers while nondispositional monadic predicates ascribe properties that are not powers in the same sense.

IV

On the view of properties I want to propose, while properties are typically not powers of the sort ascribed by dispositional predicates, they are related to such powers in much the way that such powers are related to the causal effects which they are powers to produce. Just as powers can be thought of as functions from circumstances to causal effects, so the properties on which powers depend can be thought of as functions from properties to powers (or, better, as functions from sets of properties to sets of powers). One might even say that properties are second-order powers; they are powers to produce first-order powers (powers to produce certain sorts of events) if combined with certain other properties. But the formulation I shall mainly employ is this: what makes a property the property it is, what determines its identity, is its potential for contributing to the causal powers of the things that have it. This means, among other things, that if under all possible circumstances properties X and Y make the same contribution to the causal powers of the things that have them, X and Y are the same property.

To illustrate this, let us take as our example of a property the property of being 'knife-shaped' — I shall take this to be a highly determinate property which belongs to a certain knife in my kitchen and to anything else of exactly the same shape. Now if all that I know about a thing is that it has this property, I know nothing about what will result from its presence in any circumstances. What has the property of being knife-shaped could be a knife, made of steel, but it could instead be a piece of balsa wood, a piece of butter, or even an oddly-shaped cloud of some invisible gas. There is no power which necessarily belongs to all and only the things having this property. But if this property is combined with the property of being knife-sized and the property of being made of steel, the object having these properties will necessarily have a number of powers. It will have the power of cutting butter, cheese and wood, if applied to these substances with suitable pressure, and also the power of producing various sorts of sense impressions in human beings under appropriate observational conditions, and also the power of leaving an impression of a certain shape if applied to soft wax and then withdrawn, and so on. The combination of the property of being knife-shaped with the property of being made of glass will result in a somewhat different set of powers, which will overlap with the set which results from its combination with the property of being made of steel. Likewise with its combination with the property of being made of wood, the property of being made of butter, and so on.

Let us say that an object has power P conditionally upon the possession of the properties in set Q if it has some property r such that having the properties in Q together with r is causally sufficient for having P, while having the properties in Q is not by itself causally sufficient for having P. Thus, for example, a knife-shaped object has the power of cutting wood conditionally upon being knife-sized and made of steel; for it is true of knife-shaped things, but not of things in general, that if they are knife-sized and made of steel they will have the power to cut wood. When a thing has a power conditionally upon the possession of certain properties, let us say that this amounts to its having a *conditional power*. Our knife-shaped object has the conditional power of being able to cut wood if knife-sized and made of steel. The identity condition for conditional powers is as follows: if A is the conditional power of having power P conditionally upon having the properties in set Q, and B is the conditional power of having P' conditionally upon having the properties in set Q', then A is identical to B just in case P is identical to P' and Q is identical to Q'. Having introduced this notion of a conditional power, we can express my view by saying that properties are clusters of conditional powers. (I shall count powers *simpliciter* as a special case of conditional powers.) I have said that the identity of property is determined by its causal potentialities, the contributions it is capable of making to the causal powers of things that have it. And the causal potentialities that are essential to a property correspond to the conditional powers that make up the cluster with which the property can be identified; for a property to have a causal potentiality is for it to be such that whatever has it has a certain conditional power.

This account is intended to capture what is correct in the view that properties just are powers, or that all properties are dispositional, while acknowledging the truth of a standard objection to that view, namely that a thing's powers or dispositions are distinct from, because 'grounded in', its intrinsic properties.[10]

Before I give my reasons for holding this view, I should mention one prima facie objection to it. Presumably the property of being triangular and the property of being trilateral do not differ in the contributions they make to the causal powers of the things that have them, yet it is natural to say that these, although necessarily coextensive, are different properties. It seems to me, however, that what we have good reason for regarding as distinct are not these properties, as such, but rather the concepts of triangularity and trilaterality, and the meanings of the expressions 'triangular' and 'trilateral'. If we abandon, as I think we should, the idea that properties are the meanings of predicate expressions, and if we are careful to distinguish concepts from what they are concepts of, I see no insuperable obstacle to regarding the properties themselves as identical.

V

My reasons for holding this theory of properties are, broadly speaking, epistemological. Only if some causal theory of properties is true, I believe, can it be explained how properties are capable of engaging our knowledge, and our language, in the way they do.

We know and recognize properties by their effects, or, more precisely, by the effects of the events which are the activations of the causal powers which things have in virtue of having the properties. This happens in a variety of ways. Observing something is being causally influenced by it in certain ways. If the causal potentialities involved in the possession of property are such that there is a fairly direct causal connection between the possession of it by an object and the sensory states of an observer related to that object in certain ways, e. g., looking at it in good light, we say that the property itself is observable. If the relationship is less direct, e. g., if the property can affect the sensory states of the observer only by affecting the properties of something else which the observer observes, a scientific instrument, say, we speak of inferring that the thing has the property from what we take to be the effects of its possession. In other cases we conclude that something has a property because we know that it has other properties which we know from other cases to be correlated with the one in question. But the latter way of knowing about the properties of things is parasitic on the earlier ways; for unless the instantiation of the property had, under some circumstances, effects from which its existence could be concluded, we could never discover laws or correlations that would enable us to infer its existence frrom things other than its effects.

Suppose that the identity of properties consisted of something logically independent of their causal potentialities. Then it ought to be possible for there to be properties that have no potential whatever for contributing to causal powers, i. e., are such that under no conceivable circumstances will their possession by a thing make any difference to the way the presence of that thing affects other things or to the way other things affect it. Further, it ought to be possible that there be two or more different properties that make, under all possible circumstances, exactly the same contribution to the causal powers of the things that have them. Further, it ought to be possible that the potential of a property for contributing to the production of causal powers might change over time, so that, for example, the potential possessed by property A at one time is the same as that possessed by property B at a later time, and that possessed by property B at the earlier time is the same as that possessed by property A at the latter time. Thus a thing might undergo radical change with respect to its properties without undergoing any change in its causal powers, and a thing might undergo radical change in its causal powers without undergoing any change in the properties that underlie these powers.

The supposition that these possibilities are genuine implies, not merely (what might seem harmless) that various things might be the case without its being in any way possible for us to know that they are, but also that it is impossible for us to know various things which we take ourselves to know. If there can be properties that have no potential for contributing to the causal powers of the things that have them, then nothing could be good evidence that the overall resemblance between two things is greater than the overall resemblance between two other things; for even if A and B have closely resembling effects on our senses and our instruments while C and D do not, it might be (for all we know) that C and D share vastly more properties of the causally impotent kind than do A and B. Worse, if two properties can have exactly the same potential for contributing to causal powers, then it is impossible for us even to know (or have any reason for believing) that two things resemble one another by sharing a single property. Moreover, if the properties and causal potentialities of a thing can vary independently of one another, then it is impossible for us to know (or have any good reason for believing) that something has retained a property over time, or that something has undergone a change with respect to the properties that underlie its causal powers. On these suppositions, there would be no way in which a particular property could be picked out so as to have a name attached to it; and even if, *per impossibile*, a name did get attached to a property, it would be impossible for anyone to have any justification for applying the name on particular occasions.

It may be doubted whether the view under attack has these disastrous epistemological consequences. Surely, it may be said, one can hold that it is a contingent matter that particular properties have the causal potentialities they have, and nevertheless hold, compatibly with this, that there are good theoretical reasons for thinking that as a matter of fact different properties differ in their causal potentialities, and that any given property retains the same potentialities over time. For while it is logically possible that the latter should not be so, according to the contingency view, the simplest hypothesis is that it is so; and it is reasonable to accept the simplest hypothesis compatible with the data.

Whatever may be true in general of appeals to theoretical simplicity, this one seems to me extremely questionable. For here we are not really dealing with an explanatory hypothesis at all. If the identity of properties is made independent of their causal potentialities, then in what sense do we explain sameness or difference of causal potentialities by positing sameness or difference of properties? There are of course cases in which we explain a constancy in something by positing certain underlying constancies in its properties. It is genuinely explanatory to say that something retained the same causal power over time because certain of its properties remained the same. And this provides, *ceteris paribus*, a simpler, or at any rate more plausible, explanation of the constancy than one that says that the thing first had one set of underlying properties and then a different set, and that both sets were sufficient to give it that particular power. For example, if the water supply was poisonous all day long, it is more plausible to suppose that this was due to the presence in it of one poisonous substance all day rather than due to its containing cyanide from morning till noon and strychnine from noon till night. But in such cases we presuppose that the underlying property constancies carry with them constancies in causal potentialities, and it is only on this presupposition that positing the underlying constancies provides the simplest explanation of the constancy to be explained. Plainly this presupposition cannot be operative if what the 'inference to the best explanation' purports to explain is, precisely, that sameness of property goes with sameness of causal potentialities. It is not as if a property had the causal potentialities in question as a result of having yet *other* causal potentialities, the constancy of the latter explaining the constancy of the former. This disassociation of property identity from identity of causal potentiality is really an invitation to eliminate reference to properties from our explanatory hypotheses altogether; if it were correct then we could, to use Wittgenstein's metaphor, 'divide through' by the properties and leave the explanatory power of what we say about things untouched.

It might be objected that even if my arguments establish that the causal potentialities of a genuine property cannot change over time, they do not establish that these causal potentialities are essential to that property, in the sense of belonging to it in all possible worlds. The immutability of properties with respect to their causal potentialities, it might be said, is simply a consequence of the immutability of laws — of the fact that it makes no sense to speak of a genuine law holding at one time and not at another. And from the fact that the laws governing a property cannot change over time it does not follow, it may be said, that the property cannot be governed by different laws in different possible worlds.

Let me observe first of all that in conceding that the immutability of the causal potentialities of genuine properties is a consequence of the immutability of laws, the objection concedes a large part of what I want to maintain. It is not true in general of mere-Cambridge properties that their causal potentialities cannot change over time; for example, this is not true of *grueness* on the Barker-Achinstein definition of *grue,* where something is grue just in case it is green and the time is before T (say 2000 A.D.) or it is blue and the time is T or afterwards.[11] That genuine properties are marked off from mere-Cambridge properties by their relation to causal laws (and that it is nonsense to speak of a world in which it is the mere-Cambridge properties rather than the genuine ones that are law-governed in way that makes their causal potentialities immutable) is a central part of my view.

There is, moreover, a prima facie case for saying that the immutability of the causal potentialities of a property does imply their essentiality; or in other words, that if they cannot vary across time, they also cannot vary across possible worlds. Most of us do suppose that *particulars* can (or do) have different properties in different possible worlds. We suppose, for example, that in some possible worlds I am a plumber rather than a philosopher, and that in some possible worlds my house is painted yellow rather than white. But it goes with this that particulars can change their properties over time. It is possible that I, the very person who is writing this paper, might have been a plumber, because there is a possible history in which I start with the properties (in this case relational as well as intrinsic) which I had at some time in my actual history, and undergo a series of changes which result in my eventually being a plumber. If I and the world were never such that it was then possible for me to *become* a plumber, it would not be true that I might have been a plumber, or (in other words) that there is a possible world in which I am one. There is, in short, a close linkage between identity across time and identity across possible worlds; the ways in which a given thing can be different in different possible worlds depend on the ways in which such a thing can be different at different times in the actual world. But now let us move from the case of particulars to that of properties. There is no such thing as tracing a property through a series of changes in its causal potentialities — not if it is a genuine property, i. e., one of the sort that figures in causal laws. And so there is no such thing as a possible history in which a property starts with the set of causal potentialities it has in the actual world and ends with a different set. To say the least, this calls into question the intelligibility of the suggestion that the very properties we designate with words like 'green', 'square', 'hard', and so on, might have had different causal potentialities than they in fact have.

However, this last argument is not conclusive. My earlier arguments, if sound, establish that there is an intimate connection between the identity of a property and its causal potentialities. But it has not yet been decisively established that *all* of the causal potentialities of a property are essential to it. The disastrous epistemological consequences of the contingency view would be avoided if for each property we could identify a proper subset of its causal potentialities that are essential to it and constitutive of it, and this would permit some of a property's causal potentialities, those outside the essential cluster, to belong to it contingenty, and so not belong to it in some other possible worlds. There would, in this case, be an important difference between the trans-world indentity of properties and that of particulars — and it is a difference which there is in my own view as well. If, as I believe, the assertion that a certain particular might have had different properties than it does in the actual world (that in some other possible world it does have those properties) implies that there is a possible history 'branching off' from the history of the actual world in which it acquires those properties, this is because there is, putting aside historical properties and 'identity properties' (like being identical to Jimmy Carter), no subset of the properties of such a thing which constitutes an individual essence of it, i. e., is such that, in any possible world, having the properties in that subset is necessary *and sufficient* for being that particular thing. To put this otherwise, the reason why the possible history in which the thing has different properties must be a branching-off from the history of the actual world is that the individual essence of a particular thing must include historical properties. Now I am not in a position to object to the suggestion that properties differ from particulars in having individual essences which do not include historical properties and which are sufficient for their identification across possible worlds; for I hold that the totally of a property's causal potentialities constitute such an individual essence. So a possible alternative to my view is one which holds that for each property there is a proper subset of its causal potentialities that constitute its individual essence. Such a view has its attractions, and is compatible with much of what I say in this paper; in particular, it is compatible with the claim that within any possible world properties are identical just in case they have the same causal potentialities. But I shall argue in Section IX that this view is unworkable, and that there is no acceptable alternative to the view that all of the causal potentialities of a property are essential to it.

VI

As was intended, my account of properties does not apply to what I have called mere-Cambridge properties. When my table acquired the property of being such that Gerald Ford is President of the United States, which it did at the time Nixon resigned from the presidency, this presumably had no effect on its causal powers. Beds that were slept in by George Washington may command a higher price than those that lack this historical property, but presumably this is a result, not of any causal potentialities in the beds themselves, but of the historical beliefs and interests of those who buy and sell them. And grueness, as defined by Goodman, is not associated in the way greenness and blueness are with causal potentialities. (In this sense, which differs from that invoked in Section V, something is grue at a time just in case it is green at that time and is first examined before T, say, 2000 A.D., or is blue at that time and is not first examined before T.) It can happen that the only difference between something that is grue and something that is not is that one of them has and the other lacks the historical property of being (or having been) first examined before the time T mentioned in Goodman's definition of *grue*; and presumably this does not in itself make for any difference in causal potentialities. It can also happen that two things share the property of being grue in virtue of having properties that have different potentialities — that is, in virtue of one of them being green (and examined before T) and the other being blue (and not so examined).

There is an epistemological way of distinguishing genuine and mere-Cambridge properties that is prima facie plausible. If I wish to determine whether an emerald is green at t, the thing to do, if I can manage it, is to examine the emerald at t. But examination of a table will not tell me it is such that Gerald Ford is President of the United States, or whether it is fifty miles south of a burning barn. And if I am ignorant of the date, or if t is after T (the date in Goodman's definition), examination of an emerald will not tell me whether it is grue. Likewise, while scrutiny of a bed may reveal a plaque claiming that it was slept in by George Washington, it will not tell me whether this claim is true. Roughly, if a question about whether thing has a property at a place and time concerns a genuine nonrelational property, the question is most directly settled by observations and tests in the vicinity of that place and time, while if it concerns a mere-Cambridge property it may be most directly settled by observations and tests remote from that place and time, and observations and tests made at that place and time will either be irrelevant (as in the case of the property of being such that Jimmy Carter is president) or insufficient to settle the question (as in the case of grue).

It would be difficult to make this into a precise and adequate criterion of genuineness of property, and I do not know whether this could be done. But I think that to the extent that it is adequate, its adequacy is explained by my account of properties in terms of causal powers. Properties reveal their presence in actualizations of their causal potentialities, a special case of this being the perception of a property. And the most immediate and revealing effects of an object's having a property at a particular place and time are effects that occur in the immediate vicinity of that place and time. To be sure, we cannot rule out on purely philosophical grounds the possibility of action at a spatial and/or temporal distance. And the more prevalent such action is, the less adequate the proposed epistemological criterion will be. But there do seem to be conceptual limitations on the extent to which causal action can be at a spatial or temporal distance. It is doubtful, to say the least, whether there could be something whose causal powers are *all* such that whenever any of them is activated the effects of its activation are spatially remote from the location of the thing at that time, or occur at times remote from the time of activation.

Causation and causal powers are as much involved in the verification of ascriptions of mere-Cambridge properties as in the verification of ascriptions of genuine ones. But in the case of mere-Cambridge properties some of the operative causal powers will either belong to something other than the object to which the property is ascribed, or will belong to that object at a time other than that at which it has that property. Thus if I verify that a man has the property of being fifty miles south of a burning barn, it will be primarily causal powers of the barn, and of intervening stretch of land (which, we will suppose, I measure), rather than the causal powers of the man, that will be responsible for my verifying observations.

VII

It will not have escaped notice that the account of properties and property identity I have offered makes free use of the notion of a property and the notion of property identity. It says, in brief, that properties are identical, whether in the same possible world or in different ones, just in case their coinstantiation with the same properties gives rise to the same powers. This is, if anything, even more circular than it looks. For it crucially involves the notion of sameness of powers, and this will have to be explained in terms of sameness of circumstances and sameness of effects, the notions of which both involve the notion of sameness of property. And of course there was essential use of the notion of a property in my explanation of the notion of a conditional power.

It is worth observing that there is a distinction between kinds of powers that corresponds to the distinction, mentioned earlier, between genuine and mere-Cambridge properties.[12] Robert Boyle's famous example of the key can be used to illustrate this.[13] A particular key on my key chain has the power of opening locks of a certain design. It also has the power of opening my front door. It could lose the former power only by undergoing what we would regard as real change, for example, a change in its shape. But it could lose the latter without undergoing such a change; it could so do in virtue of the lock on my door being replaced by one of a different design. Let us say that the former is an intrinsic power and the latter a mere-Cambridge power. It is clear that in my account of properties the word 'power' must refer only to intrinsic powers. For if it refers to mere-Cambridge powers as well, then what seems clearly to be a mere-Cambridge property of my key, namely being such that my door has a lock of a certain design, will make a determinate contribution to its having the powers it has, and so will count as a genuine property of it. But it seems unlikely that we could explain the distinction between intrinsic and mere-Cambridge powers without making use of the notion of a genuine change and that of a genuine property. And so again my account of the notion of a property in terms of the notion of a power can be seen to be circular.

How much do these circularities matter? Since they are, I think, unavoidable, they preclude a reductive analysis of the notion of a property in terms of the notion of causality. But they by no means render my account empty. The claim that the causal potentialities of a property are essential to it, and that properties having the same causal potentialities are identical, is certainly not made vacuous by the fact that the explanation of the notion of a causal potentiality, or a conditional power, must invoke the notion of a property. As I see it, the notion of a property and the notion of a causal power belong to a system of internally related concepts, no one of which can be explicated without the use of the others. Other members of the system are the concept of an event, the concept of similarity, and the concept of a persisting substance. It can be worthwhile, as a philosophical exercise, to see how far we can go in an attempt to reduce one of these concepts to others — for both the extent of our success and the nature of our failures can be revealing about the nature of the connections between the concepts. But ultimately such attempts must fail. The goal of philosophical analysis, in dealing with such concepts, should not be reductive analysis but rather the charting of internal relationships. And it is perfectly possible for a 'circular' analysis to illuminate a network of internal relationships and have philosophically interesting consequences.

VIII

According to the theory of properties I am proposing, all of the causal potentialities possessed by a property at any time in the actual world are essential to it and so belong to it at all times and in all possible worlds. This has a very strong consequence, namely that causal necessity is just a species of logical necessity. If the introduction into certain circumstances of a thing having certain properties causally necessitates the occurrence of certain effects, then it is impossible, logically impossible, that such an introduction could fail to have such an effect, and so logically necessary that it has it. To the extent that causal laws can be viewed as propositions describing the causal potentialities of properties, it is impossible that the same properties should be governed by different causal laws in different possible worlds, for such propositions will be necessarily true when true at all.

It is not part of this theory, however, that causal laws are analytic or knowable a priori. I suppose that it is analytic that flexible things bend under suitable pressure, that poisonous things cause injury to those for whom they are poisonous, and so on. But I do not think that it is analytic that copper is an electrical conductor, or that knife-shaped things, if knife-sized and made of steel, are capable of cutting butter. Nor does it follow from the claim that such truths are necessary that they are analytic. Kripke has made a compelling case for the view that there are propositions that are necessary a posteriori, that is, true in all possible worlds but such that they can only be known empirically.[14] And such, according to my theory, is the status of most propositions describing the causal potentialities of properties. The theory can allow that our knowledge of these potentialities is empirical, and that it is bound to be only partial. But in order to show how, in the theory, such empirical knowledge is possible, I must now bring out an additional way in which the notion of causality is involved in the notion of a property.

One of the formulations of my theory says that every property is a cluster of conditional powers. But the converse does not seem to me to hold; not every cluster of conditional powers is a property. If something is both knife-shaped and made of wax, then it will have, among others, the following conditional powers: the power of being able to cut wood conditionally upon being knife-sized and made of steel (this it has in virtue of being knife-shaped), and the power of being malleable conditionally upon being at a temperature of $100°F$ (this it has in virtue of being made of wax). Intuitively, these are not common components of any single property. By contrast, the various conditional powers a thing has in virtue of being knife-shaped — for example, the power of being able to cut wood conditionally upon being knife-sized and made of steel, the power of being able to cut butter conditionally upon being knife-sized and made of wood, the power of having a certain visual appearance conditionally upon being green, the power of having a certain other visual appearance conditionally upon being red, and so on — are all constituents of a single property, namely the property of being knife-shaped. The difference, I think, is that in the one case the set of conditional powers has, while in the other it lacks, a certain kind of causal unity. I shall now try to spell out the nature of this unity.

Some subsets of the conditional powers which make up a genuine property will be such that it is a consequence of causal laws that whatever has any member of the subset necessarily has all of its members. Thus, for example, something has the power of leaving a six-inch-long knife-shaped impression in soft wax conditionally upon being six inches long if and only if it has the power of leaving an eight-inch-long knife-shaped impression in soft wax conditionally upon being eight inches long. Now some conditional powers will belong to more than one property cluster; thus, for example, there are many different shape properties that give something the power of being able to cut wood conditionally upon being made of steel. But where a conditional power can be shared by different properties in this way, it will belong to a particular property cluster only if there is another member of that cluster which is such that it is a consequence of causal laws that whatever has that other member has the conditional power in question. And at the core of each cluster there will be one or more conditional powers which are such that as a consequence of causal laws whatever has any of them has all of the conditional powers in the cluster. For example, if something has, conditionally upon being made of steel, the power of leaving a knife-shaped impression in soft wax, then it cannot fail to be knife-shaped, and so cannot fail to have all of the other conditional powers involved in being knife-shaped. I suggest, then, that conditional powers X and Y belong to the same property if and only if it is a consequence of causal laws that either (1) whatever has either of them has the other, or (2) there is some third conditional power such that whatever has it has both X and Y.

Returning now to the conditional power of being able to cut wood conditionally upon being made of steel and the conditional power of being malleable conditionally upon being at a temperature of $100°F$, it seems to me that these do not qualify under the proposed criterion as belonging to a common property. It is obviously not true that whatever has one of them must have the other. And it does not appear that there is any third conditional power which is such that whatever has it must have the two conditional powers in question.[15]

If I am right in thinking that the conditional powers constituting a property must be causally unified in the way indicated, it is not difficult to see how knowledge of the causal potentialities of properties can develop empirically. The behavior of objects, that is, the displays of their powers, will reveal that they have certain conditional powers. Once it is discovered that certain conditional powers are connected in a lawlike way, we can use these to "fix the reference" of a property term to the cluster containing those conditional powers and whatever other conditional powers are related to them in the appropriate lawlike relationships.[16] And we can then set about to determine empirically what the other conditional powers in the cluster are.

IX

As I observed earlier, my theory appears to have the consequence that causal laws are logically necessary, and that causal necessity is just a species of logical necessity. While to some this may be an attractive consequence, to many it will seem counterintuitive. It does seem to most of us that we can conceive of possible worlds which resemble the actual world in the kinds of properties that are instantiated in them, but differ from it in the causal laws that obtain. My theory must maintain either that we cannot really conceive of this or that conceivability is not proof of logical possibility.

Anyone who finds both of these alternatives unacceptable, but is persuaded by the arguments in Section V that the identity of properties is determined by their causal potentialities, will look for ways of reconciling that conclusion with the view that there can be worlds in which some of the causal laws are different from, and incompatible with, those that obtain in the actual world. I want now to consider two ways in which one might attempt to achieve such a reconciliation. First, it might be held that while propositions describing the causal potentialities of properties are necessarily true if true at all, there are other lawlike propositions, namely those asserting lawlike connections between conditional powers, which are contingent and so true in some possible worlds and false in others. According to this view, when we seem to be conceiving of worlds in which the same properties are governed by different laws, what we are really conceiving of are worlds in which the same conditional powers stand to one another in different lawlike connections than they do in the actual world, and so are differently clustered into properties. Second, it might he held that my condition for the identity of properties across possible worlds is too strict. The theory I have advanced might be called the 'total cluster theory'; it identifies a property with a cluster containing all of the conditional powers which anything has in virtue of having that property, and maintains that in any possible world anything that has that property must have all of the members of that cluster. One might attempt to replace this with a 'core cluster theory', which identifies the property with some proper subset of the conditional powers something has in virtue of having that property. On this theory, it is only some of the causal potentialities possessed by a property in the actual world, namely those constituted by the conditional powers in its core cluster, that are essential to it — so it is possible for the same property to have somewhat different causal potentialities in different possible worlds, because of different laws relating the conditional powers in its core cluster with other conditional powers.

I do not believe, however, that either of these attempted reconciliations is sucessful. The first involves the suggestion that it is at least sometimes a contingent matter whether two conditional powers belong to the same property, and hence that there could be a world in which some of the same conditional powers are instantiated as in this world, but in which, owing to the holding of different laws, these are differently clustered into properties. The difficulty with this is that the specification of a conditional power always involves, in two different ways, reference to properties that are instantiated in our world and which, *ex hypothesi*, would not be instantiated in the alternative world in question. It involves reference to the properties on which the power is conditional, and also to the properties in the instantiation of which the exercise of the power would result. For example, one of the conditional powers in the property of being knife-shaped is the power, conditionally upon being made of steel, of leaving a knife-shaped impression if pressed into soft wax and then withdrawn. This conditional power, although not by itself identical to the property of being knife-shaped, could not be exercised without that property being instantiated. Neither could it be exercised without the property of being made of steel being instantiated. And a conditional power could not be instantiated in a world in which the causal laws would not allow an exercise of it. So in general, a conditional power could not be instantiated in a world in which the causal laws did not permit the instantiation of the properties whose instantiation would be involved in its instantiation or in its exercise.

Nothing I have said precludes the possibility of there being worlds in which the causal laws are different from those that prevail in this world. But it seems to follow from my account of property identity that if the laws are different then the properties will have to be different as well. And it does not appear that we have the resources for describing a world in which the properties that can be instantiated differ from what I shall call the 'actual world properties', that is, those that can be instantiated in the actual world. We have just seen that we cannot do this by imagining the conditional powers that exist in this world to be governed by different laws, and so to be differently grouped into properties.

It might seem that we can at least imagine a world in which *some* of the properties that can be instantiated are actual world properties while others are not. But a specification of the causal potentialities of one property will involve mention of other properties, a specification of the causal potentialities of those other properties will involve mention still other properties, and so on. If there could be a world in which some but not all of the actual world properties can be instantiated, this could only be because those properties were causally insulated, as it were, from the rest — that is, were such that their causal potentialities could be fully specified without reference to the rest and vice versa. It seems unlikely that any proper subset of the actual world properties is causally insulated in this way — and any that are insulated from all properties we know about are thereby insulated from our knowledge and our language. But could there be a world in which the properties that can be instantiated include all of the actual world properties plus some others? This would be possible only if the two sets of properties, the actual world properties and the properties that cannot be instantiated in the actual world, were causally insulated from one another. And because of this, it would be impossible for us to say anything about the properties that cannot be instantiated in the actual world; for what we can describe is limited to what can be specified in terms of properties that can be so instantiated. What we could describe of such a world would have to be compatible with the laws that specify the causal potentialities of the actual world properties and, what we have found to be inseparable from these, the laws describing the lawlike connections between the conditional powers that constitute these properties.

Now let us consider the second attempt to reconcile the claim that the identity of a property is determined by its causal potentialities with the apparent conceivability of worlds in which the causal laws that obtain are different from, and incompatible with, those that obtain in the actual world. This involves the proposal that we adopt a 'core cluster theory' in place of the 'total cluster theory', and make the identity of a property depend on a proper subset, rather than on the totality, of the causal potentialities it has in the actual world. Like the first attempted reconciliation, this involves the idea that at least some of the lawlike connections between conditional powers hold only contingently; it is this that is supposed to make it possible for the composition of the total cluster associated with a property to differ from one possible world to another, owing to different conditional powers being causally linked with the conditional powers in the property's essential core cluster. But it would seem that the lawlike connections between those conditional powers included in the essential core cluster will have to hold of logical necessity, i. e., in all possible worlds. For if they held only contingently, then in some possible worlds they would not hold. In such a world, the individual conditional powers which in the actual world constitute the essential core of the property could be instantiated, but the property itself could not be instantiated. Even if these conditional powers could be instantiated together in such a world, their coinstantiation would not count as the instantiation of a property, and so of that property, since the requistite causal unity would be lacking. But I have already argued, in discussing the first attempted reconciliation, that it is not possible that there should be a world in which conditional powers that are instantiated in the actual world can be instantiated while actual world properties cannot be instantiated.

But if, as I have just argued, the lawlike connections between conditional powers within the essential core cluster will have to hold of logical necessity, then we are faced with a problem. Some lawlike connections between conditional powers will hold contingently (according to the core cluster theory), while others will hold as matter of logical necessity. How are we to tell which are which? It does not appear that we can distinguish these lawlike connections epistemologically, i. e., by the way in which they are known. For if, as I am assuming, there are truths that are necessary a posteriori, the fact that a connection is discovered empirically is no guarantee that it does not hold necessarily. Nor can it be said that we identify the necessary connections by the fact that they hold between conditional powers belonging to some property's essential core cluster; for this presupposes that we have some way of identifying essential core clusters, and how are we to do this if we do not already know which connections between conditional powers are necessary and which are contingent?

It might be suggested that what constitutes a set of conditional powers as constituting an essential core cluster is just its being a lawlike truth that whatever has any of its members has all of them, and that it is by discovering such lawlike truths that we identify essential core clusters. Given that the lawlike connections between members of essential core clusters hold of logical necessity, this would amount to the claim that if two conditional powers are so related that the possession of either of them is both causally necessary and causally sufficient for the possession of the other, then the lawlike connection between them holds as a matter of logical necessity, while if the possession of one is causally sufficient but not causally necessary for the possession of the other then the lawlike connection may be contingent. I have no knockdown argument against this view, but it seems to me implausible. If it is possible for it to be a contingent fact that the possession of one conditional power is causally sufficient for the possession of another, then it seems to me that it ought to be possible for it to be a contingent fact that the possession of one conditional power is both causally necessary and causally sufficient for the possession of another; that is, it ought to be possible for it to be contingently true of two conditional powers that the possession of either of them is causally sufficient for the possession of the other. So if we deny that the latter is a possibility, we should also deny that the former is.

It may be suggested that it is our linguistic conventions that make certain causal potentialities essential to a property, and so determine the makeup of a property's essential core cluster. But this cannot be so. It may in some cases belong to the conventionally determined sense of a property word that the property it designates has certain causal potentialities; while I think there is no need for property words to have such Fregean senses, and think that such words often function much as Kripke thinks natural kind terms do, I have no wish to deny that a property word can have a conventionally determined sense. But there is only so much that linguistic conventions can do; and one thing they cannot do is to dictate to reality, creating lawlike connections and *de re* necessities. Having discovered that certain conditional powers necessarily go together, and so are appropriately related for being part of an essential core cluster, we can lay down the convention that a certain word applies, in any possible world, to those and only those things having those conditional powers. But this leaves open the question of how we know that the conditional powers in question are appropriately related — that they must go together in any world in which either can be instantiated. And here appeal to convention cannot help us.

It begins to appear that if we hold that some lawlike connections are contingent, there is no way in which we could discover which of the lawlike connections between conditional powers are logically necessary and which are logically contingent, and so no way in which we could identify the essential core clusters of properties. This means that when we conceive, or seem to be conceiving, of a possible world in which the actual world properties are governed by somewhat different laws, there is no way in which we can discover whether we are conceiving of a genuine possibility. All that any of our empirical investigations can tell us is what lawlike connections obtain in the actual world; and without some way of telling which of these connections are contingent and which necessary, this gives us no information about what can be the case in other possible worlds. This makes all talk about what logically might be and might have been completely idle, except where questions of logical possibility can be settled a priori. If the core cluster theory makes the modal status of causal connections, their being necessary or contingent, epistemologically indeterminate in this way, it does not really save the intuitions which lead us to resist the total cluster theory, according to which all such connections are necessary. Unless we are prepared to abandon altogether the idea that there is a 'fact of the matter' as to whether there are logically possible circumstances in which a given property would make a certain contribution to the causal powers of its subject, I think we must accept the total cluster theory and its initially startling consequence that all of the causal potentialities of a property are essential to it.

X

If, as my theory implies, there are no situations that are logically but not causally possible, how is it that we are apparently able to conceive or imagine such situations? Saul Kripke has suggested one answer to a very similar question.[17] He holds that it is a necessary truth that heat is molecular motion, but recognizes that it seems as if we can imagine heat turning out to be something other than this. According to Kripke, this appearance of conceivability is something to be explained away, and he explains it away by claiming that the seeming conceivability of heat turning out not to be molecular motion consists in the actual conceivability of something else, namely of sensations of a certain sort, those that we in fact get from heat, turning out to be caused by something other than molecular motion. The latter really is conceivable, he holds, and for understandable reasons we mistake its conceivability for the conceivability of something that is in fact not conceivable.

But if conceivability is taken to imply possibility, this account commits one to the possibility that the sensations we get from heat might standardly be caused by something other than molecular motion (and so something other than heat); more than that, it commits one to the possibility that this might be so and that these sensations might be related to other sensations and sense experiences in all the ways they are (or have been to date) in the actual world. And since the property of having such sensations is one that is actualized in this world, this would commit one, in my view, to the claim that it is compatible with the laws of nature that prevail in the actual world that these sensations should be so caused and so related to other experiences. Now this claim may be true — if 'may be' is used epistemically. But it is hard to see how we are entitled to be confident that it is. For might there not be laws, unknown to us, that make it impossible that the standard cause of these sensations should be anything other than it is, given the way they are related to the rest of our experience? If the seeming conceivability of heat turning out to be something other than molecular motion does not prove the actual possibility of this, why should the seeming conceivability of certain sensations being caused by something other than molecular motion prove the actual, and so causal, possibility of that? And if seeming conceivability no more proves possibility in the latter case than in the former, there seems little point in distinguishing between conceivability and seeming conceivability; we may as well allow that it is conceivable (and not just seemingly conceivable) that heat should turn out to be molecular motion, and then acknowledge that conceivability is not conclusive proof of possibility. We could use the term 'conceivable' in such a way that it is conceivable that P just in case not-P is not provable a priori. Or we could use it in such a way that it is conceivable that P just in case it is epistemically possible that it is possible that P should be the case — that is, just in case P's being possible is compatible, for all we know, with what we know. These uses of 'conceivable' are not equivalent, but on both of them it is possible to conceive of what is not possible.

XI

Although many of the implications of the account I have advanced are radically at odds with Humean views about causality, it does enable us to salvage one of the central tenets of the Humean view, namely the claim that singular causal statements are 'implicitly general'. As I see it, the generality of causal propositions stems from the generality of properties, that is, from the fact that properties are universals, together with the fact which I began this essay by pointing out, namely that causal relations hold between particular events in virtue of the properties possessed by the constituent objects of those events, and the fact, which I have tried to establish in the paper, that the identity of a property is completely determined by its potential for contributing to the causal powers of the things that have it. If I assert that one event caused another, I imply that the constituent objects of the cause event had properties which always contribute in certain ways to the causal powers of the things that have them, and that the particular episode of causation at hand was an actualization of some of these potentialities. I may of course not know what the relevant properties of the cause event were; and if I do know this, I may know little about their causal potentialities. This is closely related to the now familiar point that in claiming to know the truth of a singular causal statement one is not committed to knowing the laws in virtue of which it holds.[18] Moreover, a singular causal statement does not commit one to the claim that the instantiation of the relevant properties in relevant similar circumstances always produces the effect that it did in the case at hand; for the laws governing these properties may be statistical, the powers to which the properties contribute may, accordingly, be statistical tendencies or propensities, and the causation may be nonnecessitating. Also, the claim that singular causal statements are implicitly general does not, as here interpreted, imply anything about how such statements are known — in particular, it does not imply the Humean view that causal relationships can only be discovered *via* the discovery of regularities or 'constant conjunctions'. But where the present theory differs most radically from theories in the Humean tradition is in what it claims about the modality of the general propositions, the laws, that explain the truth of singular causal propositions; for whereas on the Humean view the truth of these propositions is contingent, on my view it is logically necessary. I thus find myself, in what I once would have regarded as reactionary company, defending the very sort of 'necessary connection' account of causality which Hume is widely applauded for having refuted.[19]

Cornell University

NOTES

[1] See Jaegwon Kim, 'Causation, Nomic Subsumption, and the Concept of Event', *Journal of Philosophy* 70 (1973), 27–36. I should mention that it was reflection on this excellent paper that first led me to the views developed in the present one.
[2] Peter Geach, *God and the Soul*, Routledge and Kegan Paul, London, 1969, p. 71. See also Jaegwon Kim, 'Non-Causal Relations', *Noûs* 8 (1974), 41–52, and 'Events as Property Exemplifications', in M. Brand and D. Walton (eds.), *Action Theory*, Reidel, Dordrecht, 1976, pp. 159–177.

³ I take this example from Kim, 'Causation, Nomic Subsumption, and the Concept of Event'.
⁴ David Hume, *A Treatise of Human Nature* 1.3.14, ed. by L. A. Selby-Bigge, Oxford University Press, London, 1888, p. 170.
⁵ "When any objects *resemble* each other, the resemblance will at first strike the eye, or rather the mind, and seldom requires a second examination" (*Treatise* 1.3.1, p. 70).
⁶ John Locke, *An Essay Concerning Human Understanding*, 2 vols., 2.23.8, ed. by A. C. Fraser, Oxford University Press, London, 1894, Vol. 1, p. 398.
⁷ *Essay* 2.8.8, Vol. 1, p. 398.
⁸ What does "in virtue of" mean here? For the moment we can say that a thing has a power in virtue of having certain properties if it is a lawlike truth that whatever has those properties has that power. On the theory I shall be defending it turns out that this is a matter of the possession of the properties entailing the possession of the power (that is, its being true in all possible worlds that whatever has the properties has the power).
⁹ In speaking of "circumstances" I have in mind the relations of the object to other objects; instead of speaking of "presence in circumstances of a particular sort" I could instead speak of 'possession of particular relational properties'. Being in such and such circumstances is a mere-Cambridge property of an object, not a genuine (intrinsic) property of it.
¹⁰ After this was written I found that Peter Achinstein has advanced a causal account of property identity which, despite a different approach, is in some ways similar to the account proposed here. See his 'The Identity of Properties', *American Philosophical Quarterly* 11 (1974), 257–276. There are also similarities, along with important differences, between my views and those presented by D. H. Mellor in 'In Defense of Dispositions', *Philosophical Review* 83 (1974), 157–181, and those presented by R. Harre and E. H. Madden in *Causal Powers: A theory of Natural Necessity*, Blackwell, Oxford, 1975.
¹¹ See. S. F. Barker and P. Achinstein, 'On the New Riddle of Induction', *Philosophical Review* 69 (1960), 512–522. The definition given there is not equivalent to that originally given by Goodman, in *Fact, Fiction and Forecast*, 3rd ed., Bobbs-Merrill, Indianapolis, 1975, p. 74 (originally published by University of London Press, London, 1954), and it is the latter which is employed elsewhere in the present paper.
¹² This was called to my attention by Nicholas Sturgeon.
¹³ See Boyle, 'The Origins and Forms of Qualities', in *The Works of the Honourable Robert Boyle*, 5 vols., A. Millar, London, 1744, Vol. 2, p. 461ff.
¹⁴ See Saul Kripke, 'Naming and Necessity', in D. Davidson and G. Harman (eds.), *Semantics of Natural Language*, Reidel, Dordrecht, 1972, pp. 253–355.
¹⁵ There is another reason why these conditional powers should not count as constituting a single property: the instantiation of the second of them is causally incompatible with the activation of the first, since something that is such as to be malleable at 100°F cannot be made of steel.
¹⁶ For the notion of 'reference fixing', see Kripke, *op. cit.*, pp. 269–275.
¹⁷ *Ibid.*, pp. 331–342.
¹⁸ See, for example, Donald Davidson, 'Causal Relations', *Journal of Philosophy* 64 (1967), 691–703.
¹⁹ Earlier versions of this paper were read at Cornell University, Ithaca, N.Y., in 1975, at the University of Toronto and Temple University, Philadelphia, in 1976, and at the

University of Virginia, Charlottesville, in 1977, and a number of people have given me valuable criticisms of one or more of those versions. Special thanks are due to Richard Boyd, Robert Cummins, Lawrence Davis, Glenn Kessler, Jaegwon Kim, Richard Miller, David Reeve, Michael Slote, Robert Stalnaker, and Peter van Inwagen.

Note Added in Proof. Richard Boyd has offered the following as a counterexample to the account of properties proposed in this paper. Imagine a world in which the basic physical elements include substances A, B, C and D. Suppose that X is a compound of A and B, and Y is a compound of C and D. We can suppose that it follows from the laws of nature governing the elements that these two compounds, although composed of different elements, behave exactly alike under all possible circumstances – so that the property of being made of X and the property of being made of Y share all of their causal potentialities. (This means, among other things, that it follows from the laws that once a portion of X or Y is formed, it cannot be decomposed into its constituent elements.) It would follow from my account of properties that being made of X and being made of Y are the same property. And this seems counterintuitive. If, as appears, X and Y would be different substances, the property of being composed of the one should be different from the property of being composed of the other.

I think that this example does show that my account needs to be revised. I propose the following as a revised account which is still clearly a causal account of properties; for properties F and G to be identical, it is necessary *both* that F and G have the same causal potentialities *and* (this is the new requirement) that whatever set of circumstances is sufficient to cause the instantiation of F is sufficient to cause the instantiation of G, and vice versa. This amounts to saying that properties are individuated by their possible causes as well as by their possible effects. No doubt Boyd's example shows that other things I say in the paper need to be amended.